The General Theory of Economic Evolution

C000099008

The burgeoning field of evolutionary economics has developed as a result of the traditional failure of the discipline to explain certain phenomena that impact greatly on the economy: evolution, institutions, knowledge and technology.

This book proposes a new analytic framework for the study of the nature and causes of long run economic growth and development in market systems. It starts out by analyzing the foundations of the neoclassical tradition, before developing a thesis through micro, meso and macro domains drawing conclusions as to what can be learned from the point of view of policy analysis. Dopfer and Potts focus on an open-systems analytical framework and successfully formulate and refine the analytical foundations of a new general theory of economic evolution.

The book is unique in that its general theory of economic evolution is intended as an integrated generic framework to define the rules of an economic system, how they are coordinated, and the causes and consequences of their change. It is essential reading for scholars and students of economic evolution and is also broadly intended for anyone who might seek to better understand the complex evolutionary nature of the structure and dynamics of the knowledge-based economy in today's society.

Kurt Dopfer is Professor of Economics at the Universität St. Gallen, Switzerland.

Jason Potts is a Senior Lecturer at the School of Economics, University of Queensland, Australia.

The General Theory of Economic Evolution

Kurt Dopfer and Jason Potts

Routledge
Taylor & Francis Group

LONDON AND NEW YORK

First published 2008
by Routledge
2 Park Square, Milton Park, Abingdon, Oxon OX14 4RN

Simultaneously published in the USA and Canada
by Routledge
270 Madison Ave, New York, NY 10016

*Routledge is an imprint of the Taylor & Francis Group,
an informa business*

© 2008 Kurt Dopfer and Jason Potts

Typeset in Times New Roman by
Newgen Imaging Systems (P) Ltd, Chennai, India
Printed and bound in Great Britain by
TJ International Ltd, Padstow, Cornwall

British Library Cataloguing in Publication Data
A catalogue record for this book is available from the British Library

Library of Congress Cataloging in Publication Data
A catalog record for this book has been requested

ISBN10: 0–415–27942–9 (hbk)
ISBN10: 0–415–27943–7 (pbk)
ISBN10: 0–203–50740–1 (ebk)

ISBN13: 978–0–415–27942–0 (hbk)
ISBN13: 978–0–415–27943–7 (pbk)
ISBN13: 978–0–203–50740–1 (ebk)

Contents

Figures

Foreword

Our civilization depends, not only for its origin but also for its preservation, on what can be precisely described only as the *extended order* of human cooperation, an order more commonly, if somewhat misleadingly, known as capitalism. ... The extended order is probably the most complex structure in the universe – a structure in which biological organisms that are already highly complex have acquired the capacity to learn, to assimilate, parts of suprapersonal traditions enabling them to adapt themselves from moment to moment into an ever-changing structure possessing an order of a still higher level of complexity. ... The fact that certain structures can form and multiply because other similar structures that already exist can transmit their properties to others (subject to occasional variations), and that abstract orders can thus undergo a process of evolution in the course of which they pass from one material embodiment into others that will arise only because the pattern already exists, has given our world a new dimension: time's arrow. In the course of time new features arise which did not exist before: self-perpetuating and evolving structures which, though represented at any one moment only by particular material embodiments, become distinct entities that in various manifestations persist through time. Elements selected for multiplication are those capable of forming into more complex structures. Such a model, once it has appeared, becomes as definite a constituent of the order of the world as any material object. These orders preserve their general character only by constant change (adaptation).

FA Hayek (1988) The Fatal Conceit, pp. 6, 127, 151

Preface

This book proposes a new analytic framework for the study of the nature and causes of long run economic growth and development in market systems. We shall call this process economic evolution, and observe that although it has been occurring for hundreds of years, it has itself seemingly evolved in the past half-century or so into a percolating global network known unashamedly now as a *knowledge-based economy*.

Strictly speaking, this is of course nonsense, as all economies are knowledge based and always have been. But the signal truth of the matter is that knowledge is now a much more prominent explanation of the wealth of nations. The sheer extent of modern wealth that derives from the creation and exploitation of knowledge resources, as compared to natural resources or fixed capital, is plainly evident in *Fortune 500* rankings of individuals or companies and OECD or World Bank rankings of nations.

Yet modern economies are very much knowledge based in that the growth of knowledge is the overwhelming explanation for economic growth. This is not a new idea, and was well known to the classical economists, and famously developed by Joseph Schumpeter. Yet, as a fact, it was only widely demonstrated with the empirical discovery in the 1950s of a significant residual in the factor-based explanation of growth. From that point on, it was clear that sustained economic growth could only be systematically explained in terms of the growth of knowledge.

Yet things were not always as such. In the 1700s, the dominant explanation for the wealth of nations was the power of agricultural production to produce a surplus. Interestingly, the rather obvious fact that this was based on detailed and specific knowledge of land management, animal husbandry, crop and stock breeding, harvesting, processing and the like was mostly ignored, and instead the *factor* of land and other natural resources came to be identified with the locus and origin of value. The Physiocratic school championed this explanation. However, from the British industrial revolution onwards, it became plainly apparent that the accumulation of capital was of enormously greater significance to national wealth than either the quality of arable land or the quantity of primary production. What mattered most was transformation. This epoch was to be dubbed "capitalism" by Karl Marx in reference to the central importance of the stock of capital goods in the production of wealth. But the nineteenth century was also an epoch of massive expansion of global trade and markets that underscored the contribution of the scale and scope of markets to the creation of value.

So from the Palaeolithic to the late 1700s, the wealth of nations was secularly explained in terms of primary production from the "natural capital" of land. We may call this first epoch *resourcism*. From the industrial revolution to the twentieth century, the growth of wealth was largely to be explained as capital accumulation for secondary production.

We call this second epoch *early capitalism*. By the twentieth century, however, we entered a phase of rationalization of technologies and markets that resulted in the emergence and global coordination of large-scale manufacturing enterprises and the drive to market control through scale and scope. This third epoch is *mature capitalism*, which takes us to about the 1970s.

Since then, the explanation of modern economic growth has come to rest increasingly on knowledge and on the conditions and mechanisms that drive its growth. There are of course many precursors to this, such as for example in the development of engineering and technology in textiles, chemicals and transport. But in our fourth epoch, which is where we are now, the growth of knowledge and the re-coordination of that knowledge systematically extends to all economic domains.

We shall call this fourth epoch the phase of *enterprise* or, if a synonym is sought: *venture capitalism*. In venture capitalism, the growth of wealth is a consequence of the origination of novel ideas and their subsequent adoption and retention by other agents through a process of market-based re-coordination.

Nowadays, economic systems evolve as knowledge grows. As because knowledge continuously grows, economic systems continuously evolve. Analysis of this process we shall call *generic analysis* because it can be decomposed into analysis of *rules* and populations of *rule carriers*. These concepts shall be the building blocks of our generic analysis of economic evolution in the modern market economy in which scarcities and constraints are resolved with new knowledge, and in which wealth is predominantly created from knowledge.

General theory?

We propose a general theory of economic evolution. Yet "general theory" is perhaps a bold and certainly a presumptuous claim to make. This is especially so given both our reluctance at this early stage to formalize our approach, as well as the absence of an explicit starting point in an extant special theory (such as game theory, general equilibrium theory or selection theory) that we might then seek to generalize. Yet what we seek to generalize instead are all the "special" analytic conceptions of knowledge that populate economic analysis, such as preferences, decision heuristics, markets, competencies, skills, capabilities, learning, habits, routines, hierarchies, organization, technology, human capital, trust, general-purpose technologies, contracts, laws, institutions, constitutions and so on. These are all units of knowledge and therefore the building blocks of wealth and the locus of evolutionary change; we shall argue that, more generally, they are all rules. All economic knowledge and the growth of knowledge can be analyzed as a process of coordination and change in *rules*.

That is our general theory, namely that the analysis of rules is the explanatory basis of the nature and the causes of wealth in consequence of the coordination of rules, and that economic evolution in rules is the explanatory basis of how this wealth changes. Ours is a general theory because it is a *generic theory*. This generalizes economic analysis in at least four specific ways.

First, our theory is more general than the standard evolutionary framework (of, for example, Schumpeter or Nelson and Winter) because it integrates not just what we shall call "meso" analysis of rule and population dynamics, but also micro and macro analysis of complex generic systems. It therefore ranges from embodied cognition and the travails of agent learning to the process of long run development and the problems of growth policy across a single analytic framework. Our framework generalizes evolutionary economics by linking—via meso—its micro and macro components.

Second, it is more general than the neoclassical framework because it incorporates a generic level of analysis rather than assuming generic invariance. This means that processes of coordination and change that involve change in the ideas and knowledge of the economic order, such as entrepreneurship, innovation and technological change are naturally endogenous to the framework. Our framework generalizes the view of the economy that focuses only on prices and quantities to a more general view of both micro individuals and macro systems to account for the underlying knowledge (or rules) that generated those operational outcomes and the implications of generic (i.e., rule) invariance.

Third, it is more general than standard "operational" theories of the firm or the macro-economy because it incorporates what we call 0th order "constitutive" and 2nd order "mechanism" rules as well as 1st order generic rules for operations. It is geared not just to analysis of the actions of firms or nations at a point in time, but also their capabilities to render a different environment or adapt to a changing environment. We therefore seek to extend economic analysis from exclusive focus on the operational outcomes of given knowledge (i.e., resource scarcity and "operational" choice) to a more general analysis of the generic rules that generated and that change these conditions.

Fourth, our framework is more general than technological, industrial, institutional, behavioral or strategic analyses of economic coordination and growth because it develops an integrated framework of subject and object rules. Economic evolution is not just the progress of new technologies, but the wider process of subject–object co-evolution as people and other micro units become "generically different" by originating, adopting and retaining novel rules. In this process, both behaviors and technologies co-evolve and mutually adapt to each other, a process that invariably results in both micro and macro structural change. Indeed, while economic evolution is primarily defined at the micro and meso level as generic change, it is primarily defined at the macro level as the co-evolution of subject rules in agents and object rules in the generic environment. Our framework generalizes the special subject-based or object-based theories of the economic system into a more general subject–object co-evolutionary process.

Our general theory of economic evolution is therefore intended as an integrated generic framework to define the rules of an economic system, how they are coordinated, and the causes and consequences of their change. This book is therefore aimed primarily at scholars and students of economic evolution, but is broadly intended for anyone who might seek to better understand the complex evolutionary nature of the structure and dynamics of the knowledge-based economy in this modern age of venture capitalism.

Overview

We have organized this book so as to first set out the analytical foundations of the generic approach, and then to develop these through the micro, meso and macro analytical domains, and with generic policy analysis to conclude. The reader should however be forewarned that this book hews closely to an analytic exposition of concepts and framework, and is therefore mostly abstract (in a new language of our own creation) and entirely bereft of empirical analysis, case studies, formalization, models, specific critique, topical discussion, pithy examples, and even systematic literature review. We are not especially proud of this, but prefer that subsequent focus on literature, empirical analysis, formalism, methodology, modeling, history or policy should proceed in a specialized manner, and ideally by scholars and researchers who know more about formalism, empirics, etc., than we do. Our overarching concern, instead, has been to focus on what we know best—which is open-system analytic frameworks—in order to formulate and refine the analytical foundations of a general generic theory of economic evolution.

Thus, we begin in Chapter 1, with the general analytical foundations of evolutionary economics. We construct this from the ontological foundation of *evolutionary realism* and the open system epistemic considerations of knowledge in subjects. We then construct a general rule taxonomy of two major classes of rules—subject and object, although with subject rules classified as cognitive or behavioral and object rules classified into social and technical rules—and three orders of rules—constitutional, operational and mechanism. The concept of a rule trajectory is then defined in three phases of origination, adoption and retention. These dimensions of rules are the conceptual building blocks of generic analysis and the analytic foundation of evolutionary economics.

In Chapter 2, we provide an overview of the *micro meso macro* framework of generic economic analysis. We explain the fundamental differences between classical, neoclassical and our generic framework of evolutionary economics, and then assemble this into a systematic methodology of micro meso macro analysis. This furnishes a comprehensive analytic representation of the deep complexity of the economic system.

In Chapter 3, we develop a generic analysis of the *micro unit*. We distinguish between the human subject *Homo sapiens Oeconomicus* and the agency, which is a socially organized system of agents. We emphasize the properties of economic agents with respect to the use of knowledge and their propensities and capabilities to develop new knowledge and the implications this has. A key observation is that agencies (e.g., firms) logically exist in order to carry more complex knowledge. We then examine the generic micro trajectory as the process by which a micro unit, either agent or agency, originates, adopts and retains a novel rule. A micro unit as a carrier of knowledge is the elementary unit of evolutionary economics and the micro trajectory is the elementary process of economic evolution.

In Chapter 4, we develop our framework of *meso analysis*, which is the growth (diffusion) of a population of carriers adopting a novel rule. We examine the three phases of a meso trajectory as origination (or innovation), adoption (or generic market process) and retention (or institution). We discuss the properties of a meso unit with respect to its analytic status as a population and a carrier of variety, and then its conceptual interpretation as a market process, and of the scale and velocity of that process as a meso trajectory. From this population perspective, we then examine generic strategy over the dynamic of a meso trajectory.

In Chapter 5, we turn to the coordination of the *whole economy*. We are defining the nature of a coordinated macro state at both the deep and surface levels, which we call generic macro order and generic equilibrium respectively. This defines the ideal generic conditions of the macro knowledge base. From here, we define macro coordination failure and explain its inevitability in consequence of a progressing meso trajectory, along with the deep (generic) value of market systems in resolving this problem. We seek to examine in Chapter 5 the process of macro re-coordination in the course of a macro trajectory as the total effect and consequence of a single meso trajectory. Toward generalization of this, we then consider the process of multiple or co-evolving meso trajectories as "clusters" in which many associated rules evolve at once. Empirically considered this is certainly the general condition, as economic evolution is plainly a process of many rules changing simultaneously. Yet we analytically regard co-evolution as a logical extension of the analysis of single rule coordination and change.

In Chapter 6, we extend the analysis of macro coordination to *macro dynamics* by defining as "regime" an analytical entity that embraces the entire macro trajectory and the resultant re-coordination process. The process of long run growth and development is therefore analyzed as composed of sequences of regimes and regime transitions along which new knowledge becomes both a platform for new knowledge and a mechanism for its further creation. Knowledge builds knowledge, and the consequence is economic evolution, both as an extent structure of knowledge and as a historical trajectory of knowledge. From this historically conceptualized generic macro perspective, we then re-examine the standard macro theories of coordination, self-organization and development.

In Chapter 7, we address the implications of our framework for *generic policy*. We argue for a fundamental distinction between generic and operant policy, and that evolutionary policy must be focused on generic intervention. We then further discriminate between three levels of generic intervention and argue that only 0th and 2nd order policy is legitimate. We conclude that economic evolution ultimately depends on both individual freedoms and capabilities for micro units to become generically different, and on social mechanisms for the re-coordination of these differences.

Our conclusion, therefore, is that the study of economic evolution cannot be effectively reduced to the study of micro processes (as in evolutionary game theory) nor can it be analyzed entirely at an aggregative macro level (as in modern growth theory), but ultimately requires an integrated micro, meso and macro framework. We require *micro analysis* to study how individual carriers originate, adopt and retain novel rules, and to analyze the change in micro structure that results. We require *meso analysis* to study how populations of rules change and the transformations in industries, markets and institutions that result. We require *macro analysis* to study how meso units themselves are coordinated into a macro whole and the historical logic of growth and development as sequences of macro trajectories.

Yet the analytic basis of integration is that all of these changes can be represented in terms of *generic analysis* of coordination and change in rules. This is a qualitatively different approach to the *operational analysis* normally pursued in economics that focuses upon the price and quantity measures associated with transactions and transformations. But for any systematic inquiry into the nature and causes of the wealth of nations, we believe that an analytic framework centered about the concept of rules is the proper basis for both a *general analytic framework for evolutionary economics* and a *general theory of economic evolution*.

Acknowledgments

We have benefited beyond measure from the encouragement, support and incisive discussion and critique of many great people, all of whom are directly and of course legally responsible for any coherent and lucid ideas that may have survived our subsequent renderings. Our sincere thanks to Mark Perlman, John Foster, Stan Metcalfe, Ulrich Witt, Georg D. Blind, Stephan Böhm, Peter Earl, Kate Morrison, Jack Vromen, Richard Wagner, Uwe Canter, Andreas Pyka, Jan Schnellenbach, Phil Mirowski, Markus Schwaninger, Chris Freeman, Geoff Hodgson, Bart Nooteboom, Doyne Farmer, Paolo Saviotti, Gerard Silverberg, Paul Nightingale, Peter Allen, Virginia Acha, Paul Ormerod and Bridget Rosewell.

Many thanks also to the participants of the Schumpeter Society conference 2002 (where this project was first presented), 2004, 2006; the Brisbane Club workshop 2001 (where this project originally began), 2003, 2005; the CRIC workshop 2004; the interviewees of Potts & Morrison's 2004 USA and Europe tour; UQ students of ECON7900 & ECON7540 2002–6; doctoral seminar students of Dopfer 2002–6; and thesis students of Dopfer and Potts who have worked hard and imaginatively on meso projects. Special thanks also to the kind hospitality of research visits to SFI (US), NWU (US), MPI (DE), CRIC (UK), SPRU (UK), GMU (US), UWA (AU), CU (AU), UNE (AU); the ARC Centre of Excellence in Creative Industries and Innovation at QUT, and for research grants from the ACCS (via ARC) and for the "Zürich-workshop" from the former UBS CEO Robert Sutz. Last, but certainly not least, to the boundless editorial faith of Routledge that what we were really doing was writing a textbook.

KD and JP

1 Analytical foundations of evolutionary economics

- Introduces the need for a new analytic framework for evolutionary economics
- Proposes an evolutionary ontology from which to derive such a framework
- Introduces economic evolution as a subjective and objective phenomenon
- Proposes ontologically derived analytic foundations in rules, carriers, operations and trajectories
- Concludes that these concepts can underpin evolutionary economic analysis

1.1 Mechanism and evolution

The history of evolutionary economics is the history of a long struggle of escape from the mechanistic analysis of the economic system. We find doubts about the mechanistic nature of economic phenomena reflected already in the work of Adam Smith who highlighted the central importance of the growth of knowledge to the wealth of nations, and this recognition of the power of knowledge has continued through the works of Malthus, Marx, Veblen, Marshall, Schumpeter, Keynes, Hayek, Penrose, Shackle, Georgescu-Roegen, Boulding, Day, Nelson & Winter and the many others who have sought to explain the growth of knowledge and the dynamics of the economic process as more than just the outworking of a market mechanism, but as something more complex, organic and emergent. Evolutionary economists ultimately believe that human agency and its moral instincts of empathy and imagination are at the root of not just the wealth of nations, but also its continual regeneration and evolution. A mechanistic analysis is inadequate for this, and so new frameworks are ventured. Yet these historically have been multiple. In consequence, what lies beyond mechanistic analysis has not always been clear.

In prime instance, the "evolutionary" of evolutionary economics is the notion that "what lies beyond" mechanistic analysis is evolutionary analysis as modeled on evolutionary biology in general or selection models such as replicator dynamics in particular. However, others have argued that thermodynamics, and especially open system thermodynamics, is what lies beyond mechanistic analysis. Others argue that network or complexity theory is the appropriate generalization, and others epistemics and the growth of knowledge. Yet others argue that institutions or technologies are the appropriate foundations. This penumbra can of course be extended and refined much further. Moreover, these are rarely exclusive categories, but rather contain a great deal of analytic conjecture and empathy, and therefore accommodation and ambiguity.

In consequence, evolutionary economics is best defined by what it is not—i.e., it is not a mechanistic analysis of economic coordination and change. It is not the study of the consequence of things already known, nor of their exogenous disturbance. This is why evolutionary economists ever seek to go beyond, for example, mechanistic growth models, and why they widely regard equilibrium models as naïvely mechanistic solutions to coordination problems. Yet explicit analytical foundations cut, as it were, from whole cloth are still notably absent in evolutionary economics.

There has been a great deal of recent debate and conjecture about the nature of such foundations.[1] The result is a loose analytic consensus that may be summarized about the representation of the economy as a complex open system, or more specifically, as a non-linear, quasi-entropic, differentially replicative, partially stochastic, non-integral, non-equilibrium, boundedly rational, learning-focused, behaviorally conditioned, self-organizational, strategically interactive, environmentally composed, path-dependent, institutionally structured, co-evolutionary, discovery-based, enterprise-driven, technology- and resource-dependent, topologically complex-adaptive ongoing process of variation, selection and replication in the growth of knowledge.

There are many ways to conceptualize what lies beyond mechanistic analysis, but all of them are ways of understanding a growth-of-knowledge process. In this book, we seek to resolve this analytic multiplicity into a single unified framework that we call *micro meso macro*, which we shall introduce in Chapter 2. Our starting point, however, is to recognize that if we seek to go beyond mechanistic foundations, then we shall need new analytic foundations. Yet there are many such possibilities within the ambit of the growth of knowledge, and so we shall also need new evaluative criteria. But what?

The most natural starting point, it seems to us, is to turn away initially from theoretical exegesis and formalistic abstraction, and instead to focus upon the empirical reality of evolution in the economy. Herein, evolutionary economics ultimately seeks to explain two primitive observations: (1) that the economy is largely self-coordinating; and (2) that the structure and content of the economic system is continually changing. Together, these amount to the observation of evolution and the concomitant observation of historicity and openness.

There is coordination in the economy, and there is novelty in the economy. But rather than leaping to generalized analytic frameworks—such as Universal Darwinism, general/Nash equilibrium, autopoiesis, or dissipative systems—we think it useful to first clearly establish an account of the underlying reality of economic evolution and of which the analytical framework of evolutionary economics will naturally be constructed upon. This ontology we shall call *evolutionary realism*.

What is an economy, ontologically speaking? What we do know is that it is not a machine. We know this because self-coordination and self-transformation are widely observed throughout the economic system. We also observe the continual regeneration of novel ideas with differential adoption and retention, and as a manifest product of imagination and enterprise. We also easily observe the structural transformations and turbulence this engenders. No evolutionary biologist has ever experienced evolution, but evolutionary economists can hardly but experience it. Economic evolution is manifestly observable and experiential in a way that biological evolution is not. We can easily observe entrepreneurs generating new ideas, along with the new industrial and market structures that innovations carve into the economic order.

Primary observation tells us that the economy is not a machine, but a complex open process. In consequence, mechanistic analysis has only limited powers to explain the complex open processes of coordination and change in the economy. The starting point of evolutionary economic analysis is "beyond mechanism."[2] Yet from here, where?

The best direction, in our assessment, is not abstractly *up* into a more general framework by theoretical analogy or even homology, but rather *down* into the ontology of evolutionary realism as deduced from the primary empirical observations that define the underlying reality of evolutionary economic analysis. There are many empirical generalizations that can be made of a modern economy, but we propose that relatively few are necessary and sufficient to define the empirical reality of economic evolution. We shall call these "axioms" and propose that, in fact, just three are necessary to ontologically underpin an analytic framework for evolutionary economics.

1.2   The three axioms of evolutionary realism

Metaphysics is the a priori view of reality. But ontology is the science of reality, and so differs by the effective and falsifiable criteria of empirical warrant. An ontology is therefore composed of scientific statements about the fundamental nature of reality. An evolutionary ontology for economics therefore consists of foundational propositions about what exists in an evolving economy.[3] We shall call these empirical propositions axioms.[4]

Evolutionary realism is an ontology composed of three empirical axioms: (1) bimodality; (2) association; and (3) process. Together, they represent the observation of evolution in the economic system as the continuity of some entities, the emergence of new entities, and the disappearance of other entities, along with the observation that different entities have different populations, and that each entity is connected to others in different ways. The economic system is composed of people, resources, knowledge and interactions that combine in specific ways to form a complex emergent structure. This is manifestly observable to everyone. What evolutionary economists focus on, however, is the observation that both this structure and the entities that compose it change with time. This observation is precisely why evolutionary economists reject the mechanistic analysis and its underpinning ontology, and instead seek a new foundation.

Process simply means that the economic system is located in time and that all entities have a temporal existence. Association simply means that there exists structure and that all existences are composed of their matrix of associations. The nexus of process and association is a world of structure through time, and of possible change in that structure, and is utterly native to all evolutionary economists. Bimodality means that for each idea, there can be many actualizations, and is the observation of population in the constituent economic entities of time (process) and space (association). For each technology, there can be many actualizations; for each strategy, there can be many actualizations. Or, translated into the generic category of bimodality: for each rule, there can be many carriers.

Bimodality is the empirical observation of the fundamental ontological reality (i.e., axiom 1) that the economic universe is made of many ideas and that each of these ideas has a population of actualizations of that idea. The economic system is then composed of the associations between these ideas (axiom 2) and the process of those idea structures (axiom 3). The economic world is made of specific things that connect in specific ways and these process structures continue through time. Yet this is an open universe, and so new entities can enter, new associations can be made, and new processes can happen.

The complete axiomatics of evolutionary realism can be summarized as follows:

Axiom 1: All existences are matter-energy actualizations of ideas
Axiom 2: All existences associate
Axiom 3: All existences are processes

These three ontological axioms are systematic, in that they define an independent triumvirate of interlocking observations on how the economy is coordinated and changes as an open system, namely: bimodally in terms of ideas and actualizations, associatively in terms of propensity and structure, and as a process in time. Evolutionary reality is composed of populations and structures of idea actualizations (i.e., process structures) that change with time. We shall argue that analysis of economic evolution can usefully and consistently proceed from this ontological foundation.

Following evolutionary realism, we have now an ontology that applies generally to all types of evolution, whether biological, immunological, psychological, social, economic, cultural or political. The value of this ontological conception is to make clear both the analytic commonalities and differences between otherwise different subject domains and scientific disciplines. All evolutionary processes involve the bimodality of an idea and many actualizations. This is what enables the analytic concepts of variation and selection to be applied generally to these domains, and not only to biology, but equally legitimately to evolution in immune systems, economic systems and cultural systems alike. Similarly, all evolutionary processes involve association between ideas, which is why we speak of knowledge and structure as properties of organisms and social systems alike. All evolutionary processes involve processes that render them historically contingent. A cultural or economic system is just as much an historical processes as is biological evolution.[5]

Economic evolution is therefore not "just a metaphor" from biological evolution. Rather both economic and biological evolution, along with all other evolutionary subject domains, share common properties represented by the three axioms of evolutionary realism.

1.3   Evolution in mind

However, biological evolution and economic evolution are of course directly related in the sense that economic evolution is an emergent product of biological evolution. Biological evolution began billions of years ago with the emergence of a self-replicating macromolecule (whether RNA or DNA) that, from there, unfolded the fantastic panoply of adaptations and variations that is the "branching tree of life." And on one of these many branches there emerged, relatively recently, the human species with the adaptation of minds capable of symbolic communication and cultural transmission of knowledge.[6] Thus began cultural evolution and its main driver, economic evolution. The genetic constituency of mind underpinned an emergent carrier of "generic" rules, and so began the human story, that is, "history" as located in time and marked by individuals and populations with new rules that constitute events and compose trajectories.

No one definitively knows how this happened, but whatever the initial impetus to the adaptation of the human mind that furnished these capabilities, and there are many theories on this, the effect was revolutionary in that it allowed evolutionary processes to proceed through an entirely new carrier mechanism, namely the human mind. Economic evolution is therefore emergent from biological evolution in the specific sense that the substrate of economic evolution is the human mind as the carrier and originator and regenerator of all economic rules.

Yet it remains, of course, an adapted biological feature. Economic evolution may continue apace quite independently of any change in human evolution. But, at the same time, economic evolution is not independent of the human mind any more than biological evolution proceeds independently of genes. Economic evolution is emergent from biological evolution, but it is not conditional upon it. We may of course learn much about the preponderance of human preferences and economic behaviors by studying human evolution, as many researchers are now beginning to do in various ways, yet that is rather different to supposing that it can instruct us about the conditions of economic evolution.

So, while the methodology of Universal Darwinism and other extensions of the biological model of evolution to economics have been of considerable value and importance to the development of evolutionary economics, it has made a systematic error in basically overlooking the human mind as an emergent carrier domain, leading it to an unrestricted view of replicators and an inconsistent position with respect to methodological individualism. Evolutionary economic analysis, however, is firmly based in the human subject with an adapted mind for thinking about rules. We shall examine this further in Sections 1.4 and 3.2.

Yet there are three basic concepts that, we think, need to be clearly integrated into economic analysis:

1   The human mind is internally self-referential and internally coherent. This means that the mind is not just an internal mirror of the external world, but is composed of itself and known to itself. Ergo, it is capable of imagination and experimental conjecture as well as error. A mind is a self-generating internal world, a subject.[7]
2   The human mind exists in an external world. The mind is always an open system to the extent of its exposure to stimuli and ability to process that information, but because environments will differ for different minds, agents will learn different things.[8]
3   The human mind is epistemologically bimodal, in that it knows in two ways: internally through thinking, and externally through sensory information. Internal constructs such as preferences, frames and expectations affect what the agents know, as also do external operational information such as prices and other signals. Neither can be considered primary and both interact at the locus of behavior.[9]

Evolution is the process of the adoption and embodiment of ideas into new carriers; in economic evolution, that carrier is primarily the human mind. As such, economists in general, but evolutionary economists in particular, cannot continue to be unsophisticated about the nature of this primary carrier. We need analytical foundations focused on the nature of the human mind as both a carrier of rules for operations, and as the locus for originating, adopting and retaining new rules.

Toward that end, a clear distinction is required between the subjective aspects of economic evolution—i.e., those processes that center about the human mind—and the objective aspects of economic evolution—i.e., those processes that relate to the external environment of things. Subjects are not objects because objects have no mind, and, therefore, play only a secondary role in the process of economic evolution. Objects empirically appear larger than they really are because of an overarching operational bias to conceive of the wealth of nations as the stock of actualized technical rules (i.e., capital). Of course, subjective rules are difficult to conceptualize, as are social rules, but that doesn't mean they do not exist, nor that they are unimportant.

The systematic failure to make this distinction clear, which has resulted in the casual confusion of social science with physical science and the neglect of the human mind in evolutionary sciences beyond biology, has been a major impediment to our understanding of how economic systems coordinate and change because it has failed to appreciate the role of the human mind as both a carrier and generator of generic rules.[10] Generic evolution includes cultural, social, political and economic evolution, all of which evolve over the substrate of the human mind. The human mind is, of course, an emergent product of biological evolution, but the principles of "generic" evolution are those defined by the generic parameters of the human mind as a rule-using and rule-making carrier.[11]

The human mind is, therefore, the seat of economic evolution. In consequence, the subject/object distinction, which distinguishes the rules of the mind from the rules of the environment, has a central place in evolutionary economic analysis. The analytic foundation of evolutionary economics therefore begins with the concept of generic rules developed and carried by human minds.

1.4   Analytic foundations

To do analysis, we require viable analytical units, and to be viable, they require two properties. First, they should correspond to valid general empirical assumptions (see Secion 1.2 above on empirical axioms). Second, they should be instrumentally useful in the construction of dimensional or categorical analytic concepts.

We propose that the foundations of evolutionary economic analysis can be constructed in terms of four such analytical units that have these properties of general empirical validity and instrumental usefulness, namely the concepts of *rules, carriers, operations* and *trajectory*. These shall provide, both individually and in conjunction, the analytic foundations of evolutionary economics. In Chapter 2, we then synthesize these into the building blocks of the micro meso macro framework, which we propose can, in turn, provide a general theory of economic evolution.

1.4.1   Generic rules

The economy is a process made of rules, and a rule is for operations.[12] A rule is defined as the idea that organizes actions or resources into operations. It is the element of knowledge in the knowledge-based economy and the locus of evolution in economic evolution. All economic actions or resources are the product of rules, and so all economic value derives from rules and all economic wealth is composed of rules. Economic evolution is a change in generic rules, and therefore of both value and wealth. That is why it is both creative and destructive, as Schumpeter famously indicated.[13]

All economic phenomena—whether the actions or transactions of agents, the structure of organizations, the form of commodities, or the transformations of technologies—are physically dependent on matter energy, or respectively, are subject to the entropy law.[14] We distinguish between the generic and operational domains by whether the analytic focus is on rules and their actualization in carriers (generic analysis) or on operations such as transactions or transformations (operant analysis). Accordingly, we distinguish between generic entropy (rule actualization) and operant entropy (ongoing operations).

The evolutionary ontology is of ideas, and we distinguish biological from social science by the primary classification of rules as *genetic* or *generic*. Genetic rules replicate biologically, generic rules "communicate" socially.[15] Economic evolution is the evolution of generic rules relating to the economy, which are rules relating to operations on resources. These are the cognitive and behavioral rules of the individual, the coordination of people with social rules, and the organization of matter energy with technical rules. Economic evolution is the ongoing process of coordination and change in these economic generic rules.

The concept of a generic rule can be further classified so as to account for different types of rule in the form of a generic taxonomy of *classes* and *orders* of rules. There are, we deduce, two generic dimensions to rules: (1) the classification of rules in terms of subject and object rules;

and (2) a hierarchical order to distinguish rules that constitute rules from rules that evolve rules. These two taxonomies—classes of rules and orders of rules—can provide, we believe, a comprehensive ordering of the different types of rule that compose the economic system.

The classes of rules span the domain of subject and object rules and will be denoted [CBST]. The orders of rules span the domain of constitutional, operational and mechanism rules and will be denoted [0 1 2]. At a point in time, an economic system is composed of a [CBST] × [0 1 2] matrix of generic rules. The generic state of the economy is determined by the coordination of that generic matrix. Economic evolution is change in that generic matrix.

Rule classification (1): subject and object rules

There are two classes of generic rules in the economy: subject rules and object rules.[16] Subject rules can be further divided into cognitive and behavioral rules [CB], and object rules into social and technical rules [ST]. When subject and object rules achieve coordination, such that operations are possible, then there exists the generic basis for an economic system. Economic evolution is the ongoing process of change in the coordination structure of subject and object rules.

Subject rules [CB] are the class of rules that relate to the economic agent in terms of *Homo sapiens* operating in an economic context, using economics rules and performing economic operations. We shall call this creature with generic thinking and behavior *Homo sapiens Oeconomicus*.

The rule taxonomy then distinguishes between the rules operative in the internal world of the mind, which we call cognitive rules [C], and the rules that operate the behavior of the subject, namely behavioral rules of interaction [B]. Cognitive rules exist within the mind of the agent and include rules for thinking, such as rationality and imagination, and rules for modelling the world. Behavioral rules are those that describe the actions of the agent in an external environment and include, for example, rules for interaction. Subject rules relate to an individual agent and define the internal rules of the agent's mind and the outwardly directed rules of the agent's behaviors.

Object rules [ST], on the other hand, are the class of rules for organizing things, including other people as rule carriers, that is, other subjects as objects. Object rules for organizing people (social rules, S) into social organizations include firms, networks, hierarchies, markets, laws and other institutions. Object rules for organizing matter energy (technical rules, T) are broadly defined by technology and include physical capital and commodities that embody technical rules. These are the rules for organizing physical things.

The organizational principles of firms and markets are canonical examples of social rules, and will, in many cases, correspond to what are more generally called institutions. The capabilities of a firm, for example, are embodied in these social rules, and often quite independently of the capabilities of the agents these rules organize. Technical rules are the rules that organize material objects, and are more commonly known as technologies. Technical rules work in conjunction with other rules to allow productive and consumptive transformation of physical resources.

Economic evolution is not just a simple undifferentiated process of the growth of rules (i.e., an abstracted growth of knowledge or technology process, as in the manner of "new growth theory"), but involves change in all of these rule types. Which is to say that it is not just strategies that evolve in economic evolution, nor just technical change that drives economic growth, but rather a full complement of cognitive, behavioral, social and technical rules that changes in the course of economic evolution.

Generic Rules			
Subject		Object	
Cognitive	Behavioural	Social	Technical

Figure 1.1 Rule taxonomy: subject and object rules.

Economic evolution is generic rule change. This rule change ranges from subject rules that organize the thoughts and behavior of the microeconomic agent, to object rules that organize the social and material structures of the macro economy. With economic evolution, then, it is not just things that change, but also people. Generic evolution involves change in both minds and resources. In subsequent chapters, we shall make much of this distinction and the corresponding co-evolution of subject and object rules. The central tenet of evolutionary economics, then, is that economic systems evolve as generic rules change. But the immediate analytical implication is that change in these rules will involve a complex mix of subject and object rules and, indeed, a co-evolutionary process between them. The map of the subject-object rule space should, we believe, be a priority for evolutionary economic analysis (see Figure 1.1).

This matters because there remains to this day a deep and serious confusion about the proper range and explanatory locus of subjects and objects in economic theory. Marxism and ultimately communism, for example, was based upon a complete focus on object rules (e.g., technologies and social organization), and it failed because it could neither coordinate nor evolve because it neglected the importance of subject rules. A similar critique can be made of modern economic growth theory, whether endogenous or otherwise, namely that it is entirely focused on object rules, especially physical capital, objective institutions and technology. At the other end of the spectrum, the highly subject-based aspects of economic analysis, especially the pure parts of modern microeconomics, are equally deterministic about either internal causes (e.g., behavioral, experimental or neuro-economics) or external causes (e.g., incentives, resources). This is not wrong, and indeed shall form significant building blocks of evolutionary economic analysis, but neither of these pure object-based or pure subject-based approaches forms in themselves a complete analysis of the economic system.

Economic evolution is the co-evolution of subject and object rules. It is determined by neither, but rather by the process and structure of their interaction. This structure is then continually reshaped by novel rule trajectories. Economic evolution is therefore a complex generic process at the nexus of subjects and objects. This makes an obvious difference between, for example: (a) engineering, which is the pure study of technological rules; (b) sociology, which is the pure study of social rules; (c) ethology, anthropology or behavioral psychology, which is the study of behavioral rules; and (d) cognitive psychology or neuroscience, which is the study of cognitive rules. Economics is the study of subject and object rule co-evolution, and therefore involves (at least) all of these.

Rule classification (2): orders of rules

And yet there is a further complexity to the evolutionary taxonomy of rules, in that they are also hierarchically decomposed into what we shall call *orders of rules*.

This accrues to the fact that an economic system is composed of more than just [CBST] rules for operation, which we shall now call 1st order rules. These are the rules that generically define what an economic system can operationally do and underpin its operational wealth. Yet these 1st order rules are not the sum of the generic economy, as the economic system is also composed of rules that constitute the economic system, such as the set of legal, political, social and cultural rules, or "constitutive rules," that define what is possible and permissible in the economic system. We shall call these 0th order (constitutional) rules, and shall suppose that they define the "opportunity space" of permissible 1st order operations.

However, the economic system is also composed of the set of higher order "mechanism rules" that function to originate, adopt and retain novel 1st order rules for operations.[17] We shall call these 2nd order (mechanism) rules, and shall suppose that they define the space of generic transformations in generic operations. Economic evolution is not a random process, but shaped and driven by the rules for the regeneration of new rules. At the micro level these are known as learning systems and at the macro level as innovation systems.

There are, therefore, three orders of rules in the generic taxonomy: 1st order rules as rules for operations; 0th order rules constituting the legal and institutional rules that define what is feasible and permissible; and 2nd order rules as mechanisms that change the generic space of economic operations. Economic evolution therefore occurs not just over the subject-object [CBST] rule domain, but also over the range of 0th order constitutional rules, 1st order operational rules and 2nd order mechanism rules [0 1 2] and in consequence economic evolution is generically 4×3 dimensional.

0th order rules: The constituent order of the economic system is defined by what we call 0th order rules. These refer to the premises or axioms of an economic system embedded in social, cultural, political and legal rules. To a first approximation, they are the rules that define the conditions of enterprise in the sense of what is possible and permissible and the basic rules of the whole economy. In this sense, 0th order rules are the primary or constitutional rules of the modern industrial market economy. They concern such things as the role of the state in creating and implementing systemic rules, such as the rule of law, competition policy, monetary policy, property rights, and suchlike. They also concern the collective force of empathies, sympathies and cooperative trust extended as institutions in the form of behavioral and social rules. These rules define the conditions of the evolving economic order and its permissible scope.

Constitutive or 0th order rules evolve, but not necessarily on an economically relevant timescale. They are significantly political, social, legal and cultural in their primary aspect, and therefore evolve at the speed of consensus (or domination). This is often slower than 1st order evolution, which is expedient, as 0th order rules then provides a quasi-stable background for the evolution of 1st and 2nd order rules.[18]

0th order constitutive rules	Social, legal, political, cultural, and other constituent rules that underpin generic rules for economic operations.
1st order operational rules	Generic rules originated, adopted and retained by carriers for operations.
2nd order mechanism rules	Rules for changing rules. The origination, adoption and retention of rules about origination, adoption and retention.

Figure 1.2 Rule taxonomy: orders of rules.

1st order rules: The operational order of the economic system is defined by 1st order generic rules. These 1st order rules are the set of generic capabilities of an economic agent or macro system and constitute the conventional definition of the value of a system in terms of what it can do. The sum of 1st order rules defines the resource operations of a system at a point in time. However, the stability and dynamics of this state depend also upon the state of 0th order rules and 2nd order rules that pertain, and as these change, so also will 1st order rules.[19] And this, it seems, is how the economic system evolves as a complex adaptive rule system as one new idea leads to another. The path of 1st order rules is in this way the path of economic evolution.

2nd order rules: Evolution means becoming different, and the evolution of 1st order rules depends upon a mechanism for changing those rules. That mechanism we call a 2nd order rule, or mechanism rule. The evolutionary dynamics of 1st order rules is conditional upon 0th order rules, but it is also shaped and driven by 2nd order rule-mechanism rules that involve the agent or agency in originating, adopting and retaining rules for origination, adoption and retention. These are 2nd order rules, and like 1st order rules they are also originated, adopted and retained over a rule trajectory. This can be conceptualized as a 3×3 structure as in Figure 1.3 below. This 2nd order generic matrix of rules for origination, adoption and retention will become, in Chapters 3–6, a key component of our understanding of how agents, agencies and nations evolve in consequence of the sorts of 2nd order knowledge they can develop and carry along the way. In Chapter 7 we then connect this to policy analysis in relation to education and innovation systems as 2nd order rules.

The generic economic system is composed of two classes of rules, namely subject and object rules—which can further be decomposed into subjective cognitive and behavioral rules and objective social and technical rules—and also three orders of rules—which can be decomposed into constitutive, operational and mechanism rules. Economic evolution is a process of change in 1st order rules. But, sometimes, in order to explain this process, we need resort to the explanatory power of lower-order constituent rules and higher-order mechanism rules. The upshot is that the value of an economic system lies not just in its operational capabilities, but also in its constituent and mechanism rules.

Individual agents may differ in many ways. They may differ in their constituent rules about where they locate and what they believe, or in their generic rules about what they know and what they do, or in their mechanism rules that define their capabilities to imagine, adapt and retain new ideas. Firms may differ similarly, as also may industries, regions or national economies.[20] Yet, the analytic concept of orders of rules allows us to organize that variety into the three domains of rules and to analyze economic evolution as processes of coordination and change at all three levels.

Origination of rules for origination	Origination of rules for adoption	Origination of rules for retention
Adoption of rules for origination	Adoption of rules for adoption	Adoption of rules for retention
Retention of rules for origination	Retention of rules for adoption	Retention of rules for retention

Figure 1.3 The 2nd order rule mechanism.

1.4.2   Carriers and operations

The ontological notion of a matter-energy actualization has its analytical counterpart in the notion of a carrier. All rules have carriers in the same way that all existences are composed of an idea and a matter-energy actualization of that idea. Carriers and operations are the material reality of a rule. Three main points can be stated in relation to the generic analysis of rules, carriers and operations.

First, just as an idea can have many actualizations, a rule can have many carriers. For example, a particular technology (a technical rule) can have many carriers, whether as multiple actualizations of the same product rule, or as embodied in a variety of different products. A particular behavior (a behavioral rule) can also be adopted by many different agents, and perhaps even for quite different operational purposes. A single rule can have multiple carriers and this multiplicity is the normal course of a rule trajectory.

Second, carriers can be distinguished between subject carriers (agents) and object carriers (agencies and artefacts).[21] Subject carriers are human beings with minds that function cognitively to govern social and technical behavior. Rules are carried by people as the habits of cognition and behavior that embody, or carry, rule knowledge. Object carriers, on the other hand, embody rule knowledge in organizational forms and patterns of social entities and organizations of material resources. Capital stock and physical commodities are object carriers, as are the principles that organize social systems including firms, markets and nations. Subject carriers and object carriers variously carry the rules of an economy.

Yet objects are of course never autonomous carriers, for all artefacts minimally require some subjective understanding and involvement. No man is an island and nor is any technology, as it is always connected to the mainland of human use. Subject and object carriers therefore together jointly carry the rules of an economy and, in consequence, economic evolution is always a process of co-evolution between subject and object carriers.[22]

Third, a carrier is a subject or object performing operations, and operations are of two types: transformations and transactions. Transformations encompass the range of production and consumption as processes that transform matter energy from one form into another as a process in time and space. Carriers use rules to perform transformations.

An operation may also be a transaction, which is the process of boundary crossing of rules and/or resources (i.e., atoms and/or bits) between agents and agencies.[23] This means that resources have not been transformed, but rather have changed in their functional or ownership structure as the result of a transaction. Carriers use rules to perform transactions. All economic action may therefore be construed as an operation on resources in some way as a transformation, a transaction, or both.

1.4.3   Rule trajectory

The analytic concept of a trajectory is central to evolutionary economics. A trajectory is the process unit of change, and was first given a prominent role in economic analysis by Schumpeter[24] who emphasized the disequilibriating role of the entrepreneur and the resultant process of adoption and adaptation that he called creative destruction. Schumpeterian economists ever since have centered their analysis around trajectories, and in particular technological trajectories.[25]

In neoclassical economics, the analogue of a trajectory is the path to equilibria (e.g., Pareto) or the solution of a dynamical system (e.g., Hicks).[26] In evolutionary economics, a trajectory is also a path from one state of order to another, but this process results in generic structural change in the rules, populations and associations that compose the economy. An evolutionary trajectory is not so much motion in a space as the process of change in the space.[27] A rule trajectory is the process unit of economic evolution.

A rule trajectory is the process of a novel rule becoming actualized into a carrier population. Specifically, the process of a novel generic rule can be described as it originates in one carrier, then is adopted into many carriers, then is replicated at some stable frequency. This can be represented as a rule process in three distinct phases:

Phase 1: Origination of a novel rule
Phase 2: Adoption of that rule into a population of carriers
Phase 3: Retention of that rule in a population of carriers

The analytical structure of three phases reflects the findings of many empirical studies of economic dynamics, and is in accordance with what historians of technology and institutions call a trajectory or wave. We shall call this three-phase generic process (see axiom 3 of evolutionary realism) a trajectory.[28]

A trajectory is the process by which a novel rule is originated, adopted and retained in a carrier population, such that it eventually becomes coordinated in the economic system resulting in a new economic order. This describes the process by which a novel generic rule goes from a carrier population of one to a population of many carriers. We shall describe this in Chapters 3 and 4 as the trajectory of a novel idea in a market (phase 1), through the mass adoption of the generic rule (phase 2), to the retention of a new process structure in the economy (phase 3).

The form of a trajectory is often represented as a classic logistic-diffusion curve, but our theory in no way requires that form. Indeed, it may be represented by any process with differential growth of the selective characteristics of the population and eventual carrier constraints to adoption.[29] What matters is that the phase of adoption of a rule is also a phase of differential growth, as all evolution is ultimately a process of differential growth. In Chapters 3 and 4 we shall unpack and examine this process for its effect on agents, firms, markets and institutions. For now, we simply note that this three-phase generic trajectory is the basic dynamic of economic evolution.[30]

The complete notion of trajectory defines the emergence of an entire population, such that we define a trajectory as the process of a novel rule being originated, adopted and retained into a population of carriers. However, such a trajectory is composed of a series of "micro trajectories" that represent the process by which the novel rule is originated, adopted and retained into each individual carrier composing the population. In this way, a "meso trajectory" is composed of a series of micro trajectories. The population sum of micro trajectories for a single rule through time is a meso trajectory, and a meso trajectory is the basic dynamical unit (i.e., process) of economic evolution.

1.5   Conclusion

The conventional foundations of economic analysis rest in mechanistic thinking and upon an implicit ontology of closed system invariance. Yet if economics is to become an evolutionary science it will require new analytical foundations that build upon an ontology of open system processes.

Toward this, we have proposed three empirical axioms—bimodality, association and process—in order to provide the ontological underpinnings for a suite of analytical concepts from which we may construct evolutionary economic analysis and theory. Evolutionary economic analysis therefore goes beyond mechanistic analysis and into the realm of open system analysis of coordination and change. It shares with biology the fundamental ontological premise that it is ideas (or rules in analytic language) that evolve. But in economic evolution, these rules are generic in that they are created by the human mind. For this reason, evolutionary economists emphasize that the locus of the wealth of nations is the human mind and its propensity to originate, adopt and retain new ideas.

Evolutionary economists have long maintained a tradition of arguing that endogenous economic transformation proceeds as if technologies or firms evolve, such that analogous economic forces of variation, replication and selection exist.[31] This has been a useful assumption, as it has resulted in a great deal of fruitful borrowing of models and cross-fertilization of concepts between evolutionary biology and evolutionary economics, and especially so in the Schumpeterian school of economics.[32] Yet we contend that a more formal and rigorous framework is better developed by proceeding from an ontological foundation that first generalizes both economics and biology to the empirical axioms of all evolutionary phenomena, which we propose as the three axioms of evolutionary realism. From this ontological foundation, we may then properly advance toward an analytical framework that is appropriate for evolutionary economic analysis.

The primary analytic distinction that then arises is between generic and operant domains of analysis. This corresponds to the bimodality axiom between an idea and its actualization, or, in analytic language, between a rule and its carrier. Rules enable a carrier to perform operations. The set of carriers of a rule form the rule population and this population is the result of a process called a trajectory. In Chapter 4, we shall formulate these concepts as a *meso unit* and a *meso trajectory* as the basis about which we construct the micro meso macro framework. In Chapter 3, we examine the micro structure of this process as the micro trajectory by which an agent or agency becomes generically different in consequence of a micro trajectory. But in both cases we are referring explicitly to generic change in the rule base (or knowledge base) of a carrier. Operational concerns with prices, quantities, resource scarcities and the like are of a different order of analysis. Economic evolution can be observed in the dynamics of prices and quantize and other operational variables, but it is ultimately explained by changes in generic rules.

The analytical foundation of evolutionary economics is therefore that of generic rules in carriers, and it is the nature and composition of these rules that determines the set of operations, both observed and possible. The operations of transformations and transactions on resources are then explained in terms of the generic rules that generated them, and evolutionary economics is the study of how those rules coordinate and change. The major generic analytic dimensions are therefore those of rules.

First, there are two major classes of rule: subject rules and object rules. Subject rules organize subject operations, such as thinking and behavior. Object rules organize objects, such as firms and technologies. Economic evolution is always a co-evolutionary process of subject and object rules. This is the central methodological precept of evolutionary economics.

Second, the economic order is composed of three levels of rules. The 1st order economic system of transformations and transactions operates within a 0th order system of legal, social and political rules and, in turn, is operated on by the evolutionary mechanism of

2nd order rules that originate, adopt and retain rules for origination, adoption and retention. Recognition of these three levels is crucial to theoretical analysis, as we explain in Chapters 3–6. But it is also crucial to policy analysis, as we explain in Chapter 7.

Third, the basic unit of economic evolution is a (generic) rule trajectory. This is the process of the origination, adoption and retention of a rule into a carrier. When the carrier is a single agent, we speak of a micro trajectory. When the carrier is a population, we refer to a meso trajectory, which is the standard use of trajectory as an evolutionary or generic concept. A rule trajectory results in structural change in the generic order.

Economic evolution, then, is a generic process of change in the classes and orders of rules through the process of a rule trajectory. This results in changed knowledge of carriers, changed connections between rule carriers, and changed population structures, a process that Schumpeter called "creative destruction." Yet, as Hayek explained, market systems are also self-organizational processes for re-coordinating this change. In our generic view, then, economic evolution is both a self-organizing and creative-destructive process of a novel rule trajectory.

Economic systems evolve not at the point of a new idea being originated, but only when that new idea is subsequently adopted and adapted by other carriers and then retained and maintained for ongoing operational use. This is the generic evolutionary process by which the operational wealth of nations grows. Operational change in economic systems is properly explained only by generic evolution in economic rules. Since the growth of knowledge is an evolutionary process, then so too is the growth of economic systems.

2 Micro meso macro analysis

- Introduces the scope of evolutionary economics and the methodological orientation of macro
- Distinguishes the analytic foundations of classical, neoclassical economic analysis so as to elucidate the generic methodology of evolutionary economics
- Explains how the complexity of an evolving economy is analytically resolved with micro meso macro

2.1 Analysis of the economy as a whole

So far, we have furnished the analytical foundations of this framework in terms of the concepts of rules, carriers operations and trajectories. We have indicated that all evolutionary analysis is ultimately a generic analysis in the sense of the study of coordination and change in rules. Furthermore, we have indicated how this naturally leads to a micro meso macro framework that is centered about a meso unit, as a rule and its carrier population, and a meso trajectory, as the origination, adoption and retention of the rule into a population.[1] The economic system is in this way made of meso units and has both rule structure and population structure. Economic evolution is the process of generic change and re-coordination.

In this chapter, we shall introduce the analytical framework of micro meso macro in order to explain the relation between micro generic processes of an individual agent and macro processes relating to the overall generic coordination of rule populations, and, more fundamentally, the relation these both have to meso change. Our immediate purpose, however, is not to develop this in detail, as that will be the subject of Chapters 3–6, but rather to provide a broad overview of how the analytic framework fits together and to elucidate its methodological arguments and worldview. To do so, however, we must return to first principles.

What is economics? In modern micro textbooks, economics is defined as the science of choice, or some variation upon that theme. Evolutionary economics both agrees and disagrees with this. It agrees that microeconomics studies choice, but in evolutionary microeconomics choice refers to "generic choice" as a rule behavior (e.g., rule adoption), rather than an operational behavior (e.g., transaction or transformation). Evolutionary macro economics builds on generic behavior, and economics is viewed as the science of the whole economy and how it coordinates and changes. It is the thus conceived macro perspective that, we believe, is the proper focus of evolutionary economics, and in this chapter we shall endeavor to explain why.

Our generic perspective may be suitably characterized as post-classical, post-Schumpeterian and post-Hayekian.[2] It argues that the purpose of evolutionary economics is to study the generic process of coordination and change in the growth of knowledge in the whole economy. Evolutionary economic analysis is in this view, then, ultimately a macroeconomic analysis. The purpose of evolutionary economics is to study the macro-economy. This identification of primary orientation matters because it helps us to evaluate the viability of different methodological assumptions for analysis.

Evolutionary economics offers a generic analysis of agents, markets, firms, institutions, industries and other micro elements or component parts, yet not as ends in themselves, but rather for what they contribute to the analysis of the whole economy. To do macro analysis we need meso, and to do meso analysis we need micro. The purpose of evolutionary micro analysis, then, is to underpin evolutionary meso analysis, and the purpose of evolutionary meso analysis is to underpin evolutionary macro analysis, which is analysis of coordination and change in the generic order.

The fundamental questions in economics are not, in this view, the problems of choice in markets or efficiency in firms, but rather the coordination of the whole economy and how this changes. These questions are ostensibly macro questions of long run growth and devel-opment, and our micro meso macro framework is geared to addressing precisely these. We shall introduce and develop evolutionary microeconomics in Chapter 3, as well as the new domain of meso economic analysis in Chapter 4, but we do so with the ostensible aim of seeking to explain the evolution and self-organization of the generic macro order, which shall be the subject of Chapter 5.[3]

However, this is not to say that our generic version of evolutionary economics is only of value to macro concerns. For we shall develop next a generic analysis of agent behavior and entrepreneurial actions in the face of uncertainty, and then extend this to the growth of the firm, the process of competitive enterprise and the dynamics of market selection, including the implications for prices, profits, finance, organization and strategy. Moreover, we shall analyze the structure and dynamics of industries, networks and regions and so on, all of which are ostensibly microeconomic concerns. Indeed, by analyzing the economics of specific rules composing any micro system, our generic framework may be used for a wide range of empirical, theoretical and policy analysis.[4]

Yet these micro and meso considerations of generic change in individual agents, firms, industries and markets are not our ultimate analytical purpose, but rather the means to the broader end of macro analysis. Therefore, perhaps like all well-intentioned journeys, the insights and lessons learnt along the way may ultimately be of more lasting value than resolution of the final macro objective. Nevertheless, although evolutionary micro and meso analysis are well defined and coherent in themselves—and moreover may be applied usefully to the analysis of firms, markets and industries—their ultimate *raison d'être* (for economics as the discipline that deals with the economy) is analysis of the generic order of the economy as a whole.

But what is macro? One definition is to interpret liberally macro so as to refer to any plausible notion of a "whole" economic system. Evolutionary economics would then only be concerned with generic rules inside this boundary of the analytic whole. This allows us to adapt the framework of the whole economy to focus on partial aspects by treating the micro part (e.g., the firm) as if it were a "macro" whole, and still to reapply the micro meso macro framework. So although we maintain that evolutionary economics is ultimately for macro analysis, we allow that the definition of macro may be scalable to "macro units" smaller than the whole economy.

We call this partial evolutionary economic analysis, and propose that it may be a poten-tially powerful framework for the analysis of firms, industries or regions that are experienc-ing sustained organizational or technical change, or indeed any rule change, by focusing on these as meso trajectories that effect the macro of the firm or industry, and then analyzing the structure of generic equilibrium that results (see Chapter 5, Section 2).

In this way, we may apply the framework of evolutionary economic analysis to specific concerns of subject domains, such as business strategy, industrial and market dynamics or policy concerns facing regional growth, by isolating these components of the macroeconomy, and then treating them as if they were macroeconomies in themselves. This is of course in the same style as Alfred Marshall's partial equilibrium analysis and its attendant *operational ceteris paribus* assumptions. Our version of partial evolutionary analysis as a generically scalable macro makes *generic ceteris paribus* assumptions: namely, all other rules being equal. Partial generic analysis is partial, then, over the set of rules considered subject to re-coordination and change only and not generally with respect to all generic rules. However, and despite the overriding practical business and policy relevance and indeed the sheer mass of such concerns, we shall proceed to develop our macro framework as a general macro of the "whole economy" of all generic rules.

Both classical and neoclassical economics, of course, sought the same degree of generality and aspect. They both proffered their analysis as applicable to all aspects and domains of the economy and economic behavior. In what way, then, is our version of evolutionary economics different? And more importantly, in what way does it advance beyond what is already known?

We shall make our case for substantive novelty in the subsequent section, and which shall serve as an overview of this entire book to follow. But it will prove expedient to review the core principles of classical and neoclassical economics (or at least our interpretation of them) in order to show how the micro meso macro framework relates to classical and neoclassical economics, as well as specifically how and where it departs.

2.2   Classical, neoclassical and evolutionary analysis

The analytic frameworks of classical and neoclassical economics are fundamentally distinct in terms of their analytical horizon and focus, their attribution of mechanisms and the locus of the determinant laws (or rules). Evolutionary analysis shares some important relations with the classical framework as well as providing unified accounts of other aspects. Evolutionary economics is therefore not a radical break from modern economic analysis, but in many respects a return to classical themes. Classical economics—or political economy, as it was known at the time—can be summarized in four overarching points.

First, it had an implicitly long run view.[5] This was a natural consequence of the scope of their inquiry into the coordination of the whole economy and their endeavor to account for the social distribution of income and resources in terms of aggregate patterns of production and consumption, or transactions and transformations, that were deeply embedded and only slowly changing.

Second, their long run view was analyzed in terms of the coordination of aggregate resource stocks and flows. They developed a theory of aggregate production (although less of aggregate consumption) that explained the distribution of income between social classes, namely land, labor and capital, and of the income of these factors as rent, wages and profit. But this was the extent of their generic inquiry.[6]

Third, the classical economists viewed changes in technology, institutions, populations and suchlike as endogenous explanatory variables that were manifest, for example, in the division of labor and knowledge, or the structure of income with respect to ownership of resources.[7] Their overall view was that production and consumption resource aggregates were embedded in social classes (objective social rules) and in a technical context (objective technical rules) that defined a generic milieu.[8] Consequently, they viewed endogenous coordination and change in these object rules as the proper basis of economic analysis.

Fourth, the classical economists, as was typical of the best science of the time, held an objective view of the forces at work in the social and political economic system. Neoclassical economics eventually corrected this by seeking to account for subjective preferences as well, but the classical economists sought to explain the operational aspects of the economic order in terms of objective generic laws. They believed in the existence and power of the objective rules of technology, society, and even biology, and held that these would ultimately reveal and explain the potential and constraints of an economy. Moreover, they held that these laws were not unlike Newton's laws, in that they were naturally given and immutable.[9]

Classical economics, then, may be characterized by explanation in terms of:

1   A long run view
2   Aggregate resource flows between social classes of factors
3   Endogenous (generic) explanatory variables
4   Immutable objective laws.

The classical economists held a long run view of the economic system and the economic problem. They viewed the flow of income between factors (and the social classes that owned them) as the central object of analysis, and they viewed these generic structures as endogenous explanatory variables in the account of the wealth of nations. So, they understood the concept of the generic dimension to economic analysis, and, indeed, constructed their analytical framework about its natural and invariant structure.

They sought to explain the unfolding of these dynamic laws, as for example in Smith's account of the division of labor and the extent of the market, or Malthus's account of human wealth and fecundity. But they were not able to focus on this as a process that systematically involved generic novelty and radical generic uncertainty.[10] Generic (or evolutionary) economics, therefore, seeks to unfold classical analysis into the world of generic openness and to explore the consequences of that openness.

Yet that was not how economic analysis was to develop, as the revolution of neoclassical economics from the late 19th century onwards significantly redirected the course of economic analysis toward explanation, and did so in terms of:

1   A static view
2   Individual choice with respect to resources
3   Exogenous (generic) explanatory variables
4   Immutable subjective laws.

First, the neoclassical economists eschewed a long run view, and thereby an implicitly dynamic and open analytic perspective in favor of a short run static view of the economic problem. This was a strategic step to develop a proper science of the economy by basing it upon explicit and measurable market outcomes, rather than on the looser notion of social and material progress. But to achieve this, the long run focus had to first yield to a short run analysis of agent behaviors and market equilibria. This shift in time had tectonic effects upon the development of twentieth century economics, giving rise to new analytic continents of growth theory, macroeconomics, and "new classical" economics, as well as the subduction of microeconomics and decision-theoretic institutional economics.

Second, there occurred a profound shift in analytic focus from aggregate resource explanations to individual behavior. Classical explanations were between socially conceived factors such as land and landowners, capital and capitalists, labor and laborers, and with all of the political charge these conceptions carried. Neoclassical explanations were in terms of the individual and their given endowment, which included their budgetary constraints, preferences or technologies. The neoclassical economists rejected the notion that aggregate resource stocks and flows could properly explain the distribution of economic activity and income and, instead, redirected analytic explanation to individual behavior.[11] They sought explanations that were individually consistent, which is a good thing, but they left the door wide open for this interpretation to be generically representative such that agents need not analytically differ in any essential way. Thus was born *Homo Oeconomicus*, or generically invariant man.[12]

Third, neoclassical economics then endeavored to "exogenize" the classical explanatory variables relating to technology, institutions and populations by treating them as parameters without endogenous explanatory content.[13] This was, essentially, a forced move set up by the short run equilibrium framework and the explanatory focus on individual choice. The neoclassical strategy of maintaining exogenous explanatory factors is no longer a viable way forward. Neoclassical economics has done its due in providing the intellectual arsenal to combat the errors of socialism. But that is no longer the most pressing problem that modern economic systems face. Indeed, the economic problems of today look very much like the problems that the classical economists faced, namely why are some countries or regions wealthy and growing and others not? But it did certainly affect the character of economic analysis by effectively making microeconomic analysis seem as if it were a complete analysis of the economic problem, something the classical economists would perhaps have found curious, if not absurd.

Fourth, the final trans-substantiation the neoclassical economists made was to redirect the focus of economic laws away from the notion of objective laws of technology and society, and instead to center them about the cognitive and behavioral rules of the human agent. They developed a behavioral and subjective view of action and value that was intellectually and empirically superior to an objective factor-based view of labor time. This also worked to center the cognitive prior of rationality, and the institutional prior of freedom to choose and to contract, as universal rules of economic action. Truly, it seemed, the neoclassical economists had made explicit the subjective principles of objective wealth. In particular, they isolated the notion of a universal law of subjective rationality. The neoclassical economists were not dismissive at all of the notion that universal laws governed the economic system, but they insisted that these were the laws of subjects, not of objects.

Neoclassical economics was a significant departure from classical economics along a number of key analytic dimensions, all of which relate to generic revision. These can be read as follows:

1   Classical economics had a long run view of the economic problem, and was analytically focused about the social structure of resources. Neoclassical economics had a short run equilibrium view focused about the market. Generic change was therefore foreclosed.
2   Classical economics focused explanation upon these aggregates. Neoclassical economics focused explanation upon the behavior of individuals. The generic-operational relation was shifted.
3   Classical economics made the structure of technology and social organization endogenous. Neoclassical economics made it exogenous. Object rules were fixed.

4   Classical economics supposed an objective view of economic laws. Neoclassical economics insisted that the locus of the laws of the economic system were ultimately subjective. Subject rules were elevated, but still fixed.

The classical economists were aware of the centrality of generic rules (although obviously they did not call them that), but they lacked the appropriate analytical mechanisms to capture this insight. Neoclassical economics advanced by affording subject rules equal place with object rules, but otherwise abandoned this analytic insight and proceeded as if the generic domain were effectively invariant and all generic aspects were parameters.

Neoclassical economics emerged from classical economics through the systematic neutralization of the generic dimension of analysis. Evolutionary economics, in turn, builds from classical economics by systematically unpacking that same generic dimensionality. The upshot is that the analytic commitment to generic closure is the fundamental reason the neoclassical framework can never be the basis of an evolutionary analysis: for without generic openness and change, there can be no economic evolution.[14]

Yet there are important lessons from both classical and neoclassical economics that we may take for the development of evolutionary economics. From the classical economists, we retain a focus on the long run perspective. We also retain the notion that the organization of economic activities occurs in the context of a complex social and technical structure—i.e., a structure of resource holdings and a division of labor and knowledge. Furthermore, we adduce that we should treat these variables as endogenous dynamical processes, and, moreover, that the purpose of this understanding is to explain the growth of generic value, or wealth.

From neoclassical economics we learn that an analysis of the whole economy must never neglect individual choice and action because the laws of change issue from the actions of individual agents and not from the chimera of supposedly objective laws of class structure or technological determinism. We also learn from neoclassical economics that formal analytical models based on individual incentives and actions are a far superior basis for general analysis than conjured aggregates.[15] We deeply respect these principles and aim to build upon these points of classical and neoclassical economics.[16]

However, the main point of departure for evolutionary economics concerns the notion of universal objective or subjective laws. This is not an argument about whether the true laws of the economic system are objective or subjective, which is a neat split between classical and neoclassical economics. Rather, the essential point of difference concerns the notion of *invariance* in these laws, which both classical and neoclassical economics holds to as, respectively, invariant objective or invariant subjective laws. From the perspective of evolutionary economics, these laws are not invariant. Rather, they are many, and moreover they change as an open system evolutionary process.

This is not an "academic" or marginal concern, but rather goes to the heart of analysis of how economic systems grow and develop as open complex systems. To understand the deep structural dynamics of the modern economic world, we need an analytical framework that allows both its subjective and objective parts to change, and for that, we require generic analysis of the co-evolution of subject and object rules. This is, perhaps, the principle advance of evolutionary economics, as we conceive it, on classical and neoclassical economic analysis.

From this more general generic perspective, the framework of evolutionary (or generic) economics makes an analytic extension, and even resolution, of key aspects of classical and neoclassical economics. First, because an evolving economic system is presumed to be composed of both subject and object rules, evolutionary economics continues with the key insights of classical and neoclassical economics. Second, as an evolutionary framework, it insists upon the overarching empirical observation that these rules are not universal and invariant, but, perforce, precisely what can change. Yet, rather than proceeding as a critical assessment of classical and neoclassical economics, this argument can be made positive by formulating it in analytical terms as the micro meso macro framework.

2.3   The methodology of micro meso macro

The micro meso macro framework fits together as a general theory relevant from the macro perspective down, yet is best introduced analytically as constructed from the micro agent up. The elementary unit of economic evolution is the individual agent (see Section 3.2.1 below on *Homo sapiens Oeconomicus*) as a rule carrier who uses rules for operations and also originates, adopts and retains novel generic rules. The methodology of evolutionary economics is therefore based upon *generic individualism*.

The economic agent is the generic locus of the economy as both rule-maker and rule-user. The origins of value do not accrue from the mere existence of a novel rule, but from the new operations (i.e., transformations and transactions) the novel rule enables the agent to perform as the emergent value (i.e., growth of income or wealth) the rule creates and the agent realizes. In this way, evolutionary microeconomics conforms to the neoclassical doctrine of methodological individualism by locating the unit of explanation in the generic and operant properties of the individual agent.[17] However, there are two essential points upon which it differs: (1) rules change; and (2) there is a population of agents. This has micro, meso and macro dimensions.

In evolutionary microeconomics, the individual agent is composed of a system of rules. In an analogous manner, the neoclassical agent is also composed of a rule—an endogenous "law" stated in terms of rational cognition and behavior. However, in evolutionary microeconomics, these rules can and do change. Furthermore, the process by which they change is not an exogenous or complicating notion, but the prime focus of generic microeconomic analysis.

In evolutionary economics, then, there exists a population of heterogeneous agents rather than a representative agent with representative rationality and behavior. In consequence, both neoclassical and evolutionary microeconomics are methodologically individualist, in that they are analytically focused about the agent. In neoclassical economics, there is effectively one rule (the representative agent and its rationality rule) and it does not change.[18] In evolutionary microeconomics, however, there is a variety of rules and they do change.

Evolutionary mesoeconomics, in turn, addresses the rule and its carrier population. The core analytic concept here is the rule trajectory, which describes how a rule is innovated in one carrier and then subsequently adopted by many. This is a meso trajectory and the basic process of economic evolution. A meso trajectory, however, is composed of micro trajectories that describe the individual process of adoption and retention in each carrier. This study is the province of evolutionary microeconomics.

Evolutionary mesoeconomics, then, is the study of the trajectory of the population of rule carriers. The analytic unit of meso is the rule and its population. This furnishes us with an analytical framework for the study of qualitative change in the composition and structure of the rule, as well as the population structure of all other rules in the economic system. This leads naturally into a developmental theory of economic coordination and change by providing the conceptual building blocks for evolutionary macro analysis. This shall be the subject of Chapters 5 and 6.

By this stage, however, we are no longer specifically concerned with agents or operations, but with the meso unit (composed of a rule, a population and a trajectory) as the unit of analysis. Macro is then the study of the coordination of all meso as a generic order. It further follows (from axiom 1) that the coordination of the macro system can be composed into two levels: the deep coordination of how all rules fit together; and the surface coordination of how all carrier populations fit together. Evolutionary macro dynamics will be the study of how deep and surface coordination is de-coordinated and re-coordinated in consequence of a meso trajectory.

Conventionally, macro is the sum of micro. There are of course many analytically useful intermediate summations, such as a market, industry or sector, yet these are essentially ad hoc groupings of the micro parts into larger components that will then subsequently sum to the whole. In other words, there is nothing in economic theory that explains why the industries or markets fall where they do, or, then, why they change.

However, in the generic approach to evolutionary economics, there is no direct (or even indirect) aggregative relation between micro and macro. Instead, there is an aggregative relation between micro and meso, such that the sum of carriers of a rule forms a meso unit (composed of a carrier population), and then a structural relation between all meso and the macro whole. But meso is not invariant—for indeed the very definition of economic evolution is meso invariance—and so the aggregation of micro to macro has only static value and is undefined (i.e., meaningless) from the evolutionary perspective.

Instead, we come to macro not via aggregation of micro, but via the emergence and self-organization of meso populations and structures. Meso, then, is the whole of a rule, as in the population of all carriers of a rule. But it then forms a part of the macroeconomy. The economy is made of meso, and meso is made of a population of carriers. But analysis of a meso trajectory, such as that of a new technology or strategy, is only a partial generic analysis of the whole economy.

It is better to conceptualize the micro meso macro relation in terms of two methodologically distinct aspects: micro meso and meso macro.[19] The significance and centrality of meso to evolutionary economic analysis is that it is integral to both; micro is only explicable in terms of meso, and macro is only explicable in terms of meso. The micro meso relation, therefore, is that of the rule and its population of carriers. A meso trajectory describes how this population comes to be, a micro trajectory describes the process in each individual carrier, and the micro meso trajectory is a consequence of generic imagination, novelty and choice over the phases of origination, adoption and retention.[20] Yet is this methodological individualism?

From the perspective of evolutionary microeconomics, because a meso unit is ultimately explained by the behavior of individual carriers with respect to a rule, it would be better to call this *generic methodological individualism*, as it is specifically focused about the agent's behavior with respect to a generic rule, that is, the choice to originate, adopt and retain the rule, or not. This differs, then, from *operant methodological individualism*, which centers the role of agency in the analysis of the choice of transactions and transformations. The micro meso framework therefore seeks to explain the emergence of a meso population in terms of the generic behavior of individual agents with respect to extant and novel rules, and this we insist is a generic (or evolutionary) methodological individualism.

However, when we turn to the analysis of macro coordination and change, we are no longer dealing with agents as our base analytical unit, but rather it is the meso unit itself which is the analytical unit. A meso unit is of course not an individual, but a population. Meso macro, then, cannot be described as methodological individualism, but is better represented as a kind of *methodological populationism*.[21] In methodological populationism, the analysis of the macro whole is methodologically based upon the meso unit as the elemental part, but this elemental unit is not an agency, but rather a carrier population with respect to a single rule. Analytically, the basic unit that behaves is a population and will be often analytically treated as a statistical population, as is appropriate for open system analysis.

There are important empirical differences between methodological individualism and methodological populationism when viewing the same phenomena. These differences form the analytic dimensions of evolutionary economics. For example, suppose a macro-economy was made of one million agents and one thousand rules. Methodological individualism would say that the whole economy is composed of one million elementary (micro) units, but methodological populationism would say it is composed of only one thousand elementary (meso) units. Conversely, the macroeconomy may be composed of one thousand agents and one million rules. In this case methodological populationism would find the macroeconomy composed of a million meso units, not a thousand micro units. These scenarios have different implications for the number of rules each agent is carrying and the carrier population of each rule—such that in the first, each agent is carrying on average one thousand rules, whereas in the second each rule has an average carrier population of one thousand—but these are ultimately empirical matters. The point remains that the analytical units of meso macro are rule populations and not individual agents.[22]

This, in turn, is why the evolving macroeconomy is said to self-organize as rules and populations adapt to each other, rather than to equilibrate about individual operational choice.[23] This meso macro process can be explained at the micro meso level in terms of generic adoption as conditioned by the operational forces that work at that level (i.e., price and quantity adjustments).

But at the meso macro level, the process of self-organization is the emergence of a dynamical order through the coordination of rules and the coordination of populations. We shall leave detailed analysis of this to Chapter 5 below, when we arrive at the coordination problem of deep and surface macro. The upshot, however, is that the macroeconomy becomes ordered through the process of meso coordination of rules and carrier populations. The consequence, then, of a meso trajectory is the necessary re-coordination of this order at both the generic and operant levels. Evolutionary economics seeks to analyze and understand the nature of this process (i.e., trajectory) at the micro, meso and macro analytic levels.

Methodological individualism therefore is not wrong, indeed, from the micro meso perspective, it is an exquisite methodology. Yet because it neglects to account for the structural and causal properties of (rule) populations, it is insufficient for a general evolutionary analysis of the meso macro economic order. Therefore, evolutionary economics ultimately requires two methodologies—methodological individualism and populationism—in order to account for its two principal generic domains: micro meso and meso macro.

So, although the dynamics of a meso process can be analyzed in terms of the individual agent with respect to novel rules (i.e., *generic methodological individualism*), the macro process must be analyzed as the self-organization of meso units, which requires methodological populationism. Micro meso is therefore appropriately construed in terms of (generic) methodological individualism, but meso macro must be analytically approached from the perspective of methodological populationism. The framework of evolutionary economics must therefore embrace both, and is therefore irreducibly methodologically complex.

2.4   The complexity of micro meso macro

The micro meso macro framework is somewhat more complex than the standard micro macro framework, not least in that it is composed of three levels of analysis not two. But that is a consequence of the fact that the macroeconomic order is not well described as a linear aggregation of the operations of its parts, as it is a substantially more complex system than such a treatment would suggest.

Indeed, the global macroeconomy is quite possibly the most complex system in the known universe, and certainly at least as complex as the human brain or the global ecosystem. Yet although no neuroscientist would describe the mind as a simple neuron-to-behavior aggregation, and no ecologist would describe the ecosystem as a simple gene-to-ecosystem aggregation, the current mainstream paradigm of economic analysis is analogously that, namely the supposition that micro operations sum to aggregate economy.

Mathematically, this has always seemed expedient and elegant. But in practical terms relating to how macroeconomic systems coordinate and change, it is at best autistic, and at worst dangerously irrelevant, in that it utterly ignores the considerable variation, structure and complexity in the systems and populations that compose the micro meso and meso macro order. As such, we believe that the additional analytic complexity that the micro meso macro framework requires (over the micro macro framework) is more then compensated for by a deeper insight into the evolutionary and self-organizational processes that shape the future path of the macroeconomic system.

Economies are complex systems, and so their analysis cannot be simplistic, which is what the mechanistic ontology and analysis veers toward. Complex systems are always systems of rules, and the macroeconomy is (to echo Hayek) the most complex there is. The micro meso macro framework enables us to represent this complexity in an analytically viable way.

We lose no essential principles here, as we in no way reject the preferences and actions of agents as determining the course of this process, as well as its space. But rather we analytically circumscribe these as determining the scale and scope of each meso population. From there, however, we must shift our analytic focus to the interactions and self-organizations of rule populations as the building blocks of an evolutionary macro analysis.

The evolutionary economic agent is not an isolated definitive datum, nor a component of an aggregate, but is a generically sovereign social being that enjoins with other agents in the origination, adoption and retention of rules. This is simultaneously an individual and social process at once that, through the process of generic coordination, results in the emergence of new meso populations that, thereby, create new components in the macro structure and a new order in the macroeconomy. As such, both the individual agent and the meso population are building blocks of evolutionary economic analysis.

Yet rule *cum* adoption frequency is not micro, since all members of the population have this status. It is also not macro, since meso is only a component part of macro. Within the total economic system, the meso unit takes an intermediate position that both embraces micro, and is in turn embraced by macro. The concept of meso is not therefore an exotic and delicate flower to be appreciated only at the margin of economic analysis, perhaps after the real analysis of micro and macro is done. Rather, it is the rudiment of economic concepts such as market, industry and technology, all of which only make sense in relation to a meso unit as a generic rule and its carrier population.

The reason these otherwise naturally meso concepts have remained static and exogenous—even when it is observationally unambiguous that markets change, that industries change, and that technologies change, and moreover that the most immediate and pressing economic problems that agents face is in dealing with such change—is that the aggregate logic of the micro macro framework cannot have it otherwise. It is the theory not the reality that is wrong. In turn, we suggest that our version of evolutionary economic analysis can help redress this problem.

Economic evolution is a process of endogenous transformation in the rules of an economic system.[24] This necessarily means that there is change in micro agents (i.e., agents adopt new rules) and that there is change in the macro order (i.e., the population structure of activities changes). But this cannot be directly mapped from micro to macro, because at the core of change is meso.

Yet the evolution of meso rules is precisely what modern economic analysis presumes invariant or exogenous. This affords it a certain and not inconsequential analytical power in the formulation of elegant solution concepts, yet it is facile when directed toward the economic problems of change. As every entrepreneur and World Bank economist knows, it is ultimately the analysis of the problems of change that reveal the qualities of a good framework. The micro meso macro framework is, we argue, geared precisely toward the analysis of such change.

2.5   Conclusion

The micro meso macro framework endeavors to explain how macroeconomic systems evolve through generic change, that is, via the re-coordination of meso rules in consequence of micro generic choice. It argues that the economy is made of generic rules, and economic evolution is change in both these rules and their populations, and so is always a meso process. Evolutionary micro analysis, then, is the study of individual rules, carriers or systems that compose a meso unit, and evolutionary macro analysis is the study of coordination and change in the structure of all meso units as a whole.

Evolutionary economic analysis therefore differs from classical and neoclassical analysis by the introduction of a meso domain. The classical economists, as we have already examined, built their analysis upon a theory of resource aggregates, an endogenous view of "generic" factors, and a view of object laws determining resource distributions. In turn, neoclassical economists sought to explain the economic order in terms of a disaggregation of resource aggregates to individual endowments, the exogenization of all generic factors, and a universal focus on rational choice as a subjective theory of operational value. Yet both classical and neoclassical economics held, in different ways, an invariant generic view that, therefore, precluded the possibility of evolutionary analysis.

The foundation of evolutionary economics is the scope and possibility of generic coordination and change. This means a focus on generic rules rather than operational resource aggregates, an endogenization of this via the meso analytic domain, and an evolutionary theory of value from the interaction of the methodological individualism of micro meso and the methodological populationism of meso macro.

From the perspective of evolutionary analysis, the origins of value are neither uniquely subjective or objective, nor micro or macro, but arbitrated by the meso locus of all. To explain the nature of value in an open system is the ultimate purpose of evolutionary economics. To that end, it seeks to integrate both micro and macro explanations. It does this with meso.

Micro meso macro is not therefore an added analytic complexity, but rather a method of reducing the real complexity of economic evolution to just three distinct analytical domains. Once captured, they can then be further reduced to just two components: a micro meso focus about agent carriers and rules; and a meso macro focus about rule populations. Economic evolution is instigated by a novel idea and results in the evolutionary process of generic change and re-coordination. Micro meso macro is, in this view, a logically derived and ontologically warranted framework for the analysis of generic coordination and change in an open economic system.

3 Generic micro analysis

- Introduces the micro unit of analysis as agents and agencies
- Examines knowledge and value in carriers
- Analyses a three-phase micro trajectory

3.1 Introduction

The subject of this chapter is generic micro analysis, which is the study of how generic rules are carried by micro units (which we distinguish between agents and agencies), and the process by which a novel rule is originated, adopted and retained by such carriers. The economy evolves when a new idea is adopted for use by others, such that there is generic change in individual carriers. This chapter is concerned with this process at the level of the micro unit.

However, economic evolution is not just the study of this micro evolution then aggregated up, but rather a trajectory of adoption by many new carriers of a rule results in a new rule population, a process we call a meso trajectory. As explained in the previous chapter, we require this because it is the building block of evolutionary macro analysis. This chapter on generic microeconomics is not therefore the foundation of evolutionary macro analysis, but rather the building block of meso analysis, which is the subject of Chapter 4. For this reason, it is important to recognize that the process of generic change in the micro unit is an element of the emergence of a meso unit as a population of rule carriers via the process of a three-phase meso trajectory.

Evolutionary microeconomics is, in essence, a generic microeconomics. It concerns the generic subject and object rules that compose the "knowledge carrier" as the micro unit of evolutionary analysis, and analysis of the process by which such micro units generically change. It is important to immediately note that micro generic change is *not* an evolutionary process because it is not a (meso) population process. Rather, generic micro is analysis of individual generic change in the knowledge base of the micro unit. This is a process of course, as all change is, but a process of imagination, planning and experimental endeavor, for example, or of learning, habituation and other individual behaviors, including of course rationality.

This chapter seeks to account for the unit of evolutionary microeconomic analysis in the form of a rule carrier and to analyze how it changes generically. We distinguish an agent (*Homo sapiens Oeconomicus*) from an agency (e.g., a firm) as differing by the nature of the rules they can carry, and the way they originate, adopt and retain these, which is to say by their generic distinctions. Overall, we shall seek to define the analytical meaning of a micro unit and a micro trajectory from the generic perspective.

Evolutionary microeconomics provides a generic analysis of the micro unit whereas neoclassical microeconomics is essentially concerned with the operational domain of analysis, namely choices, prices and transactions. Evolutionary game theory, behavioral and experimental economics, on the other hand, with their focus on how the agent acquires novel strategies (i.e., behavioral or technical rules), conforms broadly to our version of evolutionary microeconomics.

We proceed as follows. In Section 3.2, we define the micro unit of evolutionary economic analysis, which is composed of: the agent *Homo sapiens Oeconomicus* as a rule carrier; the agency as a socially organized rule carrier; the environment of the micro carrier; knowledge and information in carriers; and orders of rules in the carrier. In Section 3.3, we introduce the notion of a micro trajectory in terms of a process of origination, adoption and retention. This micro generic process, whereby individual agents and agencies become generically different, is the building block of both the growth of knowledge and of economic evolution.

Agents have knowledge that they use for operations. When agents acquire new knowledge, they can perform new operations. This is the origin of new value, and the source of economic growth. The phenomena of economic evolution is this process as it plays out at the meso macro level of population dynamics and structural change of the economic order, but at the micro level, the micro unit in economic analysis is a knowledge carrier, such as you or I, acquiring and applying knowledge. When that knowledge changes, what we can do changes. Evolutionary economics is the study of this process as a whole, but evolutionary microeconomics begins with this generic experience at the level of the human *agent* and the organized and bounded systems they can form, which we call *agency*.

3.2   The micro unit

The micro unit of evolutionary economics is both the agent *Homo sapiens Oeconomicus* and the agency, which is an organized system of agents such as a firm. Agents and agencies are both micro units because they are primary carriers of generic rules.

In evolutionary economics, then, a micro unit has two basic properties: (1) it carries and operationally uses rules (as knowledge); and (2) it can originate, adopt and retain new rules (as new knowledge). It has knowledge, and it can acquire knowledge. A micro unit is therefore a process unit of knowledge. Different micro units therefore differ by the knowledge they carry and how they change it.

This leads us to pointedly distinguish between the micro unit as a subject agent (i.e., *Homo sapiens Oeconomicus*), and the micro unit as carrier of knowledge via a bounded system of social coordination (e.g., a firm). Both carry knowledge and are endowed with resources and exist in an environment, yet they differ with respect to the sort of knowledge they can carry and the way they acquire it. In essence, organizations do not invent ideas, people do, but often in the context of organization. The way organizations learn and retain knowledge is different from the way individual agents do, and this is a central focus of evolutionary microeconomics.[1]

However, this difference is immaterial in neoclassical micro, which makes no generic distinction between micro units. Indeed, in its pure form, it allows agents to differ only operationally (i.e., via resource endowments) in order to generate the incentive to trade.[2] Standard microeconomic analysis therefore addresses the operational coordination of agents with given preferences, technologies, institutions and resources and finds no room for generic change, but as exogenous effects. But evolutionary microeconomics is centrally concerned with both what the agent knows, and how they acquire new knowledge. This will help us explain the emergence of a meso unit along a meso trajectory as an evolutionary process of generic micro change. What matters, then, are the analytic properties of the micro unit that relate to the generation and adoption of novel generic rules.

It has been said that the methodology of evolutionary economics is best described as "dynamics first."[3] This is not a cute way of saying that evolutionary economics is not about statics, but instead makes a fundamental point about the focus of analysis as being primarily concerned with the process of change. Our framework too is "dynamics first," and this begins with our conception of micro as a generic unit of knowledge. Consequently, we are not much concerned with the operational actions of the agent, the prices they face, or with whom they trade. That may seem to have dispensed with "economics" at the outset. But that is to misunderstand the implication of "dynamics first"; or, as we prefer it: *generics first*.

When a micro unit acquires new knowledge, and so new operational capabilities, the world becomes marginally generically different. When this happens as a process or trajectory, the economic system evolves. To analyze this process, we begin with the micro unit at the point of generic "first contact," which is the mind of *Homo sapiens Oeconomicus*.

3.2.1 Homo sapiens Oeconomicus

Homo sapiens Oeconomicus (HSO) is generic man.[4] It differs from the classical notion of *Homo Oeconomicus* in the sense that it explicitly recognizes the element of *Homo sapiens*, namely the "wise man," and not just as a tool-making and tool-using animal, but as a rule-making and rule-using animal that experiences generic change. *Homo sapiens* is capable of knowledge, and *Homo Oeconomicus* is capable of economic operations. *Homo Sapiens Oeconomicus* is capable of new knowledge for new operations and, therefore, is the carrier of economic evolution.

The standard view of economic man—*Homo Oeconomicus*—focuses on a single quality, namely the ability to rationally deduce optimal behavior in any operational circumstance. This is often expressed in the notion that economic man responds to incentives, with the implication that if you know the structure of incentives facing an agent, then their behavior will be predictable by reasoning through their self-interest. This is an inherently sensible proposition that makes economic analysis powerfully applicable to any incentive-structured context. However, by bringing the operational structure of incentives to the foreground, the agent disappears into the background as a placeholder for anything that behaves strategically with respect to incentives, whether a gene, a mouse, a person, a corporation or a nation. The power of neoclassical microeconomics (including game theory) is that it entirely abstracts from *Homo sapiens* to focus on generalized rationality.

The cost, however, is that it dispenses with what we do already know about human cognition and behavior from related sciences of evolutionary biology, anthropology, psychology, neuroscience, sociology and ethology, in prime instance. In the past few decades, there have been significant attempts to redress this abstraction with the empirical realism of behavioral economics, experimental economics and now neuro-economics, all of which seek to account for the particular features of *Homo sapiens* that impact upon their economic behavior and inherent preferences. This is a welcome turn, and indeed these new domains of microeconomics clearly fit within the ambit of evolutionary microeconomics. Yet because they begin essentially as corrections to an extant problem, namely the lack of specifically human properties in the economic agent, they subsequently tend to systematically miss the broader differences between the human economic agent (*Homo sapiens Oeconomicus*) and other agents.

Evolutionary microeconomics is also based squarely on the empirical realism of the human agent (*Homo sapiens*) in the economic context. However, it begins with the essential difference between man and other animals as being not the operational attribute of rationality, but rather in the propensity to originate, adopt and retain novel rules. *Homo sapiens Oeconomicus* is in this sense a rule-making and rule-using animal, and it is this unique ability that explains why complex economic systems are the unique province of human systems, and, moreover, why they are capable of evolution.

Rationality and technology are not uniquely human. Rationality is trivially observed in animal (including human) behavior, wherever preferences and incentives are defined.[5] And of course, many animals make and use tools, as for example monkeys with ant-digging sticks or otters with shell-smashing rocks. But the extraordinary uniqueness of *Homo sapiens* is not the operational aspect of the use of materials for specific purpose, nor even the making of rules that can be adopted and used by other agents, but to have an awareness and contemplative (i.e., rational) *imagination* of the rule-making process.

The ability to anticipate the consequences of a rule through the creation of internal models of the world is central to generic behaviors associated with the origination, adoption and retention of a novel rule.[6] The human economic agent does not just discover rules, as if ideas were natural resources to be harvested through sufficient investment,[7] but invests in the construction of rules via internal models of the world that are then used to develop further rules for acting in that world. Rules build rules (or knowledge builds knowledge) and, in this sense, the generic structure of the economy is autocatalytic.[8]

The uniqueness of *Homo sapiens Oeconomicus* lies in these higher-order abilities as manifest in the creation of 2nd order rules for changing and developing 1st order rules. The creation and transmission of these "generic rules" is the basis of what we call culture,[9] a point that resonates across the social sciences, but it is also the foundation of economic analysis from the evolutionary perspective. Tool-making and tool-using man is of course a very special animal, in that he makes more and better tools than other animals.[10] But rule-making and rule-using man is something altogether different, namely the foundation of an emergent realm of evolution in the generic domain.[11] We have been calling such an agent *Homo sapiens Oeconomicus*, and have defined it as our irreducible economic micro unit.[12]

From the ancestral environment of the African savannah to Wall Street, or the production of antediluvian hand axes to the manufacture of semiconductors, economic man has but scaled-up and reinforced a basic propensity to originate, adopt and retain generic rules.[13] The modern economy is not a miraculous and *ab nihilo* gift of providence, but a systematic consequence of the origination, adoption and retention of rules. These rules accumulated, achingly slowly at first and over vast eons and untold generations (i.e., prehistory), but then gathered exponential pace to the present.[14] Analysis of economic history has a tendency to fixate on particular technical or institutional revolutions, such as writing, property rights, agriculture, chemical engineering or eBay. But as Whitehead said,[15] the greatest invention was the invention of invention itself. This is not a cliché, but rather an understatement. The nature and causes of the wealth of nations lie not in social governance, nor in national or even private resources, but in the human mind's abilities to originate, adopt and retain generic rules.

It is the capability of agents to become generically different that is the foundation of the growth of economic systems, whether considered over months or millennia. This ability to become generically different is the fundamental quality of *Homo sapiens Oeconomicus*. Lots of animals can carry generic rules, but only the human animal can create and carry not only rules but also rules for changing rules (i.e., 2nd order or mechanism rules).[16] For this reason, only the human animal has yet progressed to generic evolution. This means not just the creation of economic systems, for lots of animals have economic systems,[17] but for the continued evolution of those systems.

Economic man is a biological animal, albeit one with a well-developed instinct for abstraction and social coordination. Other animals have well-developed adaptations for living in cold climates, hunting fish or for flying at night. We have none of these things naturally, but instead an innate ability to originate, adopt and retain generic rules through higher-order rule capabilities (i.e., what we call 2nd order rules). The upshot is that where other animals live instinctively in what we call ecosystems, we build our own, and, more-over, what we build is ever changing. These are economic systems, and this process of change is called economic evolution. We now effortlessly live in cold climates, hunt fish and fly at night, and that has nothing to do with biological evolution of the human organism, but rather is a consequence of economic evolution in our ability to originate, adopt and retain knowledge. Economic man is a generic animal.

Conceptions of economic man are inevitably freighted with ideology, so let us be explicit. The essential point is that although man is biologically and developmentally composed of certain preferences, computational abilities and social propensities, economic man can create and adopt and retain new ideas. This ability is the product of what we call 2nd order (or mechanism) rules, and the consequence is that the economy is a naturally open system. However, this process involves the co-evolution of the subject rules of the individual agent and social rules reflecting the interests of coalitions, such as firms or nations, in which individuals are embedded. The ideology of evolutionary economics, then, is neither the perfectibility of man or society imbued in the concepts of "rational man" or "socialist man," but closer to the spirit of "renaissance man" with respect to the optimistic prospects of new knowledge and to the goodness and naturalness of both an open society and an open mind.

Homo sapiens Oeconomicus is therefore a generic carrier of rules (i.e., knowledge) and is capable of originating, adopting and retaining new knowledge, and so of becoming generically different. From the evolutionary perspective, this is the "difference that makes a difference."[18] Evolutionary microeconomics is therefore centered about the scientific analysis of how humans acquire and use "generic rules," as well as how they create new rules. Rationality is important in this process, but so too is systematic imagination and learning.

3.2.2   *The agency as socially organized carrier*

The generic ability to use and adopt knowledge is not limited to agents however, but also extends to firms, organizations, households, networks and other socially organized systems of agents, which we shall call *agencies*. Agencies are more than just aggregations of agents (and agent knowledge), but harbor emergent evolutionary competences and capabilities to both carry and use new sorts of knowledge and to originate, adopt and retain new sorts of knowledge. A simple example is that although no one who works at Boeing knows how to make an airframe, but Boeing does. Moreover, it can acquire entire new capabilities (e.g., missile guidance engineering) that no single individual could. The agency can know more than the sum of the agents that compose it, and can learn new things that no individual agent could comprehend. Indeed, the wealth of nations is built upon little else, and this emergent capability is due to the coordination of social rules (see Section 1.4.2).[19]

The evolutionary theory of the agency is therefore based upon two analytic rudiments. First, agents carry different knowledge to agencies because they are composed of different rules, namely emergent social rules [CB+S] that give them emergent capabilities over agents [CB] (see Section 1.4.2 above on the generic rule classification). Second, agencies originate, adopt and retain rules differently to agents in consequence of the social structure of a meso trajectory. Specifically, the origination process is socially organized [S^1]; the adoption process is socially organized [S^2]; and the retention process is socially organized [S^3].

An agency can therefore adopt and carry different kinds of knowledge (i.e., more socially and technically complex rules) than an agent, and it does so in a different way because an agency's micro trajectory is itself part of a socially organized process. We shall examine this distinction in Section 3.2.3 below. The key point is that agencies carry different knowledge (i.e., generic rule complexes) to agents, and acquire that knowledge in a different way.

This distinction matters because it enables us to explain why firms exist. Ronald Coase and others famously justified the existence of the firm on the operational grounds of minimizing transaction costs. But the generic reason for the existence of the firm (and other forms of social organization) is that they carry different kinds of knowledge. Specifically, they can carry more complex forms of knowledge. Firms exist not just to minimize operational transaction costs, but more fundamentally they exist to organize new knowledge (i.e., generic rules) that no individual human could coordinate. The economic system is composed of more knowledge than the sum of all individuals knows, and that difference is carried by social rules.

Three basic points can be made:

1   The theory of the firm can be analytically decomposed into a generic theory of the firm and an operational theory of the firm.
2   The generic theory of the firm then distinguishes between the firm's generic knowledge (its competence) to originate, adopt and retain rules for operations, that is, 1st order rules, and its generic knowledge (its capability): to innovate, adopt and retain new rules, that is, 2nd order rules.
3   Some novel rules will require new carriers (due to inappropriate extant 0th or 2nd order rules), while other novel rules can be adopted by existing carriers.

There is an innate materialist tendency among economic scholars and the lay public alike to attribute the drivers of the wealth of nations to the systematic effect of technological change in technical rules [CB$\underline{ST}$]. This is not untrue by any means.[20] But it does systematically overlook what is just as powerful a force, the evolution of social rules for organization of agents into agencies, namely [CB$\underline{S}$T]. Technical change moves the economy, but so too does change in the rules that organize people. Evolution in social rules, including agencies, is essential to economic evolution.

The primary force by which knowledge grows is through specialization and re-coordination. This order is developed and carried by socially organized carriers of rules, or agencies, which are, in turn, coordinated by market relations. The significance of socially organizing rules to form agencies, and the competence and capability of these systems to carry knowledge, has long been known. Indeed, it was first dramatically illustrated by Adam Smith's pin factory example. Smith is of course widely known as the founder of free market economics, but his seminal illustration of the power of markets was on how agents combine into an agency through the specialization and coordination of generic rules that improved, by orders of magnitude, the productivity of the individual agents within the pin factory through social rules to organize their knowledge.[21] The point is not the efficiency of organization, but the efficacy of social rules to coordinate agents to create knowledge that no individual possessed, that is, how to make 4,800 pins a day, when the best individual knowledge could "scarcely make but one."

This process of course depends upon technology, but also upon social rules of coordination. Smith said nothing about a coordinator, and indeed, that was his point: rules that coordinate agents into agencies, however these may occur, have power because they coordinate generic rules in agents into emergent capabilities that are advanced by no agent individually, yet are achievable, and often effortlessly, by the social organization of knowledge. Economic evolution would be severely and profoundly limited, as it is in even the smartest of other animals, if it were constrained by the generic capabilities of a single agent to carry knowledge or rules. But with the social organization of rules, these limits are transcended, and, indeed, in the course of economic evolution, this is a routine process.[22]

Agencies, then, are socially organized carriers of rules. Besides, we emphasize that this is not merely an aggregation of forces, as when a group of agents socially organize, say, to lift a log or calculate a logarithm. An agency is not simply a shorthand for a scaled-up human power that could be done by one agent if repeated x times, or in one go by x agents. Rather, the power of agency comes not from the leverage of agents into agencies, and nor even through the application of rational specialization—as for example ants will build an ant colony—but from the power of social rules to yield new possibilities and opportunities. Agencies organize agents into structures of knowledge that otherwise do not exist through any aggregation of those agents, but rather through the emergence of specific connections that yield generic value.[23]

Agencies have knowledge to solve coordination problems between individual agents (which was of course Coase's point). Yet this is foremost a problem of efficacy (i.e., about what works at all), rather than a concern of efficiency (i.e., about what works best). This is, for example, the difference between generic and operational competition—generic competition is the enterprise of originating a new way of solving an economic problem, whereas operational competition occurs when a market position is exploited.[24] For evolutionary economists, the value of markets is the value of generic competition in novel rules.[25] But evolutionary economists also recognize that agencies have additional capabilities to grow knowledge of a higher-order complexity than that of individual agents.

Much of the knowledge base of an economy is carried in social agencies. It is incumbent upon evolutionary economists, then, to account for the extent of that knowledge, and how it changes. Toward this end, the evolutionary theory of the firm is based upon the presumption that, in an open system, all generic positions of knowledge, profit and rent eventually decay and so firms must constantly innovate in order to compete and prosper. In this world of ongoing enterprise competition, generic microeconomics seeks to explain the elements of emergent complex social structure that results.

3.2.3 *Generic knowledge and value in micro units*

We now turn to the question of (a) the nature of the knowledge base of the micro unit, and (b) the value of a micro unit from the evolutionary perspective. Yet we suggest that the generic framework can provide some structure and perhaps clarity to this discussion by highlighting two key analytic distinctions.

Knowledge and information are distinct concepts, but they stand in a process relation to each other. Information is first accessed or acquired, but when it is retained for ongoing use it becomes knowledge. Not all information therefore becomes knowledge. However, there are two analytic levels of information and knowledge: generic and operational.

Generic information is information about a rule or the codified form of the rule. Generic knowledge is the rule as adopted and retained by the carrier for use. Generic knowledge is the core of the knowledge base of a micro unit, whether agent or agency, and is the result of a three-phase micro process (which we discuss in Section 3.3).

Operational information is information (i.e., signals or messages) about the economic environment, such as about resource conditions, prices, plans, etc. Operational knowledge is the use of that information in the application of generic rules.

A micro unit therefore has both generic information and knowledge, and operational information and knowledge.[26] The knowledge base of the agent or agency is composed of both generic knowledge and operational knowledge, but is centered, from the evolutionary perspective, about generic knowledge. Generic and operational information, however, resides in the environment, whether this is in other agents and agencies or "in the market." Knowledge is in the micro unit, information is in the market (or meso) environment.

The micro unit uses information, and must continually seek to acquire new information, but it is made of private knowledge, which is, following our distinction, of two sorts: generic or "rule" knowledge determining what it can do, and operational knowledge determining how it does it. Agents have different knowledge because they receive different information and process it in different ways. Agents may also respond to the same operational information differently because they have different knowledge. Yet for coordination to be possible and for information (generic and operational) to be communicated, micro units must share common knowledge or understanding.[27]

But for communication, knowledge must be encoded as information and then decoded into knowledge by another agent, a process that naturally induces variation and differential replication.[28] Knowledge and information are therefore two states of the same evolutionary process of micro units with a complex and variable knowledge base. The knowledge of the micro unit is analytically composed of cognitive, behavioral, social and technical rules, but it is also analytically composed of generic and operational knowledge. Change in operational information induces operational adjustments, and analysis of that process is the subject of neoclassical economics. But change in generic knowledge induces generic re-coordination of rules, and that process is best analyzed with evolutionary economics.

Micro units are difficult to value from the evolutionary perspective because, in essence, quality in a closed system is not identical to quality in an open system. This is an entirely practical concern, namely on the proper market value of a firm or even agent in an evolving economy, but one with deep analytical implications, as it forces us to confront the question of the value of knowledge and the components of this value. Our method is to ask again the question from the generic perspective in order to account for the value of not just rules for operations—i.e., 1st order rules composing the knowledge base—but also for the value of 0th order constitutional rules and 2nd order mechanism rules whose value is only revealed in an open dynamic system context. We call this framework *generic accounting*.

The central idea is that the *evolutionary value* of a micro unit is attributable not just to its 1st order operational rules (which is the basis of standard operational accounting), but also to both its 0th order rule environment and the 2nd order mechanism rules it has developed.

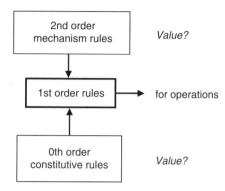

Figure 3.1 The rule structure of a micro unit.

For the micro agent or agency, 0th order rules are effectively given, or at least are difficult to change without movement to another market, city or country, or by the entrepreneurial creation of a new firm with its own "culture." A micro unit may of course endeavor to change the generic environment by lobbying parliament or writing pointed memos, but 0th order rules are generally endemic to a micro unit's operation. However, 2nd order rules are well within the generic control of a micro unit and variable in its evolutionary potential.[29] A micro unit is therefore composed of three classes of rules and subject to selective evaluation on all three. The value of a carrier is not exclusively predicated on its current operational income from 1st order rules, but also by its complement of 0th order and 2nd order rules (see Figure 3.1).

The 0th order value of a micro unit depends upon its position with respect to constitutive rules. Coordination can be achieved by a carrier positioning itself in a favorable political, legal and cultural environment, or by the reconstruction of that environment for the same end. Carriers that can reconstruct their constitutional environment to fit their 1st order capabilities have an evolutionary advantage. At one extreme this constitutes rent seeking, at the other, innovation. Either way, 0th order reconstitution or generic adaptation to 0th order rules is a relevant aspect of the evolutionary valuation of micro units.

But the main value (or knowledge) difference between micro units accrues to their 2nd order differences to originate, adopt and retain new rules. Some people and firms are very good at this, others are not. Some can do all aspects well, others are more specialized. Some agents and agencies invest heavily in this capability, and others little. This makes no difference from the static analytic perspective, but makes a huge difference from the evolutionary perspective. People and firms differ systematically not just by what they are allowed to do and what they can do (i.e., 0th and 1st order rules), but also by what they are capable of learning to do (i.e., 2nd order rules). A micro unit with 2nd order capabilities to originate and adopt new ideas is of different generic value to a micro unit that lacks these abilities.

In consequence, a micro unit is generically accounted for not just by its 1st order rules for operations (which is the focus of operational accounting), but also by the context of 0th order rules that constitute its position, and the 2nd order rules that define its adaptive capabilities to originate, adopt and retain new 1st order rules. Evolutionary accounting therefore seeks a systematic appreciation of the generic value of 0th and 2nd order rules across the balance sheets of people, companies and nations alike, and not just their 1st order knowledge capital. Markets are not irrational when they value a new company with a novel idea or unique market position or a new business model significantly above what its P/E ratio (a purely 1st order operational metric) would justify. Rather they are attempting to value its 0th and 2nd order rule components.[30]

The complexity of the economic system therefore lies not just in the generic rules and operational systems they form, but also in the computational overhead of constitutive and mechanism rules. Indeed, we should not be surprised to learn that, like DNA, most generic rules are "non-coding." The actual complexity of the generic order of 0th, 1st and 2nd order rules will be perhaps significantly larger (computationally measured) than the apparent complexity and value of the operational market order of the agent's 1st order rules.

Evolutionary microeconomics therefore seeks to unpack this value by accounting for the value of 0th and 2nd order rules with respect to the 1st order knowledge base of the carrier. 1st order rules make for competence, but 0th order rules define the "generic rents" available to that competence, and 2nd order rules make for new "generic profits" through the capability to originate, adopt and retain new ideas. Generic rents are defined as income from the use of existing rules; generic profit is the income from the origination of novel rules. The upshot is that the value of the knowledge base of the micro agent is more than just what they can deliver to a given market, but also their competitive capabilities and competence to meet new markets with new knowledge.

We can summarize our position so far as such: there are two micro units in evolutionary economic analysis—the human agent, and the agency of humans. These are evolutionary micro units because they carry knowledge and can originate, adopt and retain new knowledge. The nature of this knowledge is complex, as it consists of both generic and operational components which are themselves composed of subject and object components. Furthermore, the valuation of this knowledge is also complex, as it must account not just for operational knowledge, but also for the rules that constitute permissible actions (i.e., 0th order rules) and also the rules that grow knowledge (i.e., 2nd order rules). From the evolutionary perspective, then, a micro unit is a complex analytic entity composed of a matrix of orders [0 1 2] and classes [CBST] of rules.

Yet such recognition is just the beginning of evolutionary economic analysis, as a micro unit can also change its knowledge base through the origination, adoption and retention of a novel rule such that the micro unit becomes generically different. The process by which this occurs is called a micro trajectory and it results in a micro unit becoming generically different, changing both the knowledge base and value of the micro unit. This generic difference is the elementary and process unit of economic evolution.

3.3   The generic micro trajectory

Economic evolution originates in a micro trajectory, as the process by which a micro unit acquires a new generic rule and thus changes its knowledge base. Economic evolution is the meso process by which a population of carriers acquires a novel rule, but at the micro level this is the process, that is, micro trajectory, of a single agent originating, adopting and retaining new knowledge. The micro trajectory is the component of a population that unfolds in the dynamic of a meso trajectory.

A micro trajectory traces the process of a novel generic rule as originated, adopted and retained for use by a micro unit. All knowledge in the economy passes this way. Evolutionary psychologists tell us that the human mind enters the world not as a "blank slate" but pre-programmed with a complex suite of evolved instincts and behaviors that developmentally and experimentally calibrate to the environment.[31] Yet this is not true in economic evolution, where new carriers must actively acquire all the rules they will use. They do so as a three-phase micro trajectory.

We have indicated that a micro trajectory consists of an agent or agency originating, adopting and retaining a rule, yet this is not generally so. In most cases, what is originated, adopted and retained is not a rule but a *rule complex* of subject and object rules. An innovation that results in the diffusion of a new rule through a carrier population often involves some complement of cognitive and behavioral rules for new ways of thinking or new actions, and of social and technical rules that reorganize people and material things. A rule complex, then, is composed of cognitive rules [C], behavioral rules [B], social rules [S] and technical rules [T]—[CBST]—and we may analytically expect to observe micro co-evolution between the subject and object components of the rule complex as subject rules adapt to object rules and vice versa.

Each rule complex will be structurally unique in the weighting and significance of its subject and object components. Some rule complexes will be heavily weighted by a technical rule and much less on new social rules (such as new markets or distribution), and perhaps with less significant behavioral and cognitive changes (as when updating to a new model of a familiar product). But other rule complexes may freight much more through new behavioral rules (e.g., new ways of using a familiar technology). Unless otherwise specified, we shall use the term rule below to imply a rule complex—[CBST]—that will have, in its particular composition and weighting, a characteristic generic signature. This is a similar concept to the notion of bases in nucleic acid (AGCT) in that a gene (a rule) is composed of a signature structure of its bases (its rule complex). Each rule in an economy will have a "generic fingerprint" so to speak, and each novel rule introduces further variety into the economic "rule pool."

The analytic structure of a micro trajectory is therefore that of the origination, adoption and retention of a rule complex involving a suite of subject and object rules. But the micro trajectory of "the rule" will be structured by the nature of these rule components, how they interact with each other, and how they integrate into the carrier environment. Contemporary adoption-diffusion models, however, often assume a "representative"—phase micro trajectory in the form of a binary switching model (e.g., cellular automata or network models) or by some transition function on an aggregate measure, and make no distinction between subjective and objective components of the process. Contemporary evolutionary learning models, on the other hand,[32] have a high degree of complexity and a strong focus on the problems of bounded rationality and uncertainty that renders them difficult to generalize. Between these extremes, a micro trajectory is the process of a carrier changing its generic state or knowledge base in consequence of acquiring a new rule in order to perform new operations.

We define this process by which a micro unit becomes generically different as a three-phase structure—origination, adoption, retention—over *two* types of carriers—agents and agencies—in terms of three orders of rules—0th, 1st, 2nd—and over four types of rules—[CBST]. This generic micro $3 \times 2 \times 3 \times 4$ space is analytically appropriate, we suggest, for the representation of any rule in any micro unit at any point in space and time in order to provide a useful micro foundation for meso and macro analysis of economic evolution.

3.3.1 *The origin of evolution: micro 1*

The origin of economic evolution is the origination of a novel idea in the human mind. Origination is something that always begins in agents, not in an agency, although this may of course, and often does, happen to an agent working in an agency. Generic origination is plainly supported by the ideas and behaviors of other agents, as well as the social rules that connect agents and the technical rules that supply structured resources and embedded knowledge. Indeed, without these things generic origination cannot occur. Yet although necessary, these are not germinal conditions. For the origination of a novel rule is ultimately the product of the human mind as it is a process of not just search and discovery, but also of recognition and awareness that novelty has been generated and that the idea is efficacious. Machines may learn to analyze, and firms may learn to organize creative teams, but these are both technical and social prosthesis to the root of generic novelty in the human mind. Neither machines nor organizations can muster the cognitive ability to become aware of a new idea, nor to marshal attention, imagination and energy to its cause, although they certainly may assist.

This naturally raises the question of how the human mind originates novel ideas, which requires first a distinction between global and local novelty. Global novelty in a micro meso 1 rule is the creation or discovery of a rule complex that is original: in that the rule elements it composes—C, B, S or T—are novel, or the connections between them are novel. Inventions are like this by definition, but only span the T and sometimes S space. Global generic novelty may be substantially original in its subject [CB] aspect, its object aspect [ST], or both. Specific cases will differ. Local novelty, on the other hand, consists of the origination of a generic idea in an environment subject to the condition that this generic idea has been known already in at least one other environment. Global generic novelty is the first carrier of a novel generic rule. Local novelty is the first carrier of that rule in each new environment. The analytical difference between global and local novelty is instrumental since perfect information transparency cannot be assumed generally and/or simultaneous inventions or reinventions are possible. The dynamic of the origination and diffusion of novelty may depend significantly on environmental differentials, and advanced micro meso models should allow for their specification.

There is no single theory of the origin of generic novelty in a carrier, but rather many theories of micro origination, each of which starts from different assumptions and emphasize different aspects.[33] Some theories suppose that all generic novelty pre-exists hidden within a space and that agents avail themselves of those idea resources (often modeled as improvements in some fitness measure) by searching the space. More resources devoted to search, or more efficient search methods, will be expected to yield more novel rules. This is a common treatment in both production function and agent-based modeling, as is the reverse assumption of the random arrival of generic novelty to an agent who stays, as it were, in the same place and filters a stochastic flow of novelty.[34]

At the other epistemic extreme, novelty is not discovered by search but rather emergent from an imaginative or creative act in the space of "unknowledge."[35] In this view, a novel rule is created by assembling existing elements into new combinations and seeing new connections.[36] Consequently, the greater the environmental and cognitive diversity, and the better the framing and organizing of "the sound and the fury," the greater the creation of generic novelty.[37]

Some theories of novelty generation emphasize the internal environment, such that novelty is an operation of the mind. Others emphasize the external environment, where novelty is out there to be discovered. Some emphasize the origin of novel rules as the product of "idle curiosity," or the luck of the prepared mind, while others model it as the outcome of ongoing problem solving and tinkering.[38] Others yet favor the notion that novel rules can, like everything else, be subject to controlled production processes.[39]

Therefore, so without delving into the work of psychologists and others on creativity and problem solving,[40] it is apparent that there are many different theories of the origination of a novel idea, and moreover that they range across wholly different ontological, epistemological and analytical realms.

These different approaches can be organized within a generic framework in which the origin of a novel rule is endogenously explained by the operations of extant rules. Following evolutionary realism, we insist that this is a product of the human mind interacting with its environment. The criterion for generic novelty is that the rule must produce viable operations, where the conditions of viability are tested in the carrier's environment. Micro origination is an entrepreneurial act composed not just of the creation of a new idea, but of how that idea solves a real problem and, moreover, how others might adopt that rule for the same purpose. The "act of creation" in micro 1 therefore extends beyond the "eureka" moment of a new idea to conceptions of organization, finance, market strategies and technical forms that transform an idea into a venture. Entrepreneurship, therefore, is a complex process involving more than just the origination and recognition of an idea or the discovery of an opportunity, but also making connections and building structure in order to realize that idea or opportunity, which is a point we shall emphasize in Chapter 4 in relation to meso 1.

In our framework, origination in a micro unit is conceptualized as a consequence of its 2nd order rules for origination. (We subsequently propose that micro adoption and retention can be explained by 2nd order rules for adoption and retention.) The point is that generic novelty is not a random exogenous mutation, but rather a consequence of cognitive, behavioral, social and technical rules that have themselves been originated, adopted and retained for the task.

Carriers will naturally vary in the nature and efficacy of these 2nd order origination rules. At one extreme, there will be those with no capacity to originate novel rules, or an ineffective capacity due to internal dysfunction or a poor fit with the environment. At the other extreme will be those with highly effective and viable 2nd order origination mechanisms that enable them to consistently produce high-quality novel rules. Naturally, there will be variation in the capability and effectiveness of origination rules over a population of agents, as well as in the capability to generate new origination rules. There may also be specialization about the focus of these rules, such as about a particular aspect of a problem or environment, implying that some 2nd order origination rules are adapted to work best with specific other rules (which are possibly in a different carrier). The 2nd order rule approach to micro origination therefore has appropriate analytical scope to focus upon the mechanism of novelty generation without getting swamped in the fascinating details of say neurophysiology, bounded rationality or social context, but yet without losing these essential dimensions.

So micro origination is analytically conceived as a function of the "innovation rules" of a carrier, and there will be variety in these 2nd order rules over the carrier population. But there will also be complexity in these 2nd order origination rules, as they are not just a rule but a rule complex of [CBST] rules for origination, all of which must fit together to make an effective origination mechanism. These elements may fit together with varying degrees of efficacy, implying that an origination mechanism may fail to coordinate. For example, cognitive and behavioral rules may be appropriate and viable, but technical rules may not, rendering the entire rule complex unviable. Leonardo Da Vinci had a viable concept (C) of a helicopter and he was, as an inventor, possibly ready to go for a test run for demonstration purposes (B), but he had neither aluminium and a combustion engine (T) nor the means to make others believe in the viability of his novel idea (S). Or all rules may be appropriate, but yet the entire mechanism may be ineffective if some rules are applied at an inappropriate scale or intensity.

A further aspect of 2nd order origination is that an agency will likely exhibit a more complex origination mechanism because it can both apply further social organizational rules to the task and make use of specializations of operations and knowledge within the elements of the mechanism, for example, in a R&D laboratory. These same specializations might also be achieved through other forms of social organization, such as collaborative networks, public infrastructure or market relations.

In sum, the generic approach to the origination of novelty in the micro unit emphasizes that variety is neither random nor exogenous, but the endogenous outcome of rules for origination. Carriers originate, adopt and retain knowledge about how to generate new knowledge. These origination rules exhibit variety over carriers, and selection pressure operates on this variety via the efficacy of these mechanism rules.

3.3.2   *Adoption: micro 2*

Micro phase 2 is adoption, which is an uncommon term in evolutionary theory because it is irrelevant in biology, which is sufficiently defined in terms of replication and selection. But in evolutionary economics, selection is the process of differential adoption of novel ideas. Rules that are adopted are both replicated and selected for. Rules that are not adopted are selected against. The selection mechanism in economic evolution is differential adoption (leading to differential growth of populations). But the crucial analytic point is that this is not only a process of selective ejection or winnowing, but also and primarily a process of selective import or adoption of ideas. Central to all evolutionary social science, then, must surely be the *mechanism of adoption*.

As such, the adoption of a rule is explained in evolutionary economics by the existence of 2nd order adoption rules. This is the process by which a new rule is integrated into the extant rule system. In some cases, this will slot neatly into the micro unit, in other cases it will require major refurbishment. There will also be instances where an originated rule proves ultimately unadoptable because of generic incompatibility, rule configuration problems or a lack of operational viability. But in all cases, the method of evolutionary economic analysis is to explain generic rule processes with mechanism rule processes, such that rule adoption is explained by hypothesized adoption rules.

Rules are adopted by the agent when they expect that the new rule will contribute positively to their generic capabilities and operational outcomes, whether this is measured by status, utility, profit, happiness or whatever. We therefore presume *generic choice* rather than any process of generic sublimation or imposition as a consequence of "power."[41]

Generic rules are adopted because of the expectation of operational payoff to a new rule via the ability to do something new or better. Or they may also be adopted as part of a risk-management strategy to increase variety in the portfolio of the micro unit's capabilities, even though these may only be called upon in special circumstances. Expectations and reality, however, may fail to match, and the micro unit may adopt rules that reveal unexpected consequences, for better or worse. Generic adoption is therefore not equivalent to learning, which is mostly an operational process of adaptation and feedback to and from the environment, but rather an act of conjecture about what knowledge will, in the future, be valuable.

The economics of such rule adoption are seemingly straightforward—rules have *adoption costs* in time and other resources, and *adoption benefits* in terms of changed performance and capabilities. So the rational agent adopts new rules up to the point when marginal improved performance equals marginal adoption cost. In reality, however, this is far from straightforward, for there are substantial uncertainties and "unknowledge" about both the costs and benefits. Generic adoption is therefore, fundamentally, a conjecture about value and an act of enterprise.[42] Indeed, the very fact the rule in question is novel means that expectations must be partially conjectural and without complete analysis, as by definition that is impossible when dealing with genuine novelty.

A rule is never adopted *ab nihilo* into a blank and infinitely transformable space, but always into a specific structure of other rules, which then act as a selection environment. Of course, such blank slates can be artificially created by starting a new firm or organization, but even then there will still be preconception and implicit formatting freighted through employees, technology and institutions. To be adopted, a novel rule must fit into its environment, and a failure to do so may be attributable to the rule, the environment, or both. A catalogue of reasons why a rule may or may not fit, or why some environments are better than others, would be innumerable.

Analytically, however, we can redirect the question to the mechanisms that constrain and facilitate the process of rule adoption. These are 2nd order adoption rules, and they facilitate the process of a novel rule fitting into an extant system by coordinating the changes that must happen for adoption to occur.

Yet adoption is not just about generically fitting into a system, but also establishing operational viability. This adaptive and experimental component is a further part of the adoption process because operational viability is a key selection criterion for adoption to proceed to micro 3 with retention and embedding. An idea that fits with a carrier's other ideas but is operationally non-viable, or vice-versa, may yet fail to be adopted. Its success in doing so will be guided by 2nd order adoption rules that fit the rule into the carrier by guiding its experimentation and learning.

The micro theory of generic adoption is well represented by the substantial body of research and literature on learning in evolutionary environments.[43] However, as above, learning is not always adoption, and so we insist upon analytical recognition of the generic-operant distinction. Adoption is generic learning when it is concerned with the new actions and structures of a carrier in consequence of a new rule.[44]

Generic learning or adoption changes the operational capabilities or competence of the agent or agency rendering them not just new awareness of the environment and its consequences (i.e., operational learning) but more fundamentally opening new possibilities for operations in their environment, including by way of the transformation of the environment. Learning is adaptation to a world, whereas adoption is a generically marginal process that changes the world. Learning is a process of adaptation, but adoption is a marginal process of differentiation and progress. Learning stabilizes known advances, but adoption drives them. Adoption, not learning, is therefore the core mechanism of microeconomic evolution via generic change in micro units.

Adoption, however, occurs differently in agent and agencies. Generic adoption of a novel rule in *Homo sapiens Oeconomicus* means the adoption of a novel cognitive and behavioral rule, meaning that the agent is, however marginally or significantly, now thinking and behaving in new ways. This invariably will be accompanied by new social and technical rules, and which may indeed be significant drivers of this process, yet the basis of generic change is that agents now think and behave in new ways. The adoption of rules into agencies involves all of this, as well as the social rules to organize and coordinate this process. Social rules enable a higher degree of coordination and complexity. They enable the creation and integration of new specializations, along with the power to draw upon this new distributed computation to achieve new operations.

Agencies can adopt more complex rules than agents, and so agencies have greater value than the sum of their agent and resource components.[45] The adoption of a rule into an agency may involve more than just the addition of a new element into an extant process, but the re-coordination of the entire social organization of the process that ultimately results in a new "division of labor." Adam Smith[46] explained how the existing coordination of knowledge is the basis of wealth, and evolutionary microeconomics can explain how this changes through the adoption of novel generic ideas.

When agents adopt a novel rule it gives them new capabilities, but it does not change the boundaries of the agents, such that even though they may become more valuable, the size of their brain will not change. But when an agency adopts a novel rule its boundary may change to become bigger or smaller.[47] The implication is that it may come to carry new viable specializations and competences, making for new connections with other carriers and so new structures of coordination. The implication is that there are classes of rules (complex rules) that can only be adopted by agencies because only agencies have the integrated specializations to adopt them. No one person can adopt any kind of "making a computer" rule or "getting to the moon" rule, but an agency can. The scale and scope of what sorts of rules can be adopted is therefore a function of the sorts of organizational structures (i.e., agencies) that can exist.

Rule adoption into an agent or agency is also conditional upon the ability of the carrier to cope with the uncertainty of the event, to manage the process of change and to finance the resource cost involved. A failure in any one of these domains may doom the adoption prospects of a rule. Successful adoption requires an ability to cope with uncertain outcomes and there are many ways that this may occur, from unreasonable faith in the value of an idea (i.e., gumption or enterprise) to a well-designed portfolio to hedge risk in all directions. But that alone is not enough, for the carrier must also be able to manage the changes in generic and operational order that the new rule requires, both in terms of dealing with new connections and operations as well as errors and unintended consequences, and to do so in a manner that does not destroy the extant value of the incumbent system.

The study of these 2nd order adoption rules forms a major subject domain within the personal psychology and business management literature. Further, the ability of a carrier to adopt a novel rule must in some way depend upon unencumbered savings or the acquisition of finance to cover the resource costs between adoption and eventual operational return. A rule may fit and be able to be integrated into a carrier, but yet fail to be adopted because of financial constraints ranging from a failure to secure collateral to a failure to persuade a principal of the value of the adopted rule. An evolutionary microeconomic analysis of adoption therefore seeks to account for the range of factors that both facilitate and constrain the adoption of a novel rule.

Micro 2 is analysis of how the generic adoption of a novel rule into a carrier occurs. This process differs between agents and agencies and has many systemic (non-substitutable) aspects. It is complex and specific to an environment. But it is also the core of an evolutionary microeconomics as the "transition function" by which the knowledge base of the micro unit becomes different. To adopt a new rule is to become generically different, and generic difference is the driver of economic evolution.

3.3.3   *Retention: micro 3*

Micro 3 is the phase of a carrier retaining a novel rule for ongoing use. In an agent, this may be seen as the process of habituation and embedding of the rule into the agent's cognitive and behavioral rule complex or "lifestyle."[48] It may also be the routinization of a cognitive, behavioral, social and technical rule complex into the "competence" of the firm. Retention, in both cases, is the capability to maintain value with rules for retaining ongoing operations we call 2nd order retention rules. Micro 3 is the phase of a carrier continuing to carry a rule. There are several mechanisms by which this can be achieved—for example, continuous transmission through skilled agents, accumulation by habits and routines or embedding in material artefacts. But all mechanisms have the same outcome, namely a novel rule retained in an agent or agency for ongoing use. When an agent or agency adopts and retains a rule in this way, it becomes part of a new generic population, which we shall examine in Chapter 4 below. Yet before one can become many, one must first become one. A rule is therefore retained in a carrier by a suite of 2nd order retention mechanisms that function to stabilize the knowledge base of the carrier through the normalization or habituation of the novel rule through new cognitive or behavioral habits and routines that either yield some higher operational reward or further open the space of operational possibility.

3.4   Conclusion

Evolutionary microeconomics offers a generic account of the micro unit as either an agent—*Homo sapiens Oeconomicus*—or an agency, which is a socially organized system of agents. A micro unit is a rule carrier composed of 0th, 1st and 2nd order rules that form its knowledge base both for operations (1st order rules) and for changing that knowledge base (2nd order rules). The process by which the knowledge base changes (i.e., by which the micro unit becomes generically different) is represented as a three-phase trajectory of origination, adoption and retention.

Micro units must acquire rules, and for that they require a mechanism (2nd order rules) for originating, adopting and retaining rules. This mechanism drives the process of a micro trajectory in which a novel idea is originated by the carrier, adopted into the carrier and then retained for ongoing use. All generic rules a carrier carries are acquired through a micro trajectory and thus the effectiveness of the mechanism will determine the rules it can acquire.

In evolutionary microeconomics, differences in 1st order rules across carriers (and therefore the operations of the micro unit) are explained by differences in 2nd order rules. The rule mechanism, however, is not just for acquiring the starting set of rules, but is the way in which the carrier adapts to a changing environment and competes in that environment through the enterprise of developing new generic capabilities to solve existing problems better or to solve new problems.

The distinction between agent and agency is important for evolutionary economic analysis. Agencies are more complex than agents, in that they carry more complex knowledge structures than a single agent can, and also because they originate, adopt and retain knowledge in more complex ways. However, the distinction is also important because it is agents, not agencies that are the prime locus of the origination of knowledge through search, discovery and recognition processes that are essentially cognitive.

Yet the central premise of evolutionary microeconomics is that micro units are generically different. They do not all have the same knowledge base, but differ in the 1st and 2nd order rules they carry. Moreover, these differences enable them to become more different still.

The generic approach enables a deeper understanding of the nature of the knowledge base of micro carriers and how it changes through the process of origination, adoption and retention of new generic rules. This process of becoming different, and then of re-coordinating those differences through markets, is the origin of the wealth of nations.

The implications for microeconomic analysis are clear and surely striking: it is not operant rationality that ultimately explains wealth, but rather the generic capabilities to originate, adopt and retain rules for operational use as well as to unlearn rules that are no longer operationally useful. Economies can grow because knowledge can grow, and knowledge can grow because agents can create, adopt and learn to do new things, and so can become generically different. Evolutionary microeconomics is the study of how this happens.

4   Meso analysis

- Introduces the meso analytic unit and defines the meso trajectory
- Discusses the concept of a meso population and meso variety
- Examines the relation between meso trajectories and market dynamics
- Discusses causes of the scale and velocity of meso trajectories
- Examines micro strategy over a meso trajectory

4.1   Introduction

In the previous chapter, we defined the concept of a micro unit as an individual carrier of a generic rule and a micro trajectory as the process by which the rules of a micro unit change. In this chapter, we define a meso unit as a *population* of carriers of a rule and the *trajectory* or process by which the population emerges as successive adoption of a generic rule. A meso unit is therefore composed of a generic rule, a population of micro units and is the result of an ensemble of micro trajectories. This complex process is a meso trajectory. Yet as population, it forms a single unit in the analysis of coordination of the whole economy, which is a "macro" analysis of the coordination of *all* meso units.

But we will get to that in Chapter 5. In this chapter, we examine how a meso unit emerges. This is, in effect, the analysis of how a population grows from one original carrier (i.e., the entrepreneur or innovator) to eventually stabilize with perhaps a great many carriers (i.e., the new institution). This generic process of differential population dynamics changes the "economic order." It results in agents using new knowledge in new connective ways, which results in new firms or changed firm boundaries as well as new markets or changes in existing markets. It results in new flows of profit and finance, and the resolution of technical and organizational uncertainties, as well as in changed distributions of incomes and activities. A meso trajectory is the process unit of structural change in the knowledge base of the economy, and this is an evolutionary process of the emergence of a new population as a meso unit.

This chapter therefore concerns the central themes of post-Marshallian and post-Schumpeterian economics, namely population dynamics in relation to the evolution of industries and new technologies, market dynamics and the "creative destruction" that results. But it also concerns the central themes of Austrian, Behavioral and Institutional economics, namely in the nature and dynamics of knowledge, uncertainty, profit, expectations and market institutions. Our point of synthesis is that these can all be configured as aspects of generic change in a population. For this reason, a meso unit is the central analytic unit of evolutionary economics.

We proceed as follows. In Section 4.2, we begin with the dynamics of a meso unit as a three-phase process: origination (or innovation); adoption (or the emergence of the population); and retention (or the stabilization of the population as an institution). In Section 4.3, we discuss major analytic aspects of the concept of meso. These include the implications of meso as a population and of variety within a meso population, the relation between meso and market analysis, and causes of the scale of a meso unit and the velocity of a meso trajectory. In Section 4.4, we turn back to micro meso analysis and reexamine micro generic strategy from the perspective of a meso trajectory. This involves particular reference to the behavior of entrepreneurs and firms in relation to enterprise competition, the existence of uncertainty and profit in consequence of a novel generic rule, and to the normal process of change in organizations and markets over a meso trajectory. Section 4.5 concludes.

4.2   A three-phase meso trajectory

A meso trajectory is a three-phase process of the origination of a rule as a discovery (invention), its adoption into a population of carriers as evolutionary dynamic, and its retention by that population as an (evolved) institution. A meso trajectory results in a change in the division of knowledge in the whole economy (macro) and begins with an original micro trajectory (micro). Economic evolution is the transition of the whole economy from one state of generic order to a new generic order in consequence of a meso trajectory.

The three-phase structure of a meso trajectory is homologous to the three-phase micro trajectory, in that in the first phase a novel idea is originated, in the second phase there is a process of adoption, and in the third phase the rule is retained and embedded for ongoing operations. The difference, however, is that whereas a micro trajectory all plays out within a single agent or agency, a meso trajectory proceeds over a population of micro units. Origination in micro is about imagining and recognizing an idea, but in meso origination is about getting an idea to market or public. Adoption in micro is about fitting a new rule into the *whole* internal environment of a carrier, but in meso it is a process of rule diffusion by way of new interactions with *parts* of the external environment. Retention in micro is the normalization of a rule into the new routines of a carrier, whereas in meso it is the stabilization of the new population structure as an institution.

A micro trajectory is a generic process in which a single agent acquires knowledge. A meso trajectory is the process that constitutes the basic unit relevant for describing the coordination of knowledge of the economy. The micro process is not evolution, but generic learning or adaptation. Instead, economic evolution begins with the meso process because it is here that we arrive at the process of differential growth in generic rules as actualized in carrier populations. A meso trajectory results in a change in the structure and division of knowledge in the whole economy and begins with an original micro trajectory.

4.2.1   *Meso 1: origination*

The first phase of origination—meso 1—is the phase of the innovation of the rule. This process begins, by definition, in the mind of an agent (micro 1) and is completed with the embedding of the rule for operations (micro 3). The result is the emergence of a new rule and the germinal rule population, or elementary meso unit.

The origination of a meso unit is the product of an entrepreneur engaged in innovation. The result is a challenge to extant knowledge, the proposition of new knowledge, and a new monopoly position. Schumpeter rightly called this creative destruction, for it disrupts existing operational patterns with the implications of a new idea. But with generic analysis, we can adduce a less poetic and more analytic description of this process.

First, meso 1 constitutes the "boundary crossing" of a rule from the purely private state of the originating agent to a state where it can be adopted by other micro units. A novel generic rule is not just an idea, nor even a great idea, but must be able to be adopted by other agents or agencies. This "boundary crossing" is the essential difference between a micro invention and a meso innovation, and a necessary condition for the emergence of a population of actualizations as a meso unit. A rule that cannot be generically communicated (i.e., encoded and decoded) is just a person with an idea; it is not entrepreneurship and it is not innovation. We shall consider the strategies that can be employed to control this process in Section 4.4.

Second, meso 1 is often the origination of a rule complex of subject and object rules (see Section 1.4.1 above). It therefore involves not just the innovation of a technical rule, but also cognitive, behavioral and social rules. The entrepreneur who innovates a rule for a new product or service is not just an inventor, and may not even be the inventor of the rule, but the agent or agency who makes it generic, that is, able to be adopted by others and used for operations. This will often mean that the entrepreneur makes two contributions: (1) the "discovery of the opportunity," often in the form of a new technical rule or a new use of existing technical rule; and (2) the creation and organization of the necessary accompanying rules for thinking, behavior and social organization to render the novel rule viable. This may involve campaigns of persuasion that endeavor to change other agents' thinking and behavior, the provision of organizational and financial structures to make these changes possible, and the creation of new market structures to facilitate these changes.

Third, the origination of the rule population in meso 1 is characterized by a particular market structure: namely monopoly. But this is a natural and normal form of monopoly that is a consequence of the entrepreneur creating or opening up a new market about a new generic rule and then being the first to occupy it. This is very different from a monopoly that is the result of a micro unit driving out all other carriers, and so being the last to occupy it. If it is possible for others to adopt the generic rule, and so challenge with improvements to the rule or its operational form, then there need be no welfare concern. Indeed, this is generally the precursor to competitive rivalry.

Fourth, meso 1 proceeds in a fog of uncertainty with the expectation of profit. In a competitive market economy there are few unexploited operational opportunities, yet entrepreneurship and innovation still thrive and new profit opportunities are created by introducing new generic ideas. By definition this happens in the face of uncertainty over several dimensions. The scale of uptake of the idea, the efficiency of the market, the way it will fit into and be used by carriers, the likely competition and collaborators, the time it will take, and the reflux from other institutions, are all classically or generically uncertain. That is, there is no way to calculate a rational solution *ex ante* because the data required to do so does not, by definition, exist. Rather, that information will be created *ex post* by the meso 1 process. Expected profit is not a necessary incentive to undertake this endeavor, but it is often sufficient.

The origin of profit in an economy is the consequence of the introduction of generic novelty in meso 1, and profit is therefore a fundamentally generic (or evolutionary) concept. But why does the micro unit seek out this costly, risky, uncertain, complex and difficult endeavor? Following Schumpeter, many economists presume some kind of special intrinsic motivation or personality type along the lines of a "will to action" or a preference for risk while seeking to earn income with the possibility of striking it rich. The reason entrepreneurs innovate is therefore viewed as lying somewhere between a deviant pathology and an adventurous spirit.

Yet why entrepreneurs seek profit through generic novelty has, from our perspective, more to do with rational avoidance of bad consequences than with hopeful seeking of fortune or redemption. The motive to profit is not the drive to accumulate savings and capital (*à la* Marx), nor the drive to heroic achievement (*à la* Schumpeter), but issues from rational fear of the consequences of the innovation of others.[1] A failure to innovate does not necessarily affect one's stock of savings or capital and even where there are psychological consequences of such failure, these do not impact greatly on the generic economy. However, a failure to engage in enterprise competition through continual innovation does affect the profitability of a knowledge carrier because it will result in the loss of resource flows from other carriers. Failure to innovate can result in the death of an agency, and in the long run, this is an inevitable consequence.

Analysis of meso 1 from the survivor bias of the history of technological trajectories reveals a panoply of different behaviors and strategies that eventually resulted in new institutions, industries, markets and fortunes. Analysis of meso 1 "in the wild" however reveals a much more chaotic drama in which most ideas fail, whether by a tragedy of missed timing, or a missing rule, or by a comedy of errors that seems absurd only after the event. Yet the failures of meso 1 are just as interesting and arguably more so than the successful ideas that go on to meso 2 because they reveal the many ways in which the process of economic evolution can go wrong and fail to achieve coordination.[2] Of the many who try only some will succeed in crossing the generic starting line with a rule fit for adoption.

4.2.2 *Meso 2: adoption*

Meso 2 is the adoption of a generic rule into a population of potential carriers.[3] It is, therefore, analytically defined as a population dynamic. Yet because population change is only meaningful in the context of other populations (i.e., meso change is relative to other meso) comprehensive analysis of this shall wait until meso macro analysis in Chapters 5 and 6.[4] Still, we can make five key observations about meso 2.

First, the meso population can grow only because humans can become interested in new rules and seek to learn and retain them so as to do new things and imagine new ideas. It is surely common sense these days to allow that openness to new ideas is a trivial axiom for the possibility of enterprise, but that has not always been so. The possibility of economic evolution depends upon an instinct to novelty that conditions not just the supply of the novel idea by the entrepreneur but also the demand for novelty by the potential adopter. Meso 2 arrives (innovation as first adoption) with a match between the supply of a novel idea and its first adoption in markets with demand for that rule. The key point is that conjecture, imagination and the prospect of profit were involved in both sides of that transaction. Economies can evolve because all agents can be imaginative and daring, not just entrepreneurs.[5]

Second, this is a path-dependent process in which what happened before affects what can happen next. Operationally and under perfectly competitive conditions this cannot happen, but generically it is normal in meso 2 because rules become embedded such that some come to depend on others. Selection mechanisms then operate over composites and cannot reach directly into the rule components. Yet these are far from rare occurrences but rather the endemic circumstances of generic selection thus rendering it an invariably path-dependent process. Because novelty is difficult to value agents will take cues from each other, especially those perceived to be knowledgeable, including the market outcome itself, implying a further feedback mechanism to reinforce generic path dependency.[6]

Third, and more generally considered, meso 2 is a selective process with differential growth of the rule vis-à-vis other rules. Path dependence is the selection effect of lagged structures of adoption,[7] but this is only one of the selection mechanisms operating over meso 2. The space of selection targets is outlined by the order of rules [0th, 1st, 2nd] and their class [CBST] and can strike at any permutation of these, let alone the effects of local environment in space and time, resulting in an enormous complexity of selection dynamics. During meso 2 some agents (as carriers of rules) will prosper and others will suffer, some firms will grow and others will die, some institutions will resonate and others will fade away. Meso 2 will be characterized by "interesting times."

Fourth, meso 2 is a knowledge process in which what is publicly known changes. This is a logical corollary of the definition of a meso dynamic as a series of micro trajectories, but that is a trivial observation. More important is the feedback to other agents about the value of different variations upon the rule or the effect of different contexts and other such matters that an investor (i.e., a potential adopter) will be concerned with. Meso 2 is a growth-of-knowledge process in which an entrepreneurial conjecture about the value of a generic rule is put to the test of other agents. Through this process a private idea as a novel conjecture is subjected to public scrutiny and evaluation in the form of enterprise and adoption. The outcome will be change in the understanding, behavior and expectations of some agents, which is of course how all economic knowledge grows. Meso 2 therefore begins with high uncertainty, but toward the end of the adoption process the cumulative effect of experience and experiment will have greatly reduced that uncertainty and knowledge of the rule will settle into understandings.[8]

And fifth, meso 2 is a generic adoption process in which agents acquire new capabilities and competences. This will have operational implications in the form of new transactions and transformations, and the study of these implications is central to meso 2 analysis. The meso 2 domain will be characterized by turbulence in operations. These may involve new contracts, new finance, new management, new teams, partnerships or firms, new markets or networks, new production process, new strategic directions, new legislation, new culture and eventually in all cases newly realized desires for the solution not previously offered. During meso 2 a novel rule is being tested and explored and so new operations will be occurring. Selection works on these operations, but so also does replication. Indeed, the replication of viable operations with the novel rule (i.e., novel types of transactions or transformations) is precisely what changes in meso 2. An effective measure of operational adoption dynamics must be a central theoretical and empirical plank of evolutionary economic analysis.

Generally, meso 2 is a process of competitive enterprise, or, in its noun form, *enterprise competition*. Meso 2 is by definition restless and turbulent.[9] It is a competitive process in the literal sense of a race in which no one knows who wins until the end, although with the twist that there is no end to the race, only participant or player exit. Meso 2 is the exhilarating phase of market capitalism at its best and at its worst, both creative and destructive and ordered and chaotic all at once, creating new solutions for some, and new problems for others. This is the normal run of generic competition and the cutting edge of economic evolution as ideas are tried and tested. Competitive enterprise is competition to innovate and therefore the powerhouse of economic evolution. It is a process that feeds on imagination and uncertainty and generates the real profit that underpins the real economic growth that Adam Smith, Joseph Schumpeter and Friedrich Hayek wrote about. The domain of 0th and 2nd order rules that generate the conditions and strategies of a meso trajectory therefore effectively define the space of competitive enterprise.

4.2.3   Meso 3: retention

The third phase of a meso trajectory—meso 3—is the ongoing retention of the rule in the population of carriers as the statistically stable replication of the rule through continued use. By meso 3, the rule has formed into an *institution*, such that the carrier population replicates and the structures it requires are maintained. When all those who will adopt have, we enter phase 3 of a meso trajectory: the ongoing retention of the generic rule in a population.

By meso 3, uncertainty has been transformed into risk and generic profits have been extracted. The size of the market is revealed and good strategies have been learnt. Price movements will become stochastic as the information conveyed by them is fully expropriated.[10] Stable patterns of activity will predominate and transactions costs will fall as risk premiums vanish and efficiencies of scale and scope are produced. Maintenance and service niches will open up, and expertise will be well defined. Expectations about the rule will converge, and any environmental, cultural or political implications will become pronounced. The rule will become embedded in material artefacts and human behaviors. Cognitive and behavioral rules will normalize into habits and routines, and social and technical rules will become dominant and standard. Meso 3, as such, will begin to look a lot like the world that neoclassical economics describes. Yet the difference is that this world is explained in generic analysis whereas in neoclassical analysis it is simply assumed.

The meso 3 process is the retention of the generic rule as an institution.[11] From the evolutionary perspective, an institution is defined as a rule population that statistically replicates at some stable frequency. This definition emphasizes that an institution is not just a "general rule" but refers to a stable rule population.[12] Micro and macro consequences derive from and in turn reinforce the replicative stability of the carrier population. In turn, the meso phase of retention is the self-organization of the novel meso rule to the generic set of all other rules. This is a process of mutual adjustment and local ordering to form an emergent and self-replicating micro and macro structure of rule and carrier coordination.

4.3   Aspects of meso analysis

4.3.1   Meso as population

For economic evolution to occur, many agents must originate, adopt and retain the novel generic rule. Evolutionary microeconomics is the study of how that happens each time. It addresses how an agent acquires the operational use of a new rule. However, this is the generic adaptation of the agent, not the evolution of the agent. An agent cannot evolve any more than a single gene or particular organism can evolve.[13] All they can be is differentially adapted to their environment. In economic evolution, as in all evolution, it is the carrier population that evolves, not the carrier. Evolution is a population process and meso is the analytic concept we use to represent a population.

A meso unit, therefore, has the properties of a population, which include a size and distribution of the population—i.e., variety in rules—about a population mean. We may also attribute other factors such as a rate of change or a spatial distribution.[14] "Population thinking" is integral to evolutionary biology, and many of its major concepts such as gene frequency, species and niche are all defined with respect to the concept of a population. However, with the exception of evolutionary game theory, "population thinking" is almost entirely absent from neoclassical economic analysis, which is instead based about a calculus of representative agents and aggregates.

Neoclassical economic analysis has no meso domain because it has no concepts that are populations. An industry in this doctrine is not a population of firms or techniques, but a set of firms modeled by a scaled-up representative firm in the manner of an aggregate production function.[15] In evolutionary economics, an industry can be represented as the population of a rule complex characterizing that industry. The dynamics of the meso trajectory are, then, a function of the properties of the population of that rule.[16]

An industry is one obvious population concept, as are its components. A single market is another. Markets are generally understood in economics as mechanisms for equating demand and supply with price equilibria. In Austrian economics, markets are understood as processes (or institutions) for price discovery.[17] In evolutionary economics, we may deepen the Austrian definition by observing that the size of the market (and the limit to the size of the market) and the properties of the market are a function of the adoption of market rules and the properties of the resulting population. The evolution of markets as meso is a conjoint product of the trajectory and population dynamic of behavioral, social and technical rules composing a market which may equally be configured as the co-evolution of demand rules and supply rules described at each point as a population.[18]

Alfred Marshall cleared the ground for thinking of an industry as a population, but it was Edward Chamberlin and Joan Robinson who, along with the Austrian school, cleared the way for thinking of a market as a population. The concept of monopolistic competition is an implicit conception of a market as a rule population representing the variety inherent in any "commodity rule." The same concept is eminently generalized into the labor market or service markets where variety is endemic as a matter both of competitive strategy and the natural circumstances of production and consumption. As a theoretical concept, market has always been regarded as a mechanism to compute prices and has been little studied as a mechanism or rule system unto itself.[19] But any formulation of the computational or process structure of a market mechanism must be accompanied by a population profile and analysis of the rules composing such a distributed mechanism.

The core of an evolutionary analysis is "population thinking" and this is similarly true in economics.[20] The vantage this offers ranges over technological diffusion, institutional dynamics and the evolution of behavioral and organizational rules. It enables a study of the history of the products, technologies, institutions and behaviors that compose the economy in terms of meso trajectories of meso units that are populations. Yet a market can also be treated in the same framework as any other system of rules. To the extent that markets are like all other generic processes in the economy, namely composed of rules for operations as a carrier population, then we can seek to develop an "endogenous market theory" of economic evolution that draws upon the properties of the population of markets to advance analysis.

4.3.2 *Variety in meso*

A meso unit is a rule population and that rule population will contain variety. There are three sorts of variety that can exist in a meso unit, all of which can be traced to different forms of microstructure or different analytical perspectives on the micro components of the population.

First, there is variation in the rule itself which we call *rule variety*.[21] This is composed of the different instantiations or models of the same rule, as might be the different models of car or flavors of ice cream, etc. This is the sort of variety that occurs in monopolistic competition.

Second, there is variation in the carriers of a rule which we call *carrier variety*. This is composed of the different internal and external (rule) environments of different carriers in relation to a rule, and is the sort of variety of concern to strategic management scholars.

Third, there is *operational variety* consisting of different transactions or transformations performed by the same rule, as for example with applications of the same technology to solve different problems, or the same behavioral rule to interact with people or machines. More generally, operational variety consists of different prices for the same object, or different operational efficiency in production, and so on. Variety in a meso population is, we suggest, minimally composed in these three ways.

Fourth, an analysis of meso variety will focus on variation in the rule (i.e., within the "rule pool") and in the changes that occur in that variation over a meso trajectory. There is a well-known and heavily but accurately stylized pattern to variety over a meso trajectory, namely that it initially starts out with one novel variant (the monopoly founder) that then soon explodes to a raft of variations in proportion to the ease of entry that then compete for the same custom (i.e., adoption) before a competitive "shake-out" occurs to winnow the variants to a dominant few designs, firms or, more generally, rules.[22] This same pattern is observed in evolutionary biology and the similarity to economic evolution has been widely noted.[23] Variety is not necessarily linear and smooth, but often proceeds in the surge and repose of imagination and rationality that eventually converge with successive adoptions into a stable rule population composed of stable variations within. Variety differs over meso 1 in the generation of variety, over meso 2 in the exploration and selection from that variety, and over meso 3 in the ongoing retention of that variety. The change in variety is a measure of the change in population structure (and not just size) over the course of a meso trajectory.

Looking deeper into carrier variety at the micro level, variety can be conceived both internally and externally. Internally, an adopted rule will find itself in a micro systemic environment composed of other rules. This will in some way require adaptation in order to fit (as measured by fitness) by some change in the rule, the rule environment or both. This adaptation process therefore generates rule variety. In different environments, the rule will often serve different generic and operational purposes. Generically, it may be employed through connections to different rules, as when an "engine rule" is connected to variously a "transportation rule," an "electricity-generating rule" or a "robotics rule." Operationally, the same rule in the same carrier may be employed to perform different operations, such as when a communications-technology rule is used in production, consumption or in market activity. Variety can thus come from within.

Externally, each carrier and the context of the operations of each carrier are in a local environment that may differ substantially from other environments. The variety of local environments is a key part of the selection mechanism on rules and is rightfully complicated by the further ability of carriers to move between different such selection environments in search of opportunity, thus endogenously changing their competitive profile through 2nd order origination, adoption and retention rules to guide this process. Through a meso trajectory, rule variety may thus continue to emerge from within carriers and from the different external environments of carriers.

The economic selection mechanism is complex, yet it is into this complexity that evolutionary economic analysis can go by distinguishing between the different modes of variety that attend a rule in a meso unit and over a meso trajectory in terms of the rule itself, its carriers and its operations. This complexity is further intensified when we allow that variety expresses over a rule complex of (subjective) cognitive-behavioral and (objective) social-technical rules and simultaneously over a structure of 0th, 1st and 2nd order rules. So there are ($3 \times 4 \times 3 =$) 36 dimensions of variety in evolutionary analysis. When we collapse this variety with the assumption of generic invariance we collapse meso and arrive back at the limiting case of a representative agent in a perfect market as in general equilibrium theory in which micro and macro are indistinguishable.

The empirical mapping of such variety in both generic micro and meso analysis is certainly underway, and has achieved excellent resolution in some sectors,[24] but we are still a long way from the completion of such a map over much of economic history and even further from the continual recording of changes across the whole of the economy (see Section 5.3). Because we have yet only glimpses of the past and present map of the generic economic order, we retain only partial insights into the variety that exists over all dimensions of economic space and time. Much dedicated and thorough work has already been done by a great many scholars of the history of enterprise, business, institutions and technologies, yet this remains to be completed and extended. There is much more left to learn, both empirically and theoretically, about the forms of variety in a generic economy and how they are generated and resolved.

4.3.3 Meso and markets

An economic system is made of many generic rules, but the primary rule of a market economy is surely the market rule. Markets are not an implicit presumption in our evolutionary view, but rather markets are yet another generic rule and therefore meso unit of the economic order.[25] Markets are rules, yet they are not just another generic rule, but a rule of central concern to evolutionary economists because they are the primary rules for the organization of both generic and operational coordination.

The evolutionary view of markets, then, is of markets as generic organizational rules that produce both operational and generic coordination. An evolutionary theory of markets can therefore, we suggest, be rendered along the analytic lines of a generic approach to economics, and in seven basic ways.

First, when we speak of *the* market rule, we are referring not to a generic market rule, but to the 0th order rule of the market order. Instead, *a* market rule refers to a specific rule complex that describes the rules for transactions, trading or exchange. A posted price rule is a 1st order generic market rule, as is a Dutch auction. The market order of a country such as the Netherlands, however, is a 0th order rule. The global macro order evolves as nations variously originate, adopt and retain 0th order market rules. Yet within that process there is a further realm of generic change as macroeconomic systems originate, adopt and retain new market rules, such as the adoption of auction markets into situations where previously only posted-price markets dominated (e.g., eBay for consumer goods or spectrum auctions for public goods). Our critique of contemporary evolutionary economics is that everything seems to evolve except markets. But when markets are reconceptualized as generic rules with various rule forms, we may then proceed to analyze the evolution of markets as the evolution of any other generic rule.

Second, a market rule, from the generic perspective, is a rule complex composed of cognitive, behavioral, social and technical rules [CBST], and is, therefore, always carried by both subject and object rules. This, incidentally, is why markets are always hard to identify empirically, as they are mostly carried in an embodied form in the routine behaviors of agents and the implicit understandings of social rules and only in part by observable technical rules and objective spaces. We would of course now like nothing better than to elaborate the subject and object rules of all markets. But that, it seems, is about where evolutionary economics is up to in the development of an evolutionary theory of markets. Yet the foundational point we wish to emphasize, however, is that the generic analysis of a market always involves both subject and object components of a market rule.

Third, each market rule is a meso entity and therefore has a population. Markets have populations, and different market rules have different populations. The population of posted-price market rules is, for example, vastly greater than the population of double-action market rules, and the population of single-sided auctions is intermediate. Yet we know little about these populations, nor their relative generic change. We have little understanding yet of how population changes in market rules relate to economic growth and development. As such, it must surely be a priority of evolutionary economic analysis to endeavor to understand not just the transformation of market structure over a meso trajectory, but also the population profile of market rules (as meso units) over the course of economic development.

Fourth, some market populations involved in transactions are small and others are big, some are globally connected and others are entirely local. Some market rules such as posted-price markets have a very large population, but each market has only perhaps hundreds or thousands of connections as local users who have adopted the market rule. Then there are other market rules, such as the continuous double action of a stock market, which have millions of connections, but of which there is only a small population of the market rule, as in the set of global stock exchanges. A general generic theory of market evolution must therefore seek to account for not just the set and population of market rules, but also the population of carriers of each rule and the frequency of their market operations.

Fifth, markets are mechanisms for coordinating other rules. Market rules are, in this sense, perhaps the ultimate "general purpose technology," or at least they are definitively so in analysis of the economic system.[26] In any case, markets are generic rules for the coordination of other generic rules. Thus, the analytic implication we emphasize is that in evolutionary analysis there is a "market for markets." In other words, markets, like other generic rules, evolve. But the evolution of market rules is not like the evolution of say chip, car or toothpaste rules, because markets are mechanisms for coordinating other rules, and therefore the evolution of market rules is an endogenous feature of the evolution of economic systems.

Sixth, market evolution occurs over a meso trajectory as the structure of a market systematically changes over a meso trajectory from an initial state of market origination and monopoly to many possible final configurations by meso 3. Along the way, every agent is of course ever seeking to preserve or develop monopoly structures within this generic environment of what Chamberlin and J. Robinson called "monopolistic competition." Market evolution is, generically considered, a process in time that includes many different "competitive states." Yet analysis of these states with respect to their efficiency conditions, for example, is not and should not be the prime concern of evolutionary economics. Rather, it is analysis of how these different specific market states lead to new coordination orders that should be the central analytic concern of a generic analysis of markets both as operational market outcomes and generic market rules.

Seventh, the aggregate system of "market rules" is not just an aggregate of generic rules, as if it were, say, an aggregate of "toothpaste rules." Instead it involves the emergence of new processing powers and self-organizational complexity as due to the new coordination possibilities implied by the adoption and retention of new market rules. The evolution of market rules is, arguably, the primary generic technology of economic evolution, yet perhaps surprisingly this has not been widely recognized by either economists or historians of technology.[27] The upshot, of course, is that the evolution of market rules is the primary driver of economic development due to generic improvements in meso coordination. In consequence, analysis of the causes of economic growth should focus not just upon factor accumulation and technological change, but also on the consequence of the evolution of market rules as meso units. A market mechanism is a rule, but the market process is a co-evolving correspondence between demand rules and supply rules, which is an analytic structure we call a *generic correspondence*.[28] Each instance of a market rule represents a different coordination structure of demand rules and supply rules, and thus a different state of generic correspondence.

Generic change in rules in markets and generic change in the markets of rules is the basis of evolutionary economic analysis. Evolutionary economists therefore do not presume markets given, but seek to explain their emergence and evolution. Similarly, evolutionary economists do not assume that a market outcome (i.e., a set of exchanges) is the final arbiter of a market process, as different results may be achieved with different market rules. The evolution of market rules therefore co-evolves with the evolution of all other generic rules and, in consequence, market rules are the meso rules (and meso units) that are central to the process of coordination and change in the micro environment and macro order of an economy.

Following Schumpeter and others, evolutionary economists have mostly so far focused on the evolution of generic technological rules and their business-school brethren have concentrated on the evolution of generic organizational rules. Yet both can come together about a unified analysis of generic market rules, and in so doing integrate the old school and new school analysis of institutions with the analysis of market opportunities and their creation through the process of creating new markets.

Economic evolution is always a process of generic change, but a process of generic change is ultimately and always a process of market change. Thus, we need to learn to distinguish between the generic effects of evolution in market rules and the generic effects of the evolution of rules in markets.

4.3.4 The scale and velocity of meso

The meso unit in a market can usefully be further characterized by its generic scale and velocity. Some ideas are bigger than others, and some ideas happen faster than others. We need a way of measuring that generic quality with measures of the scale or significance of the rule and of the rate or velocity at which it is being adopted.

The scale of a trajectory refers both to the size of the carrier population and also its economic significance. The economic significance of a rule is a constructed measure composed of factors such as the cost of acquiring the rule, the price of the transformations and the value of the transactions it can make, as well as its place in the network of economic activities and the extent to which it can be substituted. The economic significance of a rule could also be composed in terms of more imponderable considerations relating to historical, cultural and political factors. In both cases, however, a definitive or even serviceable method for composing such a measure of meso scale and significance remains to be done.

Still, it is intuitively clear that some meso are bigger than others, and indeed the difference may vary over orders of magnitude. The "pop-up toaster" meso rule, for example, that began in the 1960s is large and significant, but it is tiny compared to the "internet" meso rule which also began then, even though the number of households that have adopted the toaster rule (i.e., have a pop-up toaster) and the number of households with an internet connection is perhaps now similar. Some meso are bigger than others, and we know the significance when we see it, but for analysis to advance we will need to develop objective ways of defining and measuring the comparative generic value of a meso unit.[29]

Toward this end, we conjecture that the distribution of meso scale or significance will follow a power-law distribution, such that most are small, a few are large, and an extreme few are enormous; more formally, the distribution has infinite variance and no first moments.[30] This would mean that there is no characteristic size that represents the distribution, that is, no such thing as a "representative meso." Furthermore, the process of economic evolution is scale free, that is, it evolves on all scales. Each of these trajectories is a process unit of economic evolution, and each (by definition) causes structural change in the macroeconomic system at all scales.[31]

The key point is that this is a continuous distribution and not a binary distinction between, say, stationarity and a structural break or change. Standard macro measures of structural breaks will tend only to pick up the effects of the largest of these and consign the spaces between to be stationary. But in an evolutionary model structural breaks must also happen at all scales. Trajectory by trajectory, the economy evolves and grows on all scales.

The velocity of a meso trajectory is a concept of how fast the trajectory unfolds as a measure of its growth rate through time. Some meso are faster than others, and there are two issues that arise: how we measure that, and why meso have different velocities. Velocity is simply the change in size per unit of time and, expressed in terms of previous size, can be represented as a percentage or absolute growth rate. However, while the growth rate must be positive over some part of its life, there is no natural or representative growth rate against which we may compare in order to evaluate whether it was objectively fast or slow. It is entirely relative to the velocity of other meso with which it is associated and also, as above, weighted by the "significance" of the meso rule.

As yet, there is no systematic study of the time structure of comparative meso across the economy or through history and, therefore, no analytic basis yet to propose a normalized scale.[32] We venture this would be both a useful and interesting empirical and theoretical exercise that might be instructive about why some ideas have more generic potential than others and, also, what might be done to encourage that (we return to this theme in Chapter 7 on generic policy).

As to why meso have different velocity, there are multiple factors involved. A prime consideration is that it depends on the extant size of the meso rule. Going from one to one thousand carriers may happen much faster than from one thousand to one million for obvious practical reasons. However, well-known network externality effects complicate that picture, and so the theory of generic velocity is still yet to be formally developed. A further consideration is that velocity will depend on the complexity of the adoption process over the [CBST] matrix. Some rules may require substantial changes in cognitive and behavioral rules along with new organizational forms and technical rule changes and, moreover, may not be functional until all subject and object components of the rule are in place.

So, while technical rules may be fast and easy to adopt, new behavioral rules may take much longer, effectively slowing the entire process. A novel generic rule is adopted at the velocity of its slowest component, and so the complexity of a rule over the rule taxonomy will matter. Furthermore, some rules will require substantial adaptation for adoption and operational functionality to occur, and so velocity may be slowed by the resistance of extant rules in carriers that will be required to reconfigure to some degree (including being made redundant). The level of such adaptation required and the resistance to this will differ over meso rules, and so effect meso velocity.

A generic explanation of differential velocity can therefore be analyzed in terms of the nature and distribution of effective 2nd order (or mechanism) rules for origination, adoption and retention in the population of potential carriers. Simply put, in a population with weakly developed or ineffective mechanism rules, the velocity of the meso will be much slower than in a population with well-developed and highly effective mechanism rules.[33] Moreover, the relative strengths of the mechanism-rule components matters too: in a population of innovators with well-developed rules for origination and adoption, a meso trajectory will go faster than in a population of followers, even if these followers have well-developed retention rules. An evolutionary audit of the mechanism rules of the carrier population would therefore be a useful place to start analysis of the velocity of meso adoption. While these tasks remain to be done, we may still proceed to develop generic theory based upon this endogenous explanation for the velocity of a meso in terms of the micro characteristics of the population of agents and agencies.

4.4   Micro strategy over a meso trajectory

Although micro is for meso and meso is for macro, meso analysis is also applicable to the strategic considerations of micro units in an evolving economic system—management and business studies in an enterprise economy—through analysis of *generic micro strategy* over a meso trajectory.

Micro strategy in the meso context is analysis of adaptation to generic change. Yet the standard approach to theory and analysis of strategy is based about an invariant generic world in which only operational characteristics are uncertain.[34] A firm may not know whether a rival will enter a market or cut its price, but they do know the things it can do and the expected consequences of those outcomes, and about which operational strategies can be refined with the tools of game theory. Evolutionary economics, however, is concerned with the implications of generic change, and so an analysis of strategy is focused on how a carrier survives and functions in an ever-changing generic environment.

Generic strategy is the generic choice of mechanism rules by a micro unit.[35] Different micro units will devote different resources, including none, to the development of 2nd order mechanism rules for origination, adoption and retention: these generic choices constitute the micro unit's generic strategy. This, we suggest, is the meaning of competitive advantage from the evolutionary perspective[36] as based on a micro unit's capabilities and specialization in innovation, adoption or retention. That is, even when a person or firm has an absolute advantage over all other agents in the origination, adoption and retention of rules, they will still have a comparative advantage in, say, the origination of rules, and so their generic strategy will be to specialize in that.[37] Strategy, therefore, is the choice of mechanism rules to fit the generic opportunities of the environment.

Different generic strategies have different risk–reward profiles. The most risky strategy is no strategy at all, that is, choosing not to develop any origination, adoption or retention rules, but simply to exploit existing 1st order rules for operational income. The risk is that the income stream will eventually be competed away and the micro unit will be left without a source of generic income and confined to defending operational rents through artificial restrictions on competition.

A micro unit may adopt a competitive strategy based on competence in origination and innovation, but with little development of adoption and retention mechanisms. This strategy has higher risks than a strategy focused about developing adoption mechanism rules, and which in turn has a higher risk than a strategy that seeks to develop retention mechanisms. But this strategy also has higher expectation of generic profit than a strategy focused about adoption mechanisms, which will have a mix of generic profit and generic rent. A strategy that develops mechanism rules for retention will have almost no scope for generic profit, although potentially much for operational profit.

The risk–reward profile of investment in the different mechanism rules is central to generic strategy and, as such, agents and agencies can be analytically and empirically arrayed according to their strategic profile of mechanism rules. An origination strategy of innovation is more likely to fail than a retention strategy of copying existing rules, but it is also more likely to produce novelty and value or generic profit. A retention strategy is more likely to succeed, in that it is working with well-understood generic rules, but it is unlikely to produce much generic profit as it is reusing existing ideas, although quite possibly much generic rent when these ideas are introduced into new domains.

What a firm specifically does will of course depend upon its generic knowledge as well as its generic information (see Section 3.2.3 above). Meso 1 strategy is classic entrepreneurship and meso 3 strategy is classic management. Meso 2 strategy is a mix, and so too, properly, is meso 1 and 3. No one knows how successfully to create new ideas every time any more than anyone knows how to run successful companies every time, for these are both ongoing competitive and experimental processes. But we learn as we go, and we believe that an evolutionary economic analysis can help conceptualize that process.

There are many reasons why micro units may acquire different mechanism profiles. They may have different preferences for risk, and so allocate their mechanisms accordingly. Risk lovers would stack their mechanism portfolio with innovation capabilities and risk-averse agents would tend their mechanism portfolio toward retention capabilities.

However, it is also possible that an ensemble of differently weighted portfolios could arise, not from each carrier making a rational choice, but instead from the cumulative effect of feedback with the internal and external environment, such that the profiles are individually path-dependent. A firm that invested in adoption mechanisms and received some operational payoff may then reinvest in further adoption rules, thus developing a specialization that would always have a higher payoff than additional investment in origination or retention mechanisms. In that case, it is not the initial distribution of preferences that determines the form of the mechanism ensemble, but the initial configuration of starting points. Generic path dependence in mechanism rules (and therefore competitive advantage) may result. Or the distribution of mechanism rules may be a combination of the prevailing impetus of, say, education, culture, patterns of government spending and other exogenous factors that prime micro units with capabilities to innovate, adopt or retain. In that case, the mechanism structure is the outcome of a combination of chance and necessity, and so the profile of generic strategy would be randomly compiled.

Yet the major consideration is that the value of different types of mechanism rule will change systematically over a meso trajectory and so micro strategy needs to be adapted to the phase structure of the meso rules that constitute the agents internal and external environment. Over the course of a meso trajectory we observe the following changes:

1   A novel generic rule goes from private to public over a meso trajectory.
2   Some firms will grow in meso 2 and some firms will die in meso 2, and that turbulence is natural. Death in meso 3, however, is unnatural.

3   Generic profit is defined in meso 1, extracted in meso 2 and eventually exhausted, marking the onset of meso 3. Generic profit accrues in meso 1 and 2, not meso 3.
4   Generic rent is zero in meso 1 and maximum in meso 3.
5   Rule variety rises and falls during meso 2 in consequence of market entry and selection.
6   Uncertainty goes from high in meso 1 to low in meso 3 as a novel idea comes to be experimented with and eventually understood.
7   Entrepreneurship is most valuable in meso 1 and 2, but management is most valuable in meso 3.
8   Venture finance drives meso 1 and 2, but standard savings and investment drive meso 3.

Evolutionary strategy cannot be a one-off strategy, such that due to the differential payoffs over the course of a meso trajectory. Different strategies will be required at different phases. Mechanism rules that can adapt to this will be strategically fit, and not otherwise.

Over the course of a meso trajectory, we will observe change of carrier forms in which the boundaries of existing firms change, new firms enter, and new institutions emerge. This matters to agents seeking to strategically position themselves within the shifting generic and operational forms, and also to agencies that seek to strategically shift these forms. During meso 2 new structures and processes are being ventured, both as new firms start up and new combinations are formed. Some new forms will grow by assembly, others will sprout anew. These are predictable effects, as is that some of these will fail.[38] Mechanism rules that can adapt to this generic circumstance will be strategically fit, and not otherwise. These are the challenges of generic strategy.

Economic evolution is the consequence of enterprise, and enterprise is the action that seeks to exploit a changing environment by the mechanism of introducing further change. The viable structure for any subsequent analysis must also be complex.[39] Generic strategy is about the acquisition of mechanism rules to enable a carrier to be generically complex and, moreover, to maintain that state in an open generic environment. Generic strategy enables a carrier to live in an open environment.

4.5   Conclusion

Economic evolution is the process of generic change in the economic order. The micro unit of this is a carrier—an agent or agency—originating, adopting and retaining a novel generic rule. But when a rule is adopted and retained by many micro units, it forms a rule population that we call a meso unit. The first phase of a meso trajectory is the origination of the novel rule as an innovation. Meso 2 is the phase in which the rule is adopted into a population of carriers through a trial and error process of venture and enterprise, conjecture and refutation. This will often be a turbulent process in which existing structures of firms, industries, markets and consumption patterns associated with the rule are transformed. This is the phase of market capitalism as an evolutionary mechanism. By meso 3, the carrier population has stabilized as the rule comes to form a generically structured statistically replicating rule population, or institution. The economic system evolves as new rules are originated, adopted and retained and, in this sense, a meso unit is a structural component of the economic system and the analytic nexus of economic evolution as structural change.

We subsequently examined the implications of the meso unit as the analytical core of evolutionary economics in terms of the concept of a generic population as the unit of analysis, and how this frames concepts such as market, industry and knowledge base. We also highlighted the generic differences in variety, scale and velocity that may be attributed to a meso unit, along with the implications for generic strategy, which we defined as the choice of mechanism rules to compete in a generically open economy. Yet analysis of a meso trajectory and a meso unit as a population or rule carriers is not an end in itself, but rather analysis of the process–component of the economic order. In Chapter 5, we shall define the macroeconomic order as a *coordinated structure* of meso units, and then examine how the macro order changes in consequence of a meso trajectory.

5   Macro coordination

- Defines macro order and equilibrium as deep and surface coordination of meso
- Recognizes macro coordination as co-evolution of subject and object rules
- Analyzes a macro trajectory as the de-coordination and re-coordination of a macro order
- Examines how coordination failure can occur over a macro trajectory
- Examines the co-evolution of multiple meso trajectories as clusters

5.1   Introduction

Macroeconomics is the study of the market economy as a whole, and there are two basic questions: how are the parts of the whole coordinated, and how does it change? A micro trajectory was the building block of a meso trajectory, and a meso trajectory is the building block of analysis of generic macro coordination in terms of how the whole macro economic system is coordinated in consequence of meso change, which shall be the subject of this chapter. In Chapter 6 to follow, we shall then use this general generic analysis of macro coordination as a building block (a *regime*) for analysis of macro growth and development as an ongoing historical process. But in this chapter we shall be concerned with the analysis of macroeconomic coordination in consequence of a meso trajectory.

Conventionally, macro analysis deals with operational aggregates, such as expenditure flows, as in Keynesian macro, or market transactions, as in New Classical macro. However, general equilibrium theory is only operationally general, as is Keynes's general theory. Evolutionary macro, however, seeks to go beneath these operational aggregates in order to study the underlying structure of the determinants of generic coordination of all meso as a complex evolving system. The purpose of this chapter, then, is to outline analysis of the generic structure of the whole economy. We shall seek to understand how the meso units composing that structure are coordinated and how that structure changes.

We proceed as follows. In Section 5.2, we define the generic coordination of a market economy in terms of both order and equilibrium with respect to deep and surface coordination. In Section 5.3, we examine how this order is disturbed by a meso trajectory in terms of a three-phase process of de-coordination, re-coordination and ongoing order. In Section 5.4, we shall examine several ways in which this coordination process can fail, respectively at the deep, surface and operational levels, and variously in phase 1, 2 or 3. In Section 5.5, we extend this single trajectory meso macro framework to consideration of the co-evolution of multiple rules, or what we shall call a *cluster*, both in terms of how a cluster coordinates and the ways in which it can fail to coordinate. Section 5.6 concludes.

5.2   Macro coordination

There are two fundamental states of macro coordination in the market economy. These correspond to coordination of the *deep structure* of rules—which we call generic *macro order*—and coordination of the *surface structure* of rule-populations—which we call generic *macro equilibrium*. We shall define the coordination state of macro order and equilibrium in Section 5.2.1, examine their properties in Section 5.2.2, and elaborate their subject and object dimensions in Section 5.2.3.

5.2.1   Macro order and macro equilibrium

A state of coordination exists when there is both coordination of ideas and coordination of populations of actualizations. A state of macro order exists when the matrix of associations $r_i r_j$ between the set of all generic rules $R = (r_1 \dots r_n)$ is completed. This does not mean that all rules are associated, but rather that all associations that can be made have been made. Correspondingly, a state of macro disorder holds when associations fail to occur between rules.

A state of macro equilibrium exists when all of the possibilities for actualization implied by the deep order have been exploited, such that all meso populations are in the third phase. This is defined over a given set of rules R in which each r_i is carried by a stable (meso 3) population of j carriers $r_i(c_1 \dots c_j)$. In this state, there is a given set of rules and a stable adoption frequency; all carriers who will adopt have adopted, and all adaptation and re-coordination to those adoptions has taken place. The macro equilibrium is therefore a stationary ensemble of coordinated meso 3 populations.

As a macro equilibrium, this is a *general generic equilibrium*. The state of meso equilibrium is in turn only a *partial generic equilibrium*. We therefore define a state of macro disequilibrium as corresponding to deviation from this state through a failure to actualize some of the possibilities of a deep structure. A state of macro equilibrium, however, need not proceed from a state of generic order, but rather represents the complete actualization of whatever deep structure pertains, irrespective of whether it is a state of order or not.

Macro generic coordination is described at two levels: the deep coordination of rules, and the surface coordination of populations of actualizations. Macro order is coordination at the deep level. Macro equilibrium is coordination at the surface level. The generic coordination of the whole economy is the coordination of both a complex network of rules at the deep level, and of a statistical ensemble of actualizations at the surface level. Macro generic coordination is therefore composed of both macro order and macro equilibrium.

Macro generic order occurs when the whole system of rules fit together, and for rules to fit together the associations must produce value.[1] Deep coordination is therefore operationally manifest in the structure of complementarity between operations. Deep coordination failure, then, is the property of two or more rules—i.e., a rule system—not fitting together, such that they induce no information by association. Coordination failure may involve a process of operational loss, as resources are squandered, but generically considered it is a process in which nothing generic happened. In turn, deep coordination means that something new happened, that value was created. Without deep rule coordination, value cannot exist.

Macro generic equilibrium occurs when the whole system of rule populations fit together. Populations "fit together" by adopting a frequency appropriate to the environment of other rule populations. A population of lawyers is coordinated to a population of commercial businesses as a population of foxes is coordinated to a population of hares. At the surface level, the rule population is represented as a carrier population of the micro units that compose the meso unit.[2] Surface coordination failure, then, is the failure of a rule-carrier population to "fit" appropriately with the population of associated rules. This may occur as one population stabilizes (in meso 3) too low relative to the generic potential of the associated meso environment, perhaps due to adoption failure; or symmetrically, it may overshoot a sustainable population in the meso environment.[3]

A general state of macro coordination is therefore a process structure of coordination between all meso units (and so is generic coordination) when all rules are in meso 3. In this case, all rules are coordinated with respect to other rules (such that they fit together) and all populations are coordinated with respect to each other (such that they fit together). The concepts of macro order and macro equilibrium may now serve as the benchmark for evolutionary generic analysis in that they jointly define the generic null state of "no evolution." In this, it is not unlike Schumpeter's reference to the Walrasian "circular flow" that his entrepreneurs were to creatively destroy.[4]

5.2.2 *Properties of macro order and equilibrium*

How the state of generic equilibrium or macro order comes to be is a question we shall address in subsequent sections. For now, our concern is to describe the properties and qualities of the process structure of the state of general meso coordination or macro order. The state of macro order can be defined from the generic perspective in terms of five positive properties and one normative property.

The first positive generic property of a state of macro coordination is that it has no *uncertainty* in any of its meso components. In a state of generic coordination there may be risk as to what carriers may do with their generic rules, but there is no uncertainty that they have those potential operations.[5] In a macro order, there are only risks, because all rules are assumed to be known and adapted. Uncertainty, then, is a consequence of the nature and implications of a novel generic rule being both *prima facie* unknown and knowable only through generic adoption and operational experimentation. All novelty is born into uncertainty, but by meso 3, by definition, this process has completed and every carrier knows everything they need to know. They have made their generic choices and, to the extent that the information about those choices is communicated to other carriers, then, because the generic space is known, the operational space is without uncertainty. That does not mean that the operational space will not be turbulent or ramifying, but only that it will not be subject to incalculable surprise. This is a world of growth, but not of evolution. It is a world in which the same things always happen and vary only in scale. It is a world of optimal choice of operations and optimal scale for operations.

The second positive generic property of macro coordination is that it has no *finance* in any of the meso components. In addition, this follows from the first generic property, namely if there is no uncertainty, then there is nothing to venture and so there is no need for financial entrepreneurship in creating forward contracts that are based on the (uncertain) outcomes of a novel rule.[6] Finance is an evolutionary enterprise that can only exist in the context of novel generic rules, and therefore in the face of uncertainty. Savings and investment are both generic and operational notions; but finance is a purely generic property, such that it has no role outside of an evolving economy and, in turn, no meso trajectory can happen without finance of some kind or other. Yet in a state of macro order there is no demand for finance, only a stable operational flow of savings and investment.

The third positive generic property of a macro order is that it has no income flows of *generic profit*.[7] This is because the generic profit opportunities have all been exploited in meso 1 and 2, and so by meso 3, by definition, there is only generic and operational rent to be had by differentially exploiting the idea (generic rent) or by seeking to game the market in which this generic idea plays out (operational rent, or rent seeking). Macro equilibrium is unlikely to be constituted by perfect competition in all meso, as market forms emerge from the meso process. Meso 1 is by definition monopoly, but latter market forms are essentially undetermined. Meso 3 is a partial generic equilibrium, but it is not necessarily perfect competition, and so there may well be operational profits and rents in the state of general macro equilibrium due to imperfect competition.[8]

The fourth positive generic property of a macro order is that it has *no entrepreneurship*. No one does anything generically new in the total meso 3 of a macro order.[9] Entrepreneurship is the introduction of generic novelty, and in the macro order there can be by definition no generic novelty. The generic macro order may be complex or simple, expanding or stable, but what it is not, by definition, is structurally changing in consequence of the introduction of new ideas. There are no entrepreneurs in the macro order as all have either sold up to become consumers, failed and become debtors, or traversed and become owners or managers. In all cases, the spur of entrepreneurship is but a latent potential in the macro order of total meso 3 which, by definition, has been neutralized of entrepreneurial action.

The fifth positive generic property of a macro state is that it has *stable associations* between meso units. In macro equilibrium all rules have stable carrier populations, and the associations between all rules and the connections between all carrier populations will be given as a generic structure. A macro equilibrium consists of a specific meso structure of associations and connections.[10] It is therefore impossible by definition to talk of structural change, technological change or institutional change in macro equilibrium.

The absence of generic uncertainty, finance, generic profit, entrepreneurship and structural dynamics are all positive properties of a generic macro state. They are true whatever value may be attributed to such a state. The normative (or welfare) properties of a macro equilibrium, however, are undefined. Thus, we shall invoke now a further—evolutionary— evaluative criterion, namely that given otherwise comparable states of macro equilibrium, those states that can subsequently accommodate, facilitate and process generic novelty are better than those states that cannot. It is here that we arrive at the only consistent normative position that can be taken with respect to the evaluation of a generic order and equilibrium, namely a macro state of coordination that is *ceteris paribus* "more open" is better than an order that is "less open." The value of openness or variety is a normative criterion with respect to an implicit framework in which nothing changes, yet it is the quintessential positive value of a generic evolutionary economic analysis.

The determinates of this generic state of openness that seek to maximize the extent of future openness, or the *historical possibility set*, are defined, in essence, by the extant variety in the meso macro system. The greater the variety attained and maintained in meso populations in a macro order, the greater the potential for further development from within that set.

Furthermore, as we saw in Chapter 4, the balance of 2nd order mechanism rules to originate, adopt and retain rules for origination, adoption and retention will effect the openness of a state of macro coordination. Some macro states may be weak in 2nd order mechanism rules, thus rendering change a slow process. Whereas other states of equilibrium may have strong and effective mechanism rules that facilitate fast change. That difference is a generic difference in macro states.[11] It is only in the extreme case of a macro order entirely without 2nd order rules that a macro order is rendered frozen. Yet in practise no macro order is entirely without some mechanisms of change, and so any macro equilibrium will eventually experience the creeping or abrupt effect of a meso trajectory. All macro orders, no matter how robust, will in time give way to economic evolution, as we explain in Section 5.4. In the long run, there is inevitably change.

5.2.3 Subject and object coordination in macro

The generic perspective on macro coordination means that there are three levels of coordination—deep generic, surface generic and operational—but it also means that the classes of rules—[CBST]—must be also coordinated with each other. We may treat this abstractly as the coordination of subject rules and object rules at both the deep and surface levels, and both within and with respect to each other.

The generic structure of macro coordination is therefore further divided into the coordination of deep subjective and objective structure, and surface subjective and objective structure. The macro coordination problem, then, is not just that of coordination of three distinct "vertical" levels, but also of the four "horizontal" rule types at each of the generic levels. The resolution of such a complex coordination problem is the process of economic evolution through the experimental adoption behaviors of carriers and the emergent consequence this brings. The coordination of the macro order emerges over three analytic levels in four rule dimensions at once; that's without considering the higher and lower order mechanism and constitutive rules, nor the variation within or about these rules.[12]

Subject and object rules and their relation to macro coordination are not new, but they have never really been afforded a serious macroevolutionary analysis.[13] In Marxian analysis of macro coordination, for example, objective coordination of technology and organization are self-determining (e.g., the technical laws of production) and about which the subjective elements of consciousness and behavior then coordinate. Object conditions determine subject conditions. A similar approach is found in the work of Veblen and other early Institutionalists.[14] The opposite perspective, however, is held in Keynesian and neoclassical analysis of macro coordination, where the subject is self-determining, and about which objective coordination then occurs from a set of given technological and resource possibilities.[15]

Both of these frameworks have strong elements of truth and persuasion, for the adaptation of subject behaviors to the object conditions of organizations and technologies is clearly observable. But so too is the opposite, namely the adaptation of object conditions to subject behaviors and thinking. Yet whenever a proposition and its opposite are simultaneously true, that usually means a category error. In evolutionary analysis, object conditions co-evolve with subject conditions. Subjective coordination and objective coordination are mutually determined by co-evolutionary processes of adaptation, and this coordination process occurs at both the deep level of rules and the surface level of populations at once as a self-organizing evolutionary process.

Analysis of surface subjective structure deals with the coordination of carrier populations of cognitive and behavioral rules. This involves the coordination of behavior and the division of labor, and how the skills, habits and routines in the population of economic agents "fits together." It seeks to analyze the subjective structure of the connections between populations of behavioral rules that lie beneath the material factors that are usually taken to constitute the "resources" of an economy. The surface subjective structure is the set of cognitive and behavioral rules that form the ways of thinking and ways of doing that determine, in effect, what is thought and what is done. Economies differ in these relative populations, and these differences have evolutionary significance.

Surface objective structure in turn consists of relative populations of different forms of organizational rules and technical rules, and analysis of surface objective structure is analysis of the process by which coordination is achieved over social and technical rules. This will involve the coordination of technology-adopting populations of carriers, which may include technology sectors, industries, industrial clusters or regions, which is a process that also plays out on the demand side through product life cycles and the evolution of market structures, sizes and dimensions.[16] It will also involve the appropriate sizes of market and firm populations adapting to each other. The measure of these populations of object rules that determines the sorts of operations that are organizationally and technically possible. Yet it is the interaction of these populations of object rules with the relative populations of subject rules that determines what actually happens. By all accounts, surface objective structure is the most intensely researched and best understood aspect of evolutionary analysis. Yet both surface subjective and objective structure mutually adapt through a co-evolutionary process that emerges from the deep coordination of rules that are, themselves, the outcome of the co-evolution of deep subjective and objective structure.

Deep subjective structure deals with the coordination of cognitive and behavioral rules and how they fit together as an associative logic, a level of analysis that addresses the coordination of cognitive rules, information, behavior and the division of knowledge. The structure of cognitive rules carried by agent populations and the structured complementarities required to be understood is the core of the knowledge base of the macroeconomic system. Deep subjective structure is biologically, socially and institutionally conditioned, and thereby defines the informational efficiency and shared understandings of the economic system as a "generic communication system."

Deep objective structure in turn deals with the coordination of social and technical rules and how they fit together as an associative logic. It involves the study of how the economic system fits together as a technical system in terms of analysis of production technologies, social technologies, organizational technologies, market technologies and information technologies in terms of their efficacy. The analytic concern of deep objective structure is not with the paths of the individual technical rules, for that is a meso analysis, but rather with how they all fit together as a complex system of associations between rules that organizes both people and things.

A deep structural coordination of rules is therefore a complex process structure composed of the subject orders of the mind and behavior and the object orders of people and technology. A state of generic macro coordination is therefore defined over deep and surface coordination of both subject and object rules. Rules must be coordinated at the deep level, rule-carrier populations must be coordinated at the surface level, and subject and object rules must be coordinated at both levels.

When this occurs, such that these conditions can be derived from a state of meso 3 in all rules, we have a generic macro order and equilibrium defined as a state of macro coordination.[17] And when it doesn't—such that either rules or populations don't fit together, or subject and object rules are not adapted to each other—then we have coordination failure.[18] Both are normal outcomes of the creative–destruction of a meso trajectory on a state of macro order and equilibrium.

5.3   Coordination over a macro trajectory

Analysis of macro coordination is analysis of the consequences of a meso trajectory on the macro order. It is analysis of the de-coordination, re-coordination and ongoing coordination of a novel meso trajectory on an extant macro order. We call this a macro trajectory.

Macro 1	Macro 2	Macro 3
De-coordination of order through the emergence of new meso	**Re-coordination** of order through local and global population change	**Coordination** of new order that is retained, embedded and replicated
Operational: new possibilities Surface: new population Deep: new rule	Operational: restlessness Surface: new populations Deep: new connections	Operational: new equilibrium Surface: newgeneric equilibrium Deep: new order

Figure 5.1 Macro trajectory in three phases.

A macro trajectory is analysis of a meso trajectory in terms of the total creative and destructive process of economic evolution this has on the state of macro coordination. The three coordination phases of a macro trajectory (i.e., the structural implications of a meso trajectory) are de-coordination due to origination, re-coordination due to adoption, and ongoing coordination due to retention (see Figure 5.1). This process takes a macroeconomic system from a state of order to a new state of order, or from one generic equilibrium to another, in consequence of a micro meso origination, adoption and retention process.

5.3.1   Macro 1: de-coordination

Meso 1 begins with the advent of the seminal micro trajectory, and macro 1 begins with the advent of the seminal meso trajectory, such that a novel rule is adopted and retained for ongoing use by at least one agent with the prospect of more. The emergence of a new meso trajectory will disturb the extant generic and operational order, and thus begins the process of de-coordination of the macro order of other rules due to the effect of the new rule. Every creative new idea, however beneficent and well intentioned, will have its effect only by the disruptive and destructive consequences it brings to the extant economic order.

The macro process of de-coordination therefore begins when the novel rule changes the existing relations between the component structures of the generic order, so disturbing the knowledge base of the economy by changing the extant structure of viability and opportunity. This results in the devaluation of some positions and the promotion of others.[19]

This process is evolutionary and emergent, in the sense that it percolates up from below rather than being imposed from above. It is led by the regeneration of variety in the macro population due to the novel meso population, and so then begins the process of the disintegration of previously stable structural components and leads to the initial exploration of new structural relations and associations between rules and populations, including the monopoly market position of the innovator of the generic rule. This is the beginning of the process that will, ultimately, lead to a new macro order.

In macro 1, new economic activities that involve both new transformations and new transactions are now occurring. These will then begin to change the selection environment of other rules and carriers. Some will immediately realize it and others won't, due to differences in 2nd order origination rules. But either way, de-coordination has begun and the selection process begins.

At the generic surface level, phase 1 of a macro trajectory disturbs the existing population structure of rules with a new population that results in new structures of association between rule populations. This will change the space of opportunities, both by opening new possibilities and foreclosing on existing associations.[20] New ideas will be seen to be had. New opportunities will be seen to be discovered. Existing weakness will be exposed and appropriate actions will be planned. Entrepreneurial positions will be staked. Macro de-coordination in consequence of a meso trajectory begins at the micro level due to an operational effect (say a loss of contract or a rise in price) that then triggers the onset of generic change in ideas and expectations that will percolate and ramify across the macro order as the implications of the adoption of the rule take hold.[21]

At the deep level, macro 1 involves the de-coordination of the extant logic of rule associations due to the new rule upsetting existing structures of what was known to be feasible, true or reasonable. The conventional response is at first to deny or attack it, then to adapt to it through awkward adjustments of position, then finally to assert that that was what was believed all along. Economic evolution is like the evolution of scientific knowledge in fundamentally being a growth of knowledge process with the same psychological processes involved.[22] Yet novelty breaks symmetry, and the agents that can see this early will be those who will gain control of the trajectory.[23] The gains or losses of such positions will not be revealed until macro 2, when the initial radical uncertainty or "unknowledge," as George Shackle called it, will have begun to subside into enterprise competition as the adoption process begins to take hold.

Macro 1 then begins when a new meso trajectory puts all other rules in the macro order on alert that something may have changed, and that re-coordination may be required. De-coordination is an unsettling process. But more than that, de-coordination may also be a fearful process for those affected by the new idea, and so may have to generically adapt in minor or major ways. In Chapter 1 we insisted that what makes humans unique, and what gives rise to the possibility of economic systems and economic evolution, is the propensity of humans to image and adopt new ideas. But that in no way implies that change is always welcome and effortless, and that is particularly true when that change is being foisted and driven by unseen others. Entrepreneurship is exciting and challenging, but recognizing and adapting to change can be painful and challenging. Almost all novel ideas face resistance, and that resistance can take on a highly structured and effective form when coalitions can form to block the progress of a new rule in order to protect the operational interests of existing rules, which is well recognized in for example Public Choice theory, but also to avoid the generic costs of change. Just as there are costs of using the market (i.e., transaction costs) and the outcomes of a market will depend upon the extent of those costs, so too are there costs of generic change. The outcomes of evolution, and in particular the rate and depth of macro 1 de-coordination, will therefore depend upon the level and distribution of these costs.[24] The management of these costs will naturally be the province of evolutionary economic policy, which we shall examine in Chapter 7.

5.3.2   *Macro 2: re-coordination*

Yet where the graces of liberty and enterprise shall predominate, and assuming that "generic costs" are not insurmountable, then the macro 1 phase of de-coordination shall proceed to macro 2, which is the phase of re-coordination about the new generic rule and its emerging population. Analysis of macro 2 is the study of the effects of the meso trajectory on all other meso and the re-coordination of those to fit the new meso population. Macro 2 is the evolutionary state of turbulence, complexity and self-organization.[25]

The extremes of macro 2 are bound by very different implications that we distinguish between states of marginal and total re-coordination. At the marginal extreme, the novel meso trajectory has very little impact on other rules. It would enter a self-contained and self-sustaining generic space and have little impact on current substitution or complementarity relations. It would proceed as a novel rule that adds value but had effectively no impact on anything else. In practice, this is a theoretical limit as all real (non-trivial) meso trajectories have some effect on other meso.[26] At the other extreme, the novel meso rule would engender a state of total re-coordination in all rules, such that nothing is untouched by its effect and everything requires re-coordination in some degree.[27] Examples would include the meso rule of electricity, synthetic materials or the internet. Each meso macro trajectory will fall somewhere between these extremes in proportion to the impact of the novel rule. Indeed, this is a classic scale-free distribution, with no characteristic size and no meaning to the notion of an average extent of re-coordination required. Macro 2 happens on all scales, and therefore requires all scales of theory, strategy and policy response.

As the generic economy changes in macro 2, the operational economy will be thrown, in some aspect and scale,[28] into the turbulence and regeneration of a restless market order. This will involve change in the array of prices, in the allocation of resources and the intensity at which they are used, in the distribution of income, and change in the organization of activities and in the connections between markets or sectors. This is the active phase of enterprise and competitive rivalry, the phase where everything potentially may be subject to change, and about which the nature of the subsequent eventualities remains open and emergent.

In macro 2, markets and enterprise do their work by discovering prices and, therefore, reflecting the extent of generic change and the operational constraints and opportunities available.[29] Operationally, this can mean just the fine tuning of activity levels or it may involve significant changes in transactions and transformations, including the decision to cease the operations of an existing rule and to adopt another. Generically considered, macro 2 involves change in the knowledge base of the macro order due to the changes in the knowledge base of the agents and agencies involved in the meso trajectory. This will result in change in the content and structure of economic activities that will in turn affect the level and distribution of wealth and income across the macroeconomy. Macro 2 changes things: it changes what people think and do, and also the systems they form.

The division of labor and knowledge, which is determined by the relative structure of rule populations, will change in macro 2, and with potentially far-reaching implications for the subsequent coordination of cognitive, behavioral, social and technical rules.[30] The restructuring of the content and organization of subject and object rules is an inherently complex and turbulent process that plays out as new relationships between deep structure and carrier frequency are explored and resolved.

This turbulence, however, is quite normal and natural in an open complex system in the presence of generic novelty. The macro 2 process of re-coordination will come to reveal the new deep order of associations implied by the novel rule as the outcome of an evolutionary process of differential adoption and the reformation of local structure. New deep connections between rules will come to be revealed by a parallel and open process of entrepreneurial conjecture and market refutation. This process cannot be shortened to run in less than real time.[31]

5.3.3   *Macro 3: ongoing coordination*

By the end of macro 2, most such restless doubt and uncertainty has been resolved through the cumulative effect of experience into a new normality of beliefs and operations. This is the natural path of enterprise and the basic motion of economic evolution. Macro 3 is the ongoing coordination of the new generic order as a stationary statistical ensemble. The state of macro 3 is the state of macro order and equilibrium, a process that is both ever-embedding knowledge and ever-regenerating those rules so as to retain and maintain the coordination of the once-novel generic rule within a new macro order. By macro 3, the meso rule is embedded into the macro order at all levels and it is at this stage that the broader implications of the rule play out. For example, it is in meso 3 that political retribution for the negative effects of a meso trajectory comes to the fore, as do the social and cultural motions that work to absorb and direct the new meso through familiarity and exploration. The process of retention is also facilitated by the accumulation of further market, organizational and technical innovations that progressively modularize and embed the rule in the domain of cognitive, behavioral, social and technical rules, along with the institutions that compose these. These are the natural motions of ongoing replication and coordination.

At the operational level, macro 3 will involve the retention and embedding of the new structure of transformations and transactions. At the surface generic level, macro 3 will involve the stabilization of rule populations into a new division of resources and of knowledge and the retention of a new complex generic statistical order. At the deep generic level, macro 3 will involve the ongoing process of the normalization and retention of the (new) structure of associations between rules and the ongoing stabilization and embedding of those associations through the learning of new ways.

That we do indeed learn and retain rules is evidenced in the march of evolutionary economic progress. The knowledge base of the generic order is bigger, better and more complex than it was 100 years ago, or 1,000 years ago or even one year ago. The measure of economic evolution is the operational ability to do new things and to create greater possibilities to do more new things still; by that account there has clearly been progress of recent.

But, as all growth theory teaches whether classical, neoclassical or evolutionary, wealth is generated by a stock of capital rules that are subject to entropy, and so must be continually maintained in order just to stay in the same "steady state." The generic knowledge base of an economy is similarly composed, and must also be maintained through ongoing generic investment. Operationally considered, this then requires a flow of resources but generically considered it means the maintenance and replication of rules. These are then the processes of routinization, habituation, normalization, embedding and institutionalization that are the absolute hallmarks of economic progress.[32]

A new economic order is therefore composed of two distinct trends: first, the tendency for the background stability of meso 3 to promote the regeneration of novelty; and second, the absorption and embedding of this background stability into evermore efficient operations. A new meso macro order may continue to grow through the continued improvements in efficiency and embedding it may generate, so embedding itself ever deeper in the macro order.

Yet these same conditions may provide a stable platform for the regeneration of new variety, a possibility we shall explore in Chapter 6. Our immediate analytic concern, however, is to review the process logic of a macro trajectory so as to identify where and how this coordination process may fail.[33]

5.4   Coordination failure over a macro trajectory

Generic coordination failure occurs when rules or populations fail to fit together to form a viable system. By "viable system," we mean a system capable of performing valuable operations on resources. The criterion of "fitting together" is whatever will be subject to differential adoption and replication, that is, selection, and what is being selected, therefore, are the connections between rules, rules populations and activity levels associated with the systems of meso that constitute the macro order. Generic coordination failure occurs when rules or when populations fail to connect efficaciously.[34] Operational coordination failure occurs when messages and incentives fail to connect. Our central concern, however, shall be with generic coordination failure.

There are many reasons for generic coordination failure, but they can be usefully grouped into random (i.e., exogeneric) and evolutionary (i.e., endogeneric) reasons. Coordination failure may occur due to generically exogenous events, such as change in rules and populations outside the economic system such as political, cultural, meteorological or even extraterrestrial events. These sorts of generic shocks can wreak destruction on existing states of coordination by destroying entire meso units or decimating carrier populations or radically altering the connective structures between them. A generic shock can also be positive in the same way that a mutation can sometimes be beneficial, but more often, such exogeneric shocks will induce coordination failure.

Yet despite the magnitude, regularity, extent and significance of such phenomena, we shall treat these under the analytic heading of *generic drift*.[35] Generic drift is a possible cause of coordination failure under random exogenous events, but the triggers for this are not necessarily significant in themselves. In chaos and complexity theory it has long been understood that sometimes seemingly small changes in environmental (i.e., exogeneric) conditions can trigger disproportionate changes in a system due to the ramifications of specific structures of connections and the feedback they entail. Coordination failure can thus appear spontaneous, as with the unexpected collapse of a market or sector in view of no obvious "significant" cause. However, we shall focus here on endogeneric reasons for coordination failure as they unfold systematically over the three phases of a macro trajectory. A better understanding of endogeneric coordination failure will enable us to better understand how an economic order responds to random or exogeneric shocks. As such, there are three levels at which coordination failure can occur: operational coordination failure of activity levels of transactions and transformations to mesh; surface coordination failure of generic populations to fit together; and deep coordination failure of generic rules to fit together. Operational coordination failure occurs when activity levels fail to fit together, which is what happens for example when prices signals are ineffective. It can also occur due to distortions of the price system of coordination in consequence of inappropriate or distortionary fiscal, monetary or regulatory rules. Analysis of this manner of failure forms the core of Austrian economics, constitutional political economy and, to the extent that it implies that incentives matter, is plainly in accord with the central tenets of neoclassical microeconomics. Our contribution, instead, is to unpack the generic causes of these operational outcomes. Hence, our working hypothesis is that much operational coordination failure is ultimately due to the effects of generic coordination failure (i.e., is endogeneric rather than exogeneric), and so we shall concentrate here upon these causes of arrested development or unexpected effects of a trajectory.

From the evolutionary perspective, then, operational coordination failure arises from failures of capacity adjustment between carriers of a novel rule. This occurs when the rules fit together and have been adopted in appropriate frequency, but are not operationalized effectively, resulting in an "operant business cycle" as the activity levels devoted to specific rules fluctuates. Yet for much of modern macroeconomics, this is the only sort of coordination failure that can occur.[36]

Generic coordination failure begins at the surface level when appropriate adoption frequencies do not arrive, such that there is under-adoption or over-adoption of the rule in proportion to the generic environment.[37] Too many firms competing for the same small market is one example, not enough firms competing for the same large market is another, as is the failure of investment coordination.[38] A well-executed adoption of an appropriate population of the technical rules of a rule complex but an arrested adoption of an appropriate population of behavioral or social rules is a further example. Populations can become crooked and uncoordinated in many ways. At the deep level, coordination failure occurs when a novel rule fails to make appropriate connections to other rules, in which case a rule would not fit with its generic-environment.

Again, there are many reasons for such coordination failure. The rule may be "behind its time," such that there are other more effective rules that make it unviable at any price, or it may be "ahead of its time," such that its viability would require a quite different generic set to that which currently exists. In both cases, the rule does not fit current generic circumstances. Nevertheless, a rule that doesn't fit with other rules, that is, cannot make appropriate connections, is an unviable rule under the force of selection.

Deep rule coordination failure results from failures of rule complementarity. This may be due to either second-best connections or missing connections.[39] Examples would include the failure of education systems to provide behavioral or social rules appropriate to technical rules, or the failure of sets of technical rules to form an integrated system. Every generic state of a macro order will yield a certain space for novel rules to enter, a space that is neither infinite nor continuous, but composed of "a thousand plateaus" of generic ecosystems that will accommodate some possible novel rules, but not others. Some paths are open, but not all paths. The degree of openness is crucial to evolutionary analysis of economic welfare from the generic perspective. The inherent evolutionary logic of progress in this order, as we shall see in the next chapter, offers a foundation for a new evolutionary welfare economics.

Coordination failure can occur at the deep, surface and operational levels, but such failure is monotonic in the sense that surface coordination failure cannot occur if deep coordination failure occurs, because, in that case, surface coordination is entirely undefined. Similarly, operational coordination failure presumes the existence of surface (and therefore deep) coordination.

There is a natural order to coordination structure, and so to coordination failure: operational coordination presumes surface coordination, which presumes deep coordination. Analysis of coordination failure therefore begins with deep coordination, and then proceeds back until it diagnoses the specific generic or operant point of failure. Analysis of such coordination failure can be usefully distinguished between failure in either 0th or 2nd order rules. For example, surface coordination failure due to an inappropriate adoption frequency may be consequence of missing or dysfunctional 2nd order adoption rules. Deep coordination failure due to missing behavioral rules may be due to dysfunctional 0th order public-knowledge rules. Or coordination failure due to mismatched technical or organizational rules may be due to inappropriate 0th order property-rights rules.

Coordination failure, then, can happen over three causal levels—0th, 1st and 2nd—in relation to three distinct domains of coordination failure—operational, surface and deep.

In order to analytically resolve this, we propose that a macro analysis of coordination failure should be focused primarily about the three phases of a macro trajectory and the scope for coordination failure along the way.

Deep coordination failure in meso macro 1 occurs when a rule is originated, adopted and retained at the micro and meso level, such that it forms an emergent meso population, but then fails to originate at the macro scale. A typical manifestation is the prospect of a good idea not penetrating the extant structure of coordination and unable to connect to other rules it will be selected against. There may be little outward sign of this, for the characteristic feature of such deep coordination failure is that nothing changes; de-coordination does not occur. (The failure of 2nd order origination rules, or of inertia in existing rule systems, is therefore difficult to diagnose.) A novel rule may be coordinated at the deep level by connecting to other rules, and thus engender the beginning of a de-coordination process in the macro order, but may yet fail to achieve surface coordination during meso macro 2 if populations fail to adopt appropriately.

There are many proximate operational causes for such failure, but there will also be ultimate generic causes due to failures of 2nd order adoption rules, or surface coordination failure, by which agents lack the full capability to adopt the full complement of appropriate rules (for instance adopting appropriate technical but not behavioral rules) or of failing to adopt all the necessary technical rules in a system, but only some of them. Again, this is not easy to diagnose. For example, the population of media channels may be appropriately coordinated with a population of content providers, but an overpopulation of media channels might simultaneously be understood as an under-population of content providers. There is no one true population against which all others are measured. Surface coordination failure can be recognized when populations don't fit, but to analyze where the coordination failure occurred we must look to the micro structure of the meso trajectories involved, and then seek to discover the missing or dysfunctional adoption rules.

Yet even when rules and populations are coordinated at the deep and surface level through the effective de-coordination and re-coordination processes of a macro trajectory, coordination may still fail in macro 3 if it fails to be retained.

Retention failure occurs when a rule is adopted but then fails to be usefully operationalized on an ongoing basis, and so is eventually lost. Again, there are many proximate reasons for this, but an evolutionary analysis seeks ultimate explanation in the failure of 2nd order retention rules to maintain and embed the rules for effective and efficient ongoing use. Micro explanations for this rest upon the failure of habits to form, and meso explanations rest on the failure of institutions to stabilize. The failure of macro retention, however, is a failure to embed an adopted rule so that it is systematically retained and replicated by the macro order.

In sum, macro coordination failure can occur in three ways. First, it can be a consequence of deep coordination failure due to a meso 1 innovation failing to coordinate with other meso rules and make appropriate connections. Second, it can be due to surface coordination failure in consequence of a failure of adoption frequencies, such that the respective rule populations don't fit together appropriately. The third reason is that the coordination can fail to hold, and be lost through retention failure. All of these factors have multiple reasons and causes, some of which can be traced to micro explanations, others to institutional failures, but in each case it is a generic failure of the economic system to coordinate, not an operational failure of prices or actions.

The policy implication is that it is 0th or 2nd order rules that are at fault, and so endeavors to reform such macro coordination must focus on these domains. We shall develop this argument further in Chapter 7.

5.5   The co-evolution of multiple meso trajectories as clusters

The study of coordination and coordination failure over three analytic levels and over three meso macro phases is premised on the notion that we are dealing with novel rules and meso trajectories as they happen independently and one at a time. Analytically and methodologically considered, that is the obvious place to start.

But as soon as one begins thinking about economic evolution in this way, it becomes obvious that real situations rarely involve just one novel meso rule or trajectory process *ceteris paribus*. Rather, meso evolution is typically a co-evolutionary process of multiple novel rules that are associated in some way. Indeed, the analytic abstraction of a single novel idea erupting into an otherwise stationary and invariant world of macro order is a convenient fiction, a story for tyros and textbooks, for the reality of economic evolution is always that of multiple meso trajectories at once.[40] In this sense, all economic evolution is in some degree co-evolution.

Of course in meso analysis, as in the previous chapter, this is by definition the exception, as meso analysis is a partial generic analysis, where partial means other meso trajectories assumed constant. But macro evolutionary analysis is a general generic analysis in which no other trajectories are held constant. The upshot is that most macro evolutionary coordination processes will involve multiple meso trajectories.

Yet this does not immediately proceed to an integral generic formulation in which all meso units co-evolve with all meso units as a continuous topology.[41] This is because the meso structure of macro is not a continuous field, but a complex structure of rules, some of which are more closely associated than others. We shall define a correlated or connected system of co-evolving meso trajectories as a cluster.

This may be interpreted as the co-evolution of distinct variations on a rule, such as variants on the "internal combustion engine" rule of two-stroke, four-stroke, diesel, rotary, multi-valve, etc., as a cluster of variation within a rule under common selection pressure. Or as the co-evolution of expropriations of a rule and their inherent connections, such as the co-evolution of internal combustion engines with associated rules such as automotive transport, lawn mowers, electrical generators and oil rigs, etc. This is a cluster of associated rules under common variation pressure. But whether it is driven by selection or variation pressure, in both cases we are dealing with co-evolution between rules, and so in both cases we may refer to these generally as generic clusters. As defined, then, co-evolution will also occur between producers and consumers as supply rules and demand rules co-evolve. This may occur, for example, as technology and fashion rules interact, or as new consumer lifestyles variously induce or exploit existing technological possibilities.[42] In this way, the structure of variation in a rule may co-evolve with the structure of variation in the environment.

The basis of a cluster is the system of associations between a set of different generic rules. A cluster, then, is a rule system with each element of the system a distinct trajectory, but with all trajectories correlated (i.e., co-evolving) according to the underlying matrix of associations. There are many ways of analytically representing this, but they are all essentially dynamic arrays of multi-populations on some network. As such, there are only three basic dimensions: the number of rules in the system (from $2–n$); the structure of connections between these rules (association matrix); and the carrier population of each rule (the n-vector R).

From these dimensions, other properties of the cluster can be constructed. For example, by adding a time dimension and index of phase states, the cluster can be evaluated for leading and lagging trajectory elements. Furthermore, by considering these as an ensemble, the central trajectories (such as would correspond to its eigenvectors) could be analytically evaluated. Statistical and computational techniques might then be applied to partial pieces of information in order to construct the map of co-evolving rules in the economic order. This would provide an evolutionary classification (or map) based on the generic rule structure of the economy rather than relying on operational classifications of industries, sectors and so forth. A primary map of all rule trajectories could then be further refined into clusters of trajectories identified by their co-evolution. In consequence, the enormous complexity of macroeconomic coordination and change might be more easily visualized and comprehended by a map of the co-evolutionary generic matrix.

A cluster then is a sub-system of connected rules and rule populations that co-evolve together as trajectories. Rules form into associated clusters because of rule complementarity; yet complementary rules need not necessarily form into clusters. Often these have to be coordinated or facilitated and will be conditional upon the emergence of interface standards or protocols, mutually overlapping connections or mutual dependencies, spatial proximity or regularity of interaction, cumulative joint history, and other such mechanisms for connecting two or more rules together.[43] Because of these multiple criteria, the definition of a cluster is essentially an empirical exercise and, moreover, something that itself will continue to change.

Yet we may usefully identify two broad classes of cluster in the generic economy: *producer clusters* as complex systems of co-evolving production rules; and *consumer clusters* as complex systems of consumption rules.

Producer clusters cover the ambit of what is conventionally called an industry but add a scale-free dimensionality to this by allowing clusters to be composed of clusters, and so on, accounting for the sub-components of industries, the service sectors that cross-cut industries, technology clusters and emergent industrial regions and networks. This view is already widely held among scholars of industrial dynamics and sectoral evolution.[44]

The second class of cluster is perhaps less familiar to evolutionary economists, although not so for marketing scholars. A consumer cluster is the set of correlated preferences or consumption rules across a system of carriers.[45] This principle violates the standard microeconomic axiom of independence of preference orderings, yet is a widely observed phenomenon in the meta-stability of market-demand patterns that follow from the information and rule cascades that accompany the market uptake of a new commodity or service.[46]

A cluster is made of connected or co-evolving meso trajectories, but we may also treat the emergence of a cluster itself as a three-phase cluster trajectory. However, co-evolution is not necessarily a harmonic process in which meso 1, 2 and 3 all move together. More likely is that two meso trajectories will co-evolve with each other in different stages of a meso trajectory. To this extent, the phase structure of co-evolution also matters.

Phase 1 corresponds to the emergence of the cluster with the realization of the initial set of connections between rules. This may emerge as the far-sighted leadership of a single micro agent or agency, or as an emergent outcome of the interaction of a system of carriers. These connections may be artificially induced through targeted policy intervention to create industrial parks or precincts, or they may emerge spontaneously as a result of initial historical accident, or some catalyzing factor such as a transport hub or supply of resources. Cities and other geographic concentrations and universities and other idea concentrations are the natural home of cluster emergence.[47] Clusters emerge, in essence, through the self-selection of rule carriers to associate (axiom 2) with other carriers of similar and associated rules. Knowledge gravitation by carrier mobility results in cluster formation. This can be artificially accelerated or retarded, but it is a natural process in an open generic economy.

Phase 2 of a cluster corresponds to the co-evolution in terms of the feedback between populations and the emergent coordination of these as self-organization. A cluster self-organizes by an adaptive process of increased specialization with increased co-integration. This means that the carrier firms of generic rules become more specialized about those rules while, at the same time, others create a series of niches for services into and between firms. The cluster structure will become both more specialized and more deeply integrated at once, and with the growth of the "service sector" as a natural accompaniment to economic evolution with cluster self-organization. We should also then expect to observe that most growth in new firms and jobs would appear in the cluster component that connects and services the rules rather than in the rules themselves.

Phase 3 of a cluster is the ongoing retention and stabilization of the operations of the cluster. The two extreme control states of this are, first, that the entire cluster will be absorbed into a very large (private) firm in order to "internalize" all the connections between the constituent rules and hence to more efficiently control or exploit them. Second, that the entire cluster may become controlled by government through (public) planning, regulation, sponsorship or direct ownership. This may then further be tied to policies relating to regional development, innovation, education, infrastructure and trade. Actual outcomes will invariably fall somewhere between these states, with some mix of private and public provision of connections.

In general, however, phase 3 of a cluster will result in a shift in the generic boundaries of the firms due to a changed generic structure of coordination. This is a different explanation than is provided by transaction cost theory, which is plainly an operational theory of the boundaries of a firm in terms of the relative costs of using the market. A generic explanation focuses instead on the market organization of knowledge into operationally viable carriers.

A co-evolutionary process may result in the coordination of a meso cluster or it may result in a failure of coordination. This may happen at different levels—namely of deep, surface and operational cluster order—or at different phases of a cluster trajectory—namely a failure of emergence, self-organization or retention. Analysis of cluster coordination involves the possibility of cluster coordination failure, but we should always note that cluster formation is not necessarily natural or inevitable, but a component of the growth of knowledge itself as the entrainment of emergent associations into correlated dynamics.

This is why meso macro clusters are a particularly interesting object of study in the analysis of an evolving economy. Given their role as the "connective tissue" of the macro order, and their complex and sometimes unstable emergence and development, it is also why they are a natural focus for economic policy, broadly across industry, trade, regional, competition and innovation policy domains.

With this end in mind, the generic study of cluster coordination (and failure) can be assembled from the micro meso analytics of how each trajectory behaves as a unit and then analyzed as a co-evolutionary process of two or more trajectories. This can then be coupled with a deep and surface macro model of the significance, complexity and extent of the clusters connective structure, which can then provide an analytic foundation for a new generic approach to economic growth policy through a better understanding of generic dynamics and the forces and structures that connect ideas to each other.[48]

5.6 Conclusion

This chapter has concerned the analysis of generic macro coordination in consequence of a meso trajectory. Following axiom 1 of evolutionary realism, we argued that there is a fundamental coordination distinction between the coordination of the deep order of rules and the coordination of the surface population of actualizations. This coordination could be decomposed into subject and object components. We defined the state of macro coordination under the condition of the completion of all micro and meso trajectories, and then set that as the benchmark state of generic equilibrium from which to analyze the evolutionary consequence of a meso trajectory.

We defined a macro trajectory as the effect of a meso trajectory on the system of all other rules. This was then analytically represented as a three phase process of de-coordination, re-coordination and ongoing macro coordination of both the deep generic order and the surface generic equilibrium. We examined the ways in which coordination failure can occur at each of these phases as a failure of rules or populations to connect. We then further developed this to consider the co-evolution of systems of meso rules explicitly in terms of emergent clusters of meso units and trajectories. Overall, we sought to unpack the complexity of generic coordination in an open evolving economic system in consequence of a meso macro trajectory.

We have argued in this chapter that economic evolution is a process of change and re-coordination. A meso trajectory is the driving process of change, but a macro trajectory is the process of de-coordination and re-coordination that results. This process consists of a reconfiguration of the associations between rules (deep structure) and of the populations of carriers (surface structure). When taking a microscopic perspective, we observe changes in the boundaries and capabilities and connections of micro units. When we take a macroscopic perspective, we observe the emergence of clusters. Generic macro coordination is complex. We defined generic macro order and equilibrium in terms of the analytical and operational conditions of all meso units in meso 3. But that was a portrait of a generically invariant, not evolving economy.

Schumpeter famously, and ingenuously, portrayed Walras as the greatest economist he knew, and his circular flow of general equilibrium as the natural starting point of his new analysis. He made similar motions to Marx. His point was to go beyond them. Yet his analysis only went beyond them in meso terms, much of which was focused about operational analysis. Schumpeter was what we would call a generic meso economist par excellence. Keynes is what we would call an operational macroeconomist par excellence. But who is a generic macroeconomist par excellence?

The closest to this, we think, is the later work of Hayek and some post-Keynesians.[49] And in nominating these, we would refer to their baseline as the generic circular flow of Smith's account of the division of labor and knowledge creating a state of wealth. The concept of generic macro equilibrium is an analytical formulation of the distribution of useful human knowledge in both a state of efficacious association and adoption and as a process of value. The classical economists understood this as the analytic foundation of economic analysis.

In this chapter, then, we have sought to present this conception of the coordination of the whole economy, or what Schumpeter referred to as the stationary "circular flow," as the result of micro and meso processes forming meso units for macro coordination. Such a "final" state is characterized by the absence of such evolutionary or generic properties as entrepreneurship, profit, finance, adoption, cognition, experimentation, uncertainty, failure, boundary change, structural change, connections, knowledge, population and other aspects of generic variation and selection. This state is, ultimately, characterized by the complete absence of 1st and 2nd order rule dynamics or their implications. Thus, the stationary and coordinated generic state of rule order and population equilibrium is only interesting as a benchmark for the analysis of ongoing macro coordination. For in a complex open system driven by the continuous regeneration of generic novelty of the human imagination, nothing remains still for long.

The coordination of economic systems is a consequence of human cooperation and the imagination that sustains it. But the evolution of economic systems is a consequence of human imagination and the cooperation that sustains it. The macroeconomy can, therefore, only be understood as a co-evolutionary process.

6 Macro dynamics, growth and development

- Introduces the concept of regimes and regime transitions
- Defines macro coordination and self-organization in an open system
- Proposes a theory of evolutionary growth and development

6.1 Introduction

In the previous chapter we examined the nature of macro coordination and the process of de-coordination and re-coordination in consequence of a meso trajectory as a macro trajectory. A micro trajectory was the building block of a meso trajectory and a meso trajectory was the building block of macro coordination. Here, we extend this argument to its full implications for the study of economic growth and development by considering a macro trajectory as the building block of the economic system as an open system.

The point we shall make is that economic processes of growth and development are inherently evolutionary processes. The point we shall emphasize is that this means that the future is open. Prediction is therefore impossible, but analysis is not. Indeed, we can discern clear patterns of evolutionary economic development based about generic progression.

We shall proceed as follows. In Section 6.2, we introduce the concept of a whole macro trajectory as a *regime*, and of economic history as a sequence of *regime transitions*. This will provide us with a view of the generic features of economic development in an open system and of economic history as the outcome of an evolutionary process. In Section 6.3 we gather this into a methodological and theoretical disquisition on the analysis of economic change. In Section 6.4 we then seek to apply this by considering how a general theory of generic coordination and change might underpin a general theory of macroeconomic growth and development and to the analysis of economic history.

6.2 Regimes and regime transitions

A meso trajectory, along with its micro generic transformations and total macro effect, can be considered as a new analytic unit—namely a regime—that can serve as a building block for the new science of evolutionary macroeconomics. First, we shall define the concept of a regime and the process of a regime transition and, second, we examine the necessary and sufficient conditions for macro evolution to occur not in terms of the creativity of agents, which was the micro explanation, but in terms of the nature of a macro environment in which evolution can occur. Third, we shall explain how sequences of regimes form a generic model of economic history and development. We emphasize that although there is an inherent logic within a regime governed by the logic of the rule, in a market-based economy regime sequences can never be revealed faster than in the real time of a meso trajectory and a regime transition. Regimes and regime transitions are in this way the building blocks of macroeconomic evolution.

6.2.1   Definition of regime and regime transition

A regime is defined as the complete meso unit of the rule, the structure of the carrier population and the re-coordination of the trajectory, as it affects the entire macroeconomy. A regime is therefore a unit of macro dynamics.

Regime: – rule
             – carrier population
             – trajectory

The analytic value of this concept is that it combines the structural connections of the rule to other rules (and the population to other populations) with the population dynamics of the rule in historical time. At a point in time we may conceptualize the macro order as being made of meso units, but that overlooks the distinction between meso units that have completed their trajectory and meso units that are still evolving.

A regime, then, is the term for a completed meso trajectory that forms a *structural and process component* of the macro order. A regime forms a structural component of the economy by the associations the rule makes to other rules and the connective structure of the carrier population to other rule populations. As a process component, a regime outlines the historical path of the meso unit, and, as the ongoing process of its replication, as an institution. A regime is therefore a structure, a population and a process at once as a single analytic unit. A regime, correspondingly, is the building block of generic macro analysis. This is for two broad reasons.

First, regimes are located in time as well as space and may be ordered such that one regime may follow from a previous one as a *regime sequence*: $R_i \rightarrow R_j \rightarrow R_k$. Or regime sequences may branch (bifurcate), such that: $R_{i,t0} \rightarrow R_{j,t1}$ and $R_{i,t0} \rightarrow R_{k,t1}$. Or a regime sequence may unfold along parallel co-evolving paths: $R_{i,t0} \rightarrow R_{j,t1}$ and $R_{m,t0} \rightarrow R_{n,t1}$. This suggests to us the possibility of an analytic approach to the study of macroeconomic structure and the history of economic systems as a branching "generic tree of life" in which one regime leads to another as the complex knowledge base of the economic order grows and develops. But whether conceived as a simple series or a complex branching tree, the concept of a regime as both a structure in space and a process in time provides a way of ordering the relation between the elements of an economy and therefore the structure of knowledge.

Second, from the evolutionary perspective, there is much wrong with existing classifications of the components of the macroeconomy into industries, regions or even markets, in that they often fail to represent the underlying generic structure and how it is changing. A regime is a better building block than say "industry" because it makes explicit how it fits into the economy as well as how it got there. There is no such thing as a "representative regime" any more than there is a representative agent or species. The study of regimes would constitute a much needed natural history of economic systems to complement the excellent work done by the many scholars of technological change in economic systems.

A *regime transition*, in turn, is the process by which one regime provides the conditions for the next, and so is the basic process unit of analysis of economic growth and development. Specifically, a regime transition occurs when the logic and conditions of meso macro 3 gives rise to a new meso 1. A meso trajectory is the origination, adoption and retention of a rule into a carrier population, a regime (R_i) is defined as a rule, population and trajectory and a regime transition is the path from meso macro 3 to micro meso 1 ($R^3_i \rightarrow R^1_j$) that begins a new trajectory.

Regime transitions are a central aspect of meso macro analysis from the perspective of economic progress in that they describe how one thing leads to the next. In this sense, regime and regime transition form the necessary complements of a generic theory of economic development. When we treat a meso unit in isolation and suppose that its arrival was random, as both industry and growth studies are prone to do, we completely lose sight of the unfolding relations between the deeper generic structures of knowledge that facilitate this process.

A regime viewed in isolation lacks a structural context in which it is embedded, and so the particular character of its generic competence (i.e., competitive advantage) will tend to be overlooked. But so too is a regime viewed in isolation artificially separated from the conditions under which it emerged and also the new conditions it creates as a basis for further regimes. Analysis of regime transitions must therefore seek to reveal the linkages that connect regimes such that one idea leads to the next on the unending generic loom of economic progress.

6.2.2 Conditions for economic evolution

In Chapter 1, we sought to locate the origins of economic evolution in the internal creativity of *Homo sapiens Oeconomicus* and the generic capabilities of the human mind to make and use rules. In Chapters 3 and 4, we developed this as driven by a meso 1 process of entrepreneurship and innovation as structured by operational circumstances and 2nd order origination rules. Here, however, we shall examine the generic conditions for economic evolution and the possibility of generic progress in terms of the external conditions necessary for a regime transition to occur, and thus for an economy to regenerate and so continue to evolve.

The conditions for economic evolution to occur in the form of a regime transition are complex. On the one hand, there needs to be sufficient stability in the rule population to afford a meaningful assessment of the novel rule's prospects in terms of the existing structures, specializations and markets that currently exist. This is irrespective of whether the novel rule originates as a substitute for an existing rule (in meso 3) or enters *ab nihilo* by creating something genuinely or radically new. The prospects of a substitute are meaningfully assessed with respect to the stable conditions of the incumbent rule, and the prospects of novelty are also assessed with respect to the niche that exists about a stable set of extant regimes.

Novelty only makes sense against a background of things unchanged, and so the more stable the environment the easier it is to assess and value the prospect of generic novelty. On the other hand, too much stability can engender conservatism and strong resistance to change, lowering the prospect of any novelty. However, at the other extreme, an environment with nothing but change is also a poor evolutionary environment, for although an idea may be less resisted, it will be impossible to evaluate because of the absence of any stable rules it may connect to or stable niches it may enter. An environment completely closed to the possibility of experimentation cannot possibly evolve because it can never generate variety.

Yet an environment completely open to all change can neither evolve because, lacking stable structure, there is nothing about which associations and connections may form.

As such, from the generic perspective, the most suitable environment for evolution to occur is a balance of structural order and randomness that is, as an ensemble, meta- (quasi-) stable and complex.[1] This would have sufficient stability to make evaluation and enterprise a meaningful prospect for a novel endeavor, but also enough openness to render it a possibility. There must be ability of the system to generate and accommodate variety, but also the necessary stability against which a selection process of differential replication can occur. For economic evolution to occur, a regime must end on the complex conditions necessary for a regime transition. These conditions are constituted by a state of quasi-stability, and these may or may not occur naturally. The failure of a regime to arrive in a complex state necessary for a regime transition may be traced to several generic causes.

First, novelty may fail to regenerate because of the absence of variety in the rule at meso 3. This would be manifest as the absence of variants in the market that harbor somewhat different operational capabilities and connections and although not widely adopted continue to occupy viable niches within the rule.

Second, a regime transition may fail due to inappropriate institutional circumstances (i.e., 0th order rules) at the end of meso 3. This could be due to the effects of industry or competition policy, for example, or to strategic decisions by market dominating firms to collude in generic or operational connections.

Third, a regime transition may fail due to a loss of 2nd order rules for innovation. This may be a natural consequence of the meso trajectory operating over a long period of time, such that the original entrepreneurs and innovators are no longer connected to the meso 3 state which is now dominated by 2nd order retention rules and habitual behaviors.

Fourth, a transition may fail due to an inappropriate balance of [CBST] rules. For example, by meso 3, a rule may be operationally functional in social and technical rules, but with cognitive and behavioral rules only poorly adopted and retained. While such a disconnect between subject and object rules may have little immediate impact on the continuing viability and replication of the rule; it may significantly hamper any further development. A people who will remain unfamiliar and uncomfortable with a social and material technology are unlikely to find efficient ways of integrating it into their lives, or to find imaginative new uses for it, and so regime transition may fail due to generic sclerosis.

Consequently, the properties of regimes that can make transitions are complex. They will involve a crucial balance between variety and conservation that plays out over all generic rule dimensions. Mechanisms for achieving this coordination are therefore mechanisms that must simultaneously facilitate the retention of valuable existing structure and continuous experimentation along with ongoing enterprise across all aspects of the rule. Stability and variety must be balanced such that the benefits of carrying variety and maintaining experimentation are in proportion to their cost, which is, in turn, configured with respect to the continual need to create variety in order to maintain any competitive position. The necessary condition for ongoing economic evolution, therefore, is the maintenance of complexity in all structural components of the system.[2]

A regime must be able to undergo a regime transition, so that one idea can provide the building block for the next. This condition is manifest in all manner of specific ways, but is generally manifest in a generic balance of conservation and experimentation as a quasi-stable state of complexity. Such a state of convergence makes a regime transition possible (although this is also possible in meso 2) and so the economic system can continue to evolve. Progress, then as a necessary but not sufficient condition, is what happens when the conditions for economic evolution emerge in meso 2 and 3. Economic history, then, is the ongoing generic story of these regimes and their regime transitions that connect one new idea to the next.

6.2.3   *An evolutionary theory of history*

From the generic perspective, economic history can be told as the branching sequence from one idea to the next as a regime engenders the conditions for a new regime and so on $(R_1 \rightarrow R_2 \rightarrow \ldots)$. Economic history is progressive to the extent that one idea follows from the previous as a regime transition of *generic progress* that is otherwise known as the growth of knowledge.[3] In the alternate case, in which novel ideas arrive randomly, economic history is a process of generic drift, and not progressive. This distinction between generic drift and progress is central to the difference between theories of economic growth and economic development.

A theory of development consists of regimes and regime transitions forming a development sequence as distinct from a generically random growth process. While it is widely appreciated, both intuitively and empirically, that the growth of knowledge is a process that feeds on itself, as for example one generation of computers is used to design the next, it has also thus far proven difficult to represent analytically this phenomenon in a satisfactory way, a theme we shall return to below.

The distinction between generic drift (i.e., random regimes) and progress (i.e., regime transition) is also, we suggest, central to the historicity of the evolutionary economic process. The attachment of causal connections to sequences of events by their generic relation, that is, via a regime and regime transition, advances the possibilities of an empirical evolutionary analysis. This manner of analysis was first promulgated by Schumpeter with his assembly of different cycles and trajectories into a story of regimes and regime transitions, and has been greatly developed by subsequent economic historians and theorists.[4] The framework of regimes and regime transitions can therein provide a theoretical foundation in terms of micro meso macro analysis to underpin a generic theory of economic history in terms of rules that were able to connect to other rules and regenerate the conditions for their own embedding.

In Darwinian logic, the immortality of a rule is conditional upon its ability to create a continuous line of descendants. Gene selection is therefore determined by ability to replicate into the next generation. In the generic logic of evolutionary economics, the immortality of a rule is conditional upon its ability to embed itself deeply in the structure of knowledge, such that it becomes ultimately an institution upon which other things are then built, and so will be forever replicated by the ongoing success of its emergent descendents. Generic rule immortality comes not from a replicative diffusion process *per se*, but from the new rules that may emerge and advance the complexity of the economic order in consequence of the regime stability of that rule due to its sufficient embedding. As more rules emerge from that semi-stable structure, the constituent rule becomes increasingly stable and embedded as its operations of replication are increasingly carried by the emergent rules.

For Darwinian genes (and memes), success is replication. But for generic rules, success is retention through embedding. This is a process that can be analyzed in terms of levels, orders and phases of generic rules, an analysis that may then form a suitable basis for a theory of economic history as a process of regimes and regime transitions. In this way, the logic of economic history and the evolutionary path of economic development can, we believe, be conceptualized usefully as patterns of regime sequences carving out evolutionary economic history. Yet, whatever we might come to know about the generic structure of economic history and development, this can never provide a map of the future.

The economic possibilities of future generations are unknown, not because we have not yet extrapolated all that is known, but rather because they are fundamentally unknowable, as they will be composed of rules that do not yet exist. The future is unknown and unknowable, or, in other words, the future is open. Economic evolution is an open process in that it is continually dependent on the emergence of novelty, and without this ongoing infusion of variety the process of economic evolution would grind to a halt as selection predominated. Evolution is a process of ongoing selection over continuously regenerated variety and will occur wherever variations compete for scarce resources. But these variations must be continuously regenerated, for without such a continuous regeneration mechanism evolution is just stochastic optimization.[5]

But economic history shows that time and again, the calculus of advance is generic difference, such that one idea leads to another. Small cranes are used to assemble large cranes, computers are used to design new computers, and ideas are used to create new ideas. That is how knowledge grows. A generic extrapolation in which an idea runs inextricably to diminishing marginal product is adequate as a partial analysis, but is just a starting point for a more general macro analysis of the evolution of generic rules in which one idea leads to another. Yet a generic theory of history and development that explores the consequences of past novelty says nothing necessarily about future novelty. Analysis of past patterns is not necessarily predictive in an open evolving system because the generic rules they are based upon by definition have changed. A generic analysis of economic history will reveal a pattern of regimes and transitions, but any extrapolation of those patterns is analysis in the face of generic uncertainty. The micro meso macro framework is not a predictive model, but rather an analytic structure about which to investigate a rule with specific knowledge of its generic and operant conditions.

Economic history is neither a determinist sequence of techno-logic, nor a random drift of ideas. It has both continuous structure built up through the embedding of rules into the knowledge base of the economic order, and a continual openness to new possibilities through the complexity inherent in that process. Of course, some rules embed deeper in the knowledge base than others, and some possibilities will be foreclosed due to the absence of variety and complexity in retained outcomes. Economic evolution is not a Markov process in which only the parameter values of the previous state matter to the transition to the next state, but nor do those parameters and their history completely determine the next state, as in a differential equation.[6]

An evolutionary theory of economic history is better understood as more akin to a partially directed and operationally weighted stochastic generic Markov process in which most memory is retained in the system, but not all. The rule structure of current regimes will condition the path of evolution, and yet this path will remain fundamentally open due to the consequence of novel ideas. Thus, in the evolutionary course of history there is at a present time always a "contextual determinism" paralleled by a set of "historic opportunities."[7] A generic theory of economic history must therefore seek to be more than just an account of overlapping spaces and times of generic events, and more than an aggregate operational account of correlated consequence (e.g., cliometrics). Rather, it should seek to trace the pathways and connections within regimes and across regime transitions to subsequent emergent regimes. Generic economic history is the story of such paths.

6.3   Macro coordination, evolution and self-organization

Before turning to a more detailed analysis of the macro coordination dynamics in Section 6.3.1, let us briefly recapitulate our basic theoretic position. Economic evolution is the process by which the knowledge base of the economy—i.e., the generic system—changes. This process happens as novel rules are originated, adopted and retained into carriers, so changing their operational capabilities. This creative process is necessarily destructive of some of the existing content and structure of knowledge and patterns of activity, and will rarely be efficient as it goes. Yet it is the ultimate source of the wealth of nations. Economic evolution is generic change, and when this change improves our material welfare, it is progress. Not all economic evolution is progress, but much and perhaps even most is. For the wealth of nations to grow, the generic system of knowledge must evolve.

The general theory of economic evolution is composed of a general theory of rules—i.e., of the generic domain—and of the operational consequences of change in those rules. This can be modeled at three distinct analytical levels: micro, meso and macro. From the perspective of the whole, economic evolution is the process of de-coordination of an existing macro order and re-coordination into a new macro order. The general theory of economic evolution is based upon a systematic account of the generic domain of rules as deductive procedures for operations. Our theory of rules is as follows:

- Rules are originated by human minds
- There are two major classes of rule—subject and object
- There are four minor classes of rule—cognitive, behavioral, social and technical
- There are three orders of rules—0th, 1st, 2nd
- There are three phases to a rule trajectory—1 2 3
- Each rule can have many carriers—this is the rule population
- There are two types of rule carrier—subjects (agents, agencies) and objects (socially and technically organized).

Economic evolution is the process by which a novel rule is originated at the micro level in the mind of an agent, and is then adopted by other agents over a three-phase trajectory so as to form a stable meso population in terms of all four classes of the rule. This process disturbs the existing macro order, and begins the entrainment of new order and the possibility of generic change that improves on the old order of rules. In static operational analysis this is called "Pareto" change. In evolutionary generic analysis this should be called "Marshallian," "Hayekian" or "Schumpeterian" change to reflect the possibility of new rules to progress the existing macro order.

In any case, this is an evolutionary process in the Darwinian sense. It is composed of a mechanism of variety generation, as the introduction of a new rule into the rule population, and a mechanism of selection as the differential replication of that rule through differential adoption and retention. This classical view of variation, selection and replication sits at the core of our general theory in terms of the evolution of a meso population as driven by variety within the rule, heterogeneity of carriers of the rule or as a co-evolutionary process between different rule populations.

However, economic evolution is not just a (meso) population dynamic of variation and selection, but also involves systematic micro changes in the rules that agents and agencies carry as well as self-organizing changes in the generic structure of the macro order. The micro meso macro framework provides a general conceptual underpinning for further development of analysis of the endogenous growth and transformation of the whole economy as an ongoing evolutionary process.

So far, then, we have built up a theory of economic evolution that begins with a novel idea in a single agent that then develops into a theory of the meso unit as the rule is adopted and retained by a population of carriers. Such a meso trajectory disturbs (i.e., de-coordinates) the macro order and engenders a process of re-coordination that over a macro trajectory results in a new macro order. This process occurs in parallel, as multiple meso trajectories unfold at once, and in series, as one meso trajectory leads to the next. These meso macro processes are defined respectively as the co-evolution of many meso and the process of regime transitions from one trajectory to the next, and that, in abstract, is our theory of economic evolution.

6.3.1   Macro coordination dynamics in perspective

Yet we shall not deem to call this a theory of the coordination of the whole economy, but only a start in that direction. This may seem evasive, as we have pointedly argued that the purpose of an evolutionary economics is to explain the macroeconomy as a whole, and that the reason for the elaborate construction of the evolutionary micro and meso framework, to say nothing of the ontological foundation of this, was to provide a basis for an analysis of the macro. Furthermore, this may seem weak, as surely such a sketchy and unformulated start upon a theory of macro coordination cannot compete with the already seemingly well-developed theories of the macroeconomy. Yet we maintain that these theories have not solved the problem of macro coordination and that our sketchy and abstract start does make for progress because it improves over the current situation of effectively no theory.

The statement that there is currently no general theory of coordination will surely annoy just about everyone, so let us unpack it: a general theory of allocation is not a general theory of coordination. The Walrasian framework and subsequent development of general equilibrium is a theory of allocation under given generic conditions (preferences, technologies, organization, etc.). This is not a theory of coordination of the whole economy because it presumes completely that the coordination of the rules of the economy, the carrier populations, and the associations and connections between all of these has already taken place.

It is wrong to assume that something is given and then call it a theory of that something. You cannot assume coordination, concoct a model based upon this assumption, and then declare the product a theory of coordination. At best, it's false advertising. Yet, this is precisely what the neoclassical theory of allocation does vis-à-vis coordination. General equilibrium theory entirely avoids the problems of coordination because it has no generic level, that is, there is effectively nothing to coordinate. Therefore, this is the reason it cannot deal with the question of how structure emerges, or how the process of organic growth or self-organization occurs in the macroeconomy; the assumption is that it just happens. Coordination is free in general equilibrium.

A similar critique can also be made against the Keynesian framework (although less so against Keynes's own comprehensive framework). It sought to deal with the whole economy and its problems of coordination, but again it collapsed the generic dimension to a crude caricature of generic rules, dispensing entirely with social and technical rules of organization and allowing only some representative behavioral rules relating to marginal savings and investment propensities.[8] The core of analysis was thereby transferred to the operational level of aggregate expenditure flows.

Furthermore, the general framework of input–output analysis is similarly constrained by assuming, in effect, that all generic coordination has already taken place (i.e., the matrix of inter-sector resource flows and elasticities is meaningfully known) and that analysis is only concerned with the analysis of the effect of changes in resources quantities or prices. This is in no way to critique the value of the enormous intellectual exercise involved in these frameworks. It is only to insist that they are not actually, as they sometimes imply, general theories of macro coordination.

General equilibrium theory, the neoclassical–Keynesian synthesis and input–output models are only operationally general; they are not generically general over the space of the coordination problem. This is because they all, in one way or another, effectively assume what they set out to explain. They presume that the generic level is already coordinated, and then proceed immediately to analyze the operational consequences of this.

Indeed, this practise has become so widespread and embedded that it seems perhaps strange to envisage an economic framework of the whole economy that does otherwise. So, the potential strangeness of our micro meso macro framework from the comparative analytic position, and perhaps its seeming remoteness to existing categories of analytic concepts and discourse and its elaborate development of entirely new concepts (e.g., rule, carrier, trajectory), should be understood as the attempt to provide the analytical foundations for such a theory of coordination and to do so into an analytical space that is, surprisingly, largely unpopulated.

Yet, there are of course existing frameworks that seek to explain the coordination of the whole economy. The two that stand out are Adam Smith's theory of the division of labor and knowledge, and Friedrich von Hayek's theory of the emergent order (cosmos) of the whole economy. Both of these were theories of self-organization of the many parts into an ordered whole, and it is notable that both have utterly resisted formalization and analytical development much beyond the designs of their progenitors.

Why? Because a theory of the self-organization of the whole economy must be more than just a theory of the coordination of given, if initially disordered, parts. But Smith and Hayek were not thinking of the coordination problem of the whole economy in such a simplified way because what they knew to be true, and what they took as the deeper essence of the coordination problem of the whole, was this: first, the parts themselves are never "given"; and second, the parts themselves are continually changing.

To the analytic mind, the notion of developing a rigorous theory of coordination about fundamentally undefined and (worse) protean elements is well beyond the ken of what is, even now, analytically tractable. Moreover, to pose the problem in that way is, perhaps, seeming evidence that one does not actually understand what modern neoclassical analysis is ultimately capable of explaining given enough latitude to interpret the solution to an allocation problem as the solution to a coordination problem. Adam Smith and Friedrich Hayek both disagreed with this equivalence. But Smith must be forgiven because that was a long time ago, and Hayek remains implicitly regarded as not really being a proper theorist, more a man of words and ideas than theorems and proofs:[9] the distant mutterings of academic scribblers, as it were.

Yet, this is to misunderstand the deeper problem they were trying to solve, namely the generic coordination problem of how the many rules and carrier populations of the economy come to self-organize in such a way as to engender a state of generic coordination that, upon which, the operational coordination of resources with respect to this can proceed. They were concerned with the problem of economic coordination where coordination was not presumed given, but, rather, the very problem to be resolved: macro coordination is a generic problem and an evolutionary outcome. Yet it remains largely unexplained.

There are two reasons why this deeper problem was lost or subsumed. The first, as already signalled, is that the equilibrium framework provided a powerful analytic focus toward the construction of theories that explained how distributed parts could coordinate through selection mechanisms, or market forces, in terms of the mutual adjustment of operations.

The eventual consequence was that the solution concepts of the theories of this operational process became equivalent to the solution of the generic coordination process itself. Operationally this is justifiable as a model, but generically it is entirely nonsensical. For it presumed as given and fixed what it must then seek to explain as open and changing.

The second reason was that the whole inquiry was hijacked by the rise of the political movements of socialism and communism that sought to "solve" the coordination problem through elite centralized calculation. Smith and Hayek, among many others, had clearly signalled the absurdity of this. The lasting effect, however, was that the "planning versus markets" debate was taken to be the end of the matter and the lasting substance of their contribution.

Yet their ultimate concern—a plea for the superiority of market coordination over centralized planning—has been widely misunderstood, for they both took that to be self-evident. Instead, what they sought was an account of the self-organizational process of how the division of labor and knowledge, or the complex emergent order of economic activities, itself evolves and self-organizes. That, we maintain, is still the fundamental economic problem that the generic framework of micro meso macro takes some analytic steps toward.[10]

Now perhaps it may seem odd to evolutionary economists that we would isolate Smith and Hayek in our assessment of those who have sought to analyze the evolutionary generic coordination of the whole economy, but not include the likes of Joseph Schumpeter in our pantheon—for what was his *Theory of Economic Development* if not precisely that?

Our answer, which may be unpopular or even heretical among modern evolutionary economists, is to say that Schumpeter's contributions were essentially meso. He did not actually develop his framework to the deeper question of the self-organization of the whole economy. Of course, we would not even be thinking these thoughts were it not for his great contribution in focusing the meso perspective. But, we are bound to observe that Schumpeter, as with those he built upon and those who have followed since, did effectively take self-organization as given. So while Schumpeter and others clearly did make brilliant and incisive contributions to the nature and causes of the growth and development of the whole macroeconomy through an analysis of the causes of novelty generation and the disruptive consequences this brings, they remain, in our terms, essentially analysis of meso dynamics.[11]

Schumpeterian analysis addresses the generic meso dimension and extends naturally to encompass multiple meso processes. Yet, so far, it still stops short of an analysis of the coordination of the whole. Although focused on generic analysis and the dynamics of such, it nevertheless takes self-organization (i.e., open generic coordination) as a constant.

For all the talk of creative destruction, Schumpeter still pulled up short of extending this to a general macro growth model.[12] This is especially apparent in Schumpeter's self-styled position with respect to Walras, where he supposed that once the order-destroying effects of the entrepreneur had seeded, the process of economic evolution would break the economy from its circular flow, or generic order, and all else would just follow naturally. This is Austrian and Walrasian micro theory at once. Yet it harbors the same presumptions to a theory of coordination as neoclassical economics: namely assuming that a process will happen, and then turning around and calling that a theory of coordination. Schumpeterian analysis is excellent on meso, but it is not yet a macro analysis.

Most other post-classical economists have engaged in much the same thing. Consider, for example, Allyn Young's theory of increasing returns, and Nicholas Kaldor's theory of endogenous growth.[13] These are both widely regarded by the *cognoscenti* of evolutionary economists as deep and signal contributions to the study of economic growth and development from the perspective of open evolving systems, and certainly they are. But what they are not are general frameworks of the generic coordination of the whole economy.

Young's framework emphasizes that as economies grow they become structurally different due to differential scale economies, which is most definitely true, but that is not yet a theory of how that process happens. Kaldor's framework emphasizes that structural growth involves differential growth between sectors, with some leading that process and capturing resources that then feed others. Again, this is true and deeply insightful, but it is not yet a theory of the generic coordination of the whole because it still takes the self-organization of the economy as given and then focuses on resource flows between multiple connected sectors.

We of course have no wish to prosecute special theories of something for not being general theories of everything. Our point is simply that even the deepest and most determined endeavors to analyze the generic coordination of the whole economy—and how it grows and develops, as the works of Young, Schumpeter and Kaldor certainly are—still falls short of a general theory of generic coordination of the whole economy. Kaldor, Young and Schumpeter, as typical post-classical economists, took the self-organizing approach as constant. They made deeply insightful advances into what we call meso trajectories and the dynamics of resource flows over generic models that made sophisticated discriminations between rules. But ultimately they allowed that either those rules themselves were given, as in a multi-sector model, or that the self-organizing process was given, as in the re-coordination of the economy following a generic disturbance.

Now of course none were being disingenuous or claiming more than they had, for the problem of explaining generic coordination is exceptionally hard. That we can only point to two instances of development of this (Smith and Hayek), and that these belong to arguably the greatest economists who ever lived, is testimony to that. Yet we are in no way suggesting that we have solved this problem. Indeed, nothing of the sort. But we are suggesting that our framework is a start along this path. Moreover, we believe that we have exposed the essential dimensions of the problem, namely as the coordination of meso units.

Furthermore, we observe that a general theory of generic coordination is, essentially, a general theory of complementarity between rules themselves (deep coordination) and between populations of carriers (surface coordination). It is widely appreciated that a general theory of substitution exists (namely the neoclassical framework), but it is a profound mistake, and indeed a categorical misunderstanding of the meaning of an open system, to suppose that the inverse of this is a general theory of complementarity.

Yet there currently exists no such theory in economics. Moreover, the problem is not as trivial as the inverse substitution (i.e., complementarity matrix) hypothesis would have it. It is precisely what entrepreneurs seek out for profit and consumers seek out for utility (namely new connections that have value). This is an open and ever-changing set that is continually changed by the continuous micro generic processes of adoption that change the populations of rules and so the possibilities of connections between meso.

A general theory of generic coordination must be not just a theory of what rules fit with what other rules, as if this were the mapping of a territory that could be done just once for all time. The problem is compounded by the fact that connections between populations also must be mapped and that these structures will continue to change. Maps of the human genome or even of ecosystems are only plausible because the underlying genes or species do not change on a scale comparable to how long it takes to make the map. This is not invariably true for economic evolution.

The upshot is that generic maps may be more like weather maps than cartographic maps: just as useful, but with use-by dates. This is why, however hard this task is, we must continue to seek an analytical solution. Toward this end, we propose that the micro meso macro framework can provide a viable and practical conceptual and analytic foundation for the further development of a unified evolutionary economic science.

6.3.2   *Toward an evolutionary theory of growth and development*

Marshall's districts, Schumpeter's trajectories, Penrose's firms and Nelson and Winter's industrial populations are all exemplars of the industrial and technological dynamics which formed the main path of evolutionary economic analysis over the twentieth century. There are now many excellent industry and technology studies that combine detailed historical analysis with algebraic or computational models of these meso dynamics of rules, rule systems and rule populations. A number of industries have been extensively mapped (e.g., textiles and chemicals) along with the lines of many key technologies (e.g., steel and integrated circuits).

Yet these vast bodies of work covering a broad range of time periods and industries still await a unified analytic synthesis into a comprehensive and general theory of the whole macroeconomic order. However, toward this end, there have been two main analytic paths: the historians of technology and long run economic development; and the various theories of endogenous growth.

The first path is represented by the work of Chris Freeman, Carlotta Perez, Joel Mokyr, Douglas North, Paul David, David Landes, Joseph Schumpeter and Karl Marx, all of whom seek to combine a sufficiently broad time and scope to draw out through detailed empirical analysis the generic patterns that describe the large-scale transformation of the economic system. These studies differ in focal points, including institutions, technologies, generic knowledge and the co-evolution of social and technical rules, and also in coverage, for example, concentrating on manufacturing or emergent institutions. But together, they provide a general empirical map of the generic and operational structures that have existed and changes that have occurred over the past two centuries. This map of course is still far from complete and composed with vast gaps (e.g., the service economy, consumer preferences, market technologies, China and Brazil, etc.). However, it does provide an initial map that can be used as a template for further mapping and as a guide for the development of theory.

The other path has been that of endogenous growth theory and its many incarnations. It is a modern textbook myth that growth theory consists of two phases, namely Solow's exogenous growth theory and Lucas and Romer's endogenous growth theory. For the fact is that growth and development theory from Adam Smith to Allyn Young, Karl Marx to Amartya Sen, or Jack Downie to Dani Rodrick has always been endogenous and it is Solow's exogenous model that is the outlier.[14]

Nevertheless, modern endogenous growth theory still tends to focus on very low dimensional generic variation, such as the rule for the allocation of resources to R&D. With this method, they have been able to produce models that show the implications of differential investment in the growth of knowledge and of the sorts of growth paths expected under different institutional regimes.

Yet they still have little purchase on the structural changes involved in this process, whether at the micro or macro level, because these modern endogenous growth models are essentially operational theories. That is not a bad thing in itself, and indeed is an essential component of a general evolutionary theory of economic coordination and change. Still, the fact remains that modern endogenous growth theory is essentially focused on operational re-coordination in consequence of highly stylized generic change, that is, the growth of "knowledge."

The basic problem with the exogenous growth theory of Solow et al. is that it was generically invariant; growth was a product of factor accumulation on given generic conditions. The endogenous growth theory of Lucas and Romer et al. went beyond this by allowing that new rules could enter and change the marginal productivity of other factors engendering a state of constant or increasing marginal productivity to factor accumulation. This was, and remains, an important advance, and in significant part due to its connection to invariant choice-theoretic micro foundations, but it still falls well short of a theory of meso change. It explains how micro agents can learn new things and how that can lead to an aggregate of new growth, but it has no account of the process by which that happens. In effect, it assumes that a random meso 1 goes directly to a locked-in meso 3. As an abstraction, this is not wrong. But as a theory, it leaves aside the most interesting questions: which new ideas will become embedded and how, and what else will change in consequence of that meso trajectory.

Both old and new growth theory fails to account for the generic domain and its complex, evolving, self-organizing process structure. Old growth theory is entirely about operational change on generically invariant conditions, and although new growth theory opens analysis to a two-stage growth process, it is still a long way from an account for the complex evolving generic change in the content and organization of activities, labor, knowledge and structure that characterizes modern economic evolution.

Generic endogenous growth theory emphasizes that economic growth, transformation and development involves a process in which novel generic ideas enter and restructure the economic order, and that this is not the same as a shift outward in the production function or a jump from a novel idea to a new industry, as from one equilibrium to the next without any account of the process between and beyond.

How then can the micro meso macro framework guide us further in these efforts? Generic endogenous growth theory seeks to unpack the difference between growth and development in terms of the effects of an original micro trajectory (i.e., meso 1), a meso trajectory, the operational expansion of meso 3, a regime transition from meso 3 to meso 1, and the co-evolution and self-organization of systems of meso trajectories. The whole macroeconomy evolves as a process of meso trajectories, from the origination of the novel generic idea in a mind to the retention of the adopted idea in a population of carriers and the new deep and surface structure that implies. This is the de-coordination and re-coordination of the macro order that underpins the theory of generic endogenous growth and development.

The micro meso macro framework offers a theory of the generic endogenous growth of the whole economy, not just in terms of technical rules or sufficient institutions, but across the set of cognitive, behavioral, social and technical rule classes and over the gamut of 0th, 1st and 2nd order rules. Moreover, it tracks this progress over the three phases of a rule trajectory and the transition from one regime to the next.

Micro meso macro, in this way, provides a framework for the theory of endogenous generic change and analysis of endogenous generic coordination. Economic growth is what happens when a new idea that has been successfully trailed, adapted and embedded is able to provide the basis of an operational expansion of activities. Economic evolution is the ongoing supply of such generic opportunities.

Long run economic development is, in this way, the outcome of an ongoing evolutionary process in which one new idea leads to the next, in which the meta-stability of one population leads to the possibility of a new population, and so in which new economic activities seed and disperse on the basis of this growth of knowledge process.

The evolutionary economic approach to generic endogenous growth theory aims to sharpen both empirical and theoretical analysis of how the growth of knowledge process happens in economic systems. It combines the insights of the historians of technology and institutions and the basic feedback principles of endogenous growth theory. But rather than seeking an empirical or theoretical extension of either of these, it points toward a richer and deeper *synthetic* model of the generic processes of economic evolution. Clearly, this is a natural extension of the program of appreciative theorizing that Nelson and Winter introduced in their 1982 book.

There are still many gaps in our understanding of how macroeconomic systems are coordinated and how they change. We do not yet have a map of how all cognitive, behavioral, social and technical rules fit together, nor how all constitutive, operational or mechanism rules fit together, nor a comprehensive map of the historical trajectory and continuous state of all rules.

A complete generic map would be enormously expensive to construct, involving perhaps hundreds of economists, historians, statisticians and mathematicians and thousands of research projects. However, such a generic mapping project would provide the historical baseline for future economic evolution and would, therefore, be an enormously worthwhile project for mapping and forecasting as well as "generic engineering" in both strategy and policy.

Instead, nowadays, what we have are but approximate maps of some rule classes at some locations at some points in time. These are, in turn, calibrated against generic maps of the thread and weave of the basic rules of the modern economic order in terms of specific technologies, behaviors, organizations and institutions. These are enormously useful for some strategic and policy purposes with respect to specific industrial or market dynamics, yet the map of generic structure and change remains radically incomplete both in terms of its complex structure and process dynamics.

Beginning slowly at first, but accelerating recently, evolutionary economic analysis has come to map and describe some of the generic structure of the economic order. But evolutionary economics still has a long way to go to map all the different rules considered relevant and the different types of dynamic processes at work. Interestingly, evolutionary biology is still in the same ongoing process over a century since it first started. Evolutionary economists have been describing the evolutionary structures and processes of the economic system for a long time now, and that will probably continue to increase in both coverage and inference. What changes, however, are the referents of our description and analysis in a generic theory of economic evolution. Economic systems evolve as rules change, and so the further empirical development of a generic macro theory of economic evolution must hinge not just upon the extension of evolutionary analysis to ever more rules as industries or markets. Rather, further empirical development must seek to reveal the structure of cognitive, behavioral, social and technical rules in each regime, and the 0th, 1st and 2nd order rules that define that generic structure and process. Toward this end, the micro meso macro framework provides the necessary analytical and empirical infrastructure for a foundation to generic endogenous growth theory.

6.4   Conclusion

If the generic path of economic evolution can be described in terms of novel rules being adopted by and retained into *Homo sapiens Oeconomicus*, so changing the macro order of the generic system, then so too perhaps can other "generic" rules of *Homo sapiens*—such as *H. Politicus, H. Sociologicus, H. Culturalis, H. Technologicus*, as well as Thorstein Veblen, and Nelson and Winter's concept of *H. "Routinus"* and Richard Dawkins' concept of *H. Memeticus*. These can all be viewed from the micro meso macro perspective, as they are all dealing with novel rules that enter into an environment of other rules.

From a higher plane, micro meso macro may provide the foundation of a general social and not just economic science. A new cultural rule enters into an environment of other rules and is usefully tracked both through individual people and through populations. The same is true of a political rule, a social rule or a technical rule.

We conjecture, then, that human society evolves in the same way, namely through a three-phase trajectory process involving three orders of rules and over four classes of rules. Furthermore, we suspect that it will result in the same pattern of outcome, namely a structural transition from an existing order of rules to a new order through the evolutionary process of rule variety driving differential carrier adoption leading to a new order of rule retention and therefore of micro and macro structure.

We suspect, therefore, that socio-cultural evolution will share many of the same analytic features as economic evolution. Indeed, the evolution of economic systems is both embedded in socio-cultural-technical systems and, in turn, is conditioned by these same systems as the coevolution of subject and object rules.

Economic systems evolve when new ideas enter from within or otherwise. Political, social and cultural systems evolve in the same generic or "growth of knowledge" way. Generic novelty is the ultimate cause of all economic, political, cultural and social evolution. The adoption and retention of that novelty is generic evolution. In each case, this is an original product of the human mind and a social product of the growth of knowledge.

Homo sapiens Oeconomicus does not just inhabit an environment and then adapt to it, as did Robinson Crusoe, but actively seeks to change that environment in order to explore both its generic capabilities and its generic potential. Economic man has knowledge. But it is not the case that he will never be satisfied with that knowledge, but rather that he never can be, because other agents will create new ideas and those will, eventually, compete with everything he has. The solution therefore is to continually develop new knowledge.

The study of economic evolution is the study of this process, which we think can be analyzed as a micro meso macro process. Smith and Schumpeter both saw the potential of adventurous minds to adapt to an uncertain environment and, also, for this new idea to become the resources, capital, structure and institutions of a new generic environment. They saw how these rules could also be things that could grow and evolve. Yet it was Hayek, ultimately, who saw this natural generic trajectory most clearly: namely, that economic systems evolve when a new idea creates a new environment that opens a path to create further new ideas. Economic systems evolve as a new idea becomes a micro, meso, and then macro trajectory.

7 Generic policy

- Distinguishes generic and operational policy
- Discusses three levels of generic policy
- Argues a preference for 0th and 2nd order policy

7.1 Introduction

So we now have a micro meso macro generic framework. The obvious question to ask, then, is what policy implications this framework might have. We shall not endeavor here to develop specific recommendations for various policy domains—such as competition policy, industry policy, fiscal policy, etc.—and nor shall we review the growing literature on evolutionary economic policy.[1] Instead, we shall concentrate upon the broad outlines of what a justified analytic basis for policy must be as derived from our framework.

Our starting premise is conventional: namely that all policy is intervention into the economic order to promote welfare. But such an intention announces nothing about how or where or why such intervention should be conducted. A more systematic analytic approach is we think required and we propose that this can be built upon a primary distinction between two overarching policy domains: *generic policy* that is focused on rules and *operant policy* that is focused on prices, transactions, incomes, production, etc. We identify only generic policy as legitimate, yet within that, we then further reveal three different levels of generic policy: namely 0th, 1st and 2nd order generic policy. We reject the case for 1st order policy but seek to advance 0th and 2nd order generic policy intervention in the coordination of the constituent rules and mechanisms of the economic order.

7.2 Generic and operational policy

All policy is intervention, yet there are many ways to intervene in the economic order. A crucial distinction is between policy that seeks to intervene at the generic level of rules and populations, which we call generic policy, and policy that seeks to intervene at the operational level of prices, quantities or income structures and flows, which we call operational policy.

All neoclassical and Keynesian policy analysis that ultimately seeks to intervene in markets, prices or income distributions is operational policy. Such policy is logically based on a given or invariant generic domain and seeks only to intervene in the outcomes of the economic order. However, policy that focuses on coordination and change in the underlying generic order itself, as composed of technologies, industries, institutions, mechanisms, legal, cultural and political systems, etc., is generic policy. We shall argue that evolutionary economic policy is best conceived as generic policy.

It is important to note that this conception is based upon the economic distinction between generic and operant levels of the economy and not on political conceptions of left or right, radical or conservative, etc. For there can be both "left-wing" and "right-wing" operational policy to "correct" prices or redistribute income, as well as left- and right-wing generic policy to radically change or conserve the economic order. Political-economy distinctions have no importance here at all.

Instead, what matters is the generic-operant distinction because it distinguishes cause from consequence in the pursuit of progress.[2] Operational intervention only reconfigures the outcomes of the generic order, and while this may lead to social welfare improvements, it makes no contribution to economic progress in the historical opportunity set. It is only generic policy that can effect this, both for better and for worse.

Unlike operational policy, then, generic policy always has historical context because it is always an intervention into an evolving rule system with specific states of generic coordination and current processes of generic change. History matters because history *is* generic context. Generic policy, then, is intervention into the rules and rule populations of the macro order of meso units and their trajectories. It is intervention into a complex, open and history-dependent system.

7.3 Three orders of generic policy

We may therefore distinguish three levels of generic policy as based about the three orders of rules: 0th order constitutional rules; 1st order operational rules; and 2nd order mechanism rules (see Section 1.4.2 above). Policy that seeks to effect coordination and change in constitutional rules is 0th order generic policy; policy that seeks to effect coordination and change in operational rules is 1st order generic policy; and policy that seeks to effect coordination and change in mechanism rules is 2nd order generic policy.

0th order policy seeks to intervene at the level of constitutional rules in order to change the underlying structure of property rights, competition law, legal trade agreements, environmental regulation, labor laws, monetary and financial institutions, public infrastructure, and generally all social, political and cultural institutions that affect the economic order. 0th order policy seeks to change the rules for economic coordination.

1st order policy seeks to intervene in the [CBST] rules that determine economic operations of transactions and transformations. This is either by indirect sponsorship and support through purchasing or government contract, or via direct provision of economic goods, as for example with communication, health, insurance or transport services, or the government control of specific industries, as for example oil, steel or media. 1st order policy seeks to change the rules that compose the economic system in order to provide goods that would either not otherwise be provided, or be provided at the "wrong" operational levels, whether too much or too little.

2nd order policy seeks to intervene in the mechanism rules that structure the origination, adoption and retention of 1st order rules.[3] This is intervention into the capabilities of the economic system not to produce commodities, but to develop the capabilities to generate and adopt novelty, to adapt to change and to retain and embed progress in [CBST] rules.[4] At the center of this is the education system for replicating not just known knowledge, but also the capabilities to develop further knowledge. 2nd order policy seeks to intervene to enhance the capabilities to evolve through the development of knowledge to originate, adopt and retain new knowledge. This focuses on innovation systems and other broadly Schumpeterian mechanisms to support, facilitate and drive the growth of knowledge.

These three generic orders of policy can be loosely mapped to extant schools of economic thought. Plainly, the Austrian/Hayekian/ordo-liberal school can be read into 0th order policy, the neoclassical market-failure school can be read into 1st order policy, and the Schumpeterian framework can be read into 2nd order policy. But so too can the Institutional school (of Commons, for example) be read into 0th order policy, Keynesianism into 1st order policy, and endogenous growth theory into 2nd order policy. The key point, it seems to us, is that none of these are general theories, but rather all are special theories dedicated to different levels of policy analysis. A unified generic policy framework must therefore seek to analyze and integrate these positions.

7.3.1   *Against 1st order policy*

The question, though, is what should we do? Where should policy seek to intervene, and for what purpose? This inescapably requires a normative evaluation and the principles of this can, we believe, be stated plainly and defensibly as amounting to the general illegitimacy of 1st order generic policy that seeks direct intervention in the order of market operations.

The goal of economic policy is always to seek improvements in the generic conditions of a market economy.[5] It seeks to rectify coordination failure in rules and rule populations and to facilitate the evolutionary self-organizing process of change in rules and rule populations. This is to be plainly distinguished from policy that seeks operational effect by intervening in exchange or production and the consequent patterns of price and income.

The wealth of nations is based upon the coordination of specialized knowledge in distributed agents into a complex system of operations. The freedom of individual agents to adapt and the coordination of their difference is the underlying power of the market economic order. In consequence, economic policy should be focused on intervention in the rules that generate operational outcomes, not on the operational outcomes themselves.

Yet that does not imply *laissez-faire*, for a market economy is made not just of 1st order rules, but also of 0th and 2nd order rules that coordinate what can and might happen. Generic policy should, we submit, focus only on coordination and change in constitutional and mechanism rules through the analysis and development of both 0th order and 2nd order policy.

Another way of putting this same normative assessment is that there is both evolutionary and non-evolutionary policy. Evolutionary policy seeks to facilitate processes of change and coordination in the knowledge base of economic agents and their connections by intervention into the rules that constitute and evolve this system. 0th and 2nd order policy is evolutionary policy because it seeks to affect the process of economic evolution through intervention into its structuring and regenerative mechanisms.

However, policy that seeks to intervene directly in rules for economic operations (i.e., 1st order policy) is non-evolutionary in that it seeks to control the generic economy. Worse, it then seeks to impose rational, social, cultural or religious ideals onto its functioning. In such a policy schema, the open-system virtues of property rights, or individual freedom under law, or the inherent value of education, experimentation or research are but costly inefficiencies that would ideally be eliminated in a perfectly rational system. For, in theory, a perfect 1st order system is a frictionless machine that functions smoothly to achieve given ends without seemingly unnecessary variation and duplication. Non-evolutionary policy is generally characterized by the political economy of special interest groups that seek operational rent by intervention into prices or incomes. Such policies invariably stifle generic change and the growth of knowledge by their effect on the mechanisms that generate and regenerate variety.

Evolutionary economic policy should therefore focus on 0th and 2nd order policy—i.e., intervention into 0th and 2nd order rules—because it is here that policy can have evolutionary generic effect. It does so by seeking to re-coordinate and change the constitutional order of rules that generates the environment of economic operations, and by seeking to re-coordinate and change the mechanism rules that facilitate adaptation and the regeneration of knowledge.

7.3.2   2nd order policy

The mechanism (or 2nd order) rules of an economy determine the rules that an economy can originate, adopt and retain, and so the knowledge it can grow. In classical and neoclassical analysis, this just happens, such that all knowledge is given, and only recently has human capital theory and endogenous growth theory come to plainly recognize that the regeneration and advance of knowledge is costly. For evolutionary economists, however, this is an axiom. In consequence, evolutionary economic analysis and policy has come to focus less on the efficiency of the growth of knowledge and more on its efficacy.

The analytic resolution of our generic framework is that knowledge grows (i.e., economies evolve) over a three-phase process of origination, adoption and retention. This process only happens when there are 2nd order rules underlying and making the dynamics of 1st order rules. The long run growth and development of the operational economy is a consequence of the existence and effect of mechanism rules for generically sustained growth.

Conventionally, there are two major components to this: education, as the reproduction and acquisition of existing knowledge; and innovation, as the creation of new knowledge. It is widely understood that both education and innovation policy are central for the maintenance and growth of the wealth of nations. However, the analytic connection between these different states of knowledge, namely that generic education and innovation are but different phases of the same underlying meso trajectory, is not widely appreciated. Thus, the implication that innovation, competition and education policy might all be as one has not been widely considered.

Yet from the evolutionary perspective, the appropriate policy delineations follow the three phases of a meso trajectory. *Origination policy* would focus on the mechanisms for the generation of novelty, which may center about mechanisms for creativity and research. *Adoption policy* would focus about the mechanisms of generic learning of extant knowledge, which is the vast bulk of the education system, and also, of course, knowledge of rules for learning and adoption. *Retention policy* would then focus on the embedding of reusable knowledge into elements of culture and institutions that preserve past advances. This is often cast in the manner of moral, political or cultural education or protection to retain and regenerate the values of an order.

Generic 2nd order policy is therefore knowledge policy, and this is usefully decomposed into origination, adoption and retention policy. The policy separation between education, innovation and competition is, in our view, an artificial operational distinction. It is better, we think, to evaluate these from a unified generic basis of the origination or innovation of knowledge, the adoption or growth of knowledge, and the retention or embedding of knowledge. 2nd order policy therefore seeks to grow knowledge, and so to advance future wealth, through facilitation of the mechanisms by which knowledge grows. These can be analytically decomposed into mechanisms for originating knowledge, adopting knowledge and retaining knowledge, and it is along these lines that 2nd order policy should be both formulated and evaluated.

7.3.3   0th order policy

Yet just as 2nd order mechanisms are ultimately adaptive or generic welfare enhancing mechanisms to life in an open economy, 2nd order policy is ultimately just adaptive policy constituted upon certain 0th order rule conditions that generate an open order in which such adaptive mechanisms are of value. In other words, the very possibility of the growth of knowledge and the value of 2nd order mechanisms to evolve and develop it, is ultimately conditional upon certain specific systems of constitutional rules that make this evolutionary process possible. The scope of 2nd order policy is ultimately determined, then, by the generic parameters of 0th order policy.

0th order policy is focused not just about the macro span of how all operational and mechanism rules fit together into a macro order (as we examined in Chapters 5 and 6), but about the more general and encompassing problem of how all generic political, social, legal, cultural and economic rules fit together into an interdependence of orders, that is, a way in which economic rules might fit with moral, social, political, cultural and legal rules.[6] In this view, 0th order policy therefore seeks to coordinate the generic value of the economic order with the values of other social, political or cultural orders.

For the past century or so, the central 0th order policy question has been the extent to which the market economy can be coordinated with the planned economy. This is being increasingly answered in favor of the market economy, but that is not the end of the question, which has since broadened beyond the compatibility of socialism and neoclassical efficiency to the further question of whether centrally controlled (i.e., non-democratic) states can generically evolve.

Economic growth can occur in a closed society through the operational expansion of an embedded generic structure, but economic evolution can only occur in an open society, as it requires the tolerance, and indeed encouragement, of exploration, experimentation, failure, difference, divergence and ultimately from increased variety in the component parts. This means that the social, cultural and political forces must seek to encourage, or at least not actively retard, the process of micro units becoming generically different. In this way, we may afford the interdependence of orders a more explicit and precise meaning.

An open market economy in which agents are not just operationally free to choose the commodities they will consume, but also generically free to choose the knowledge they will adopt, ultimately rests upon a social, political and cultural order in which variety is sustainable. Generic openness therefore fundamentally requires tolerance of novel ideas as a primary condition, and only excitement about novel ideas as an accelerant.[7] Such tolerance may well be constitutionally embedded in, for example, freedom of speech laws or other legislation that affords and protects the right to be different. Difference is the elemental driver of economic evolution, and societies that are tolerant of different ideas and rules carried by micro agents possess a necessary condition for economic evolution.

This can be immediately contrasted with fundamentalist models of economic order which seek to control the generic order and eradicate all wilful micro difference, be they utopian communist or socialist conceptions of the political economy, or fundamentalist religious conceptions of, for example, a Christian, Islamic or Orthodox economic order. As one, these political/cultural economic models systematically place a negative value on generic novelty due to its disruptive or contaminating effects. This is often accompanied by a suspicion of profit as illegitimate, of finance as immoral, of enterprise as rebellion, of imagination as suspect, and of property as theft. Fundamentalist models of the economic order therefore advance 0th order policy, often under the cover of operational efficiency, to eradicate all such unnecessary variety and moreover to close down the sources of such variety in individual creative freedoms.

The result is a systematically non-evolutionary 0th order policy in which the constitutional rules of the economic order are subordinated to political, religious or cultural goals. Evolutionary 0th order policy, however, seeks to achieve an interdependence of orders, such that essential individual freedoms are maintained across cultural, political and economic systems and adaptation and accommodation between such systems can occur. Common-law systems, for example, provide a flexibility to enable the legal framework to adapt to deal with novel forms of property or transactions, and democratic systems provide a flexibility and accountability for governance systems to adapt to changed generic economic conditions. The result will necessarily be complex, contingent, historically specific and always adapting, yet that organic messiness is the irreducible essence of what 0th order evolutionary policy should seek to achieve.

7.4 Conclusion

The goal of economic policy is to facilitate generic coordination and change, and it does this in two basic ways. First, through facilitating the conditions for novelty to exist, which we have identified with 0th order policy. And second, though the development of the mechanisms to achieve such change, which we have called 2nd order policy.

Open societies drive economic evolution through the creation of space for novelty and the possibility of micro units becoming generically different. Freedom is not therefore just a moral, civic or political quality, but also a fundamental economic quality in the possibility of opening the future to new generic potential. The value of freedom is the possibility of novelty, and the power of novel generic ideas is that they are what endogenous growth theorists call "non-rival," that is, they can be adopted and used by other agents without operational cost to their originator. But generic ideas are operationally costly to originate, adopt and retain. New knowledge is neither free nor given, but requires generic investment in rules resulting in the de-coordination and re-coordination of the economic order, an ongoing and natural evolutionary process that Schumpeter called "creative destruction," but which we have defined and given further analytical precision with the concept of a "meso trajectory."

And in turn, economic evolution powers open societies via the new operations that generic novelty creates. It is the possibility of novelty that is the origin of all wealth, and it is the market system—along with other institutional mechanisms of generic freedom, including rules for origination, adoption and retention—that constitutes the process of ongoing generic construction. This is the basis of all freedom, the origin of all wealth, and the central unit of evolutionary economic analysis.

Our central message is that the generic economic order is both complex and open. It is complex in that the system of associations between rules is complex. And it is open in that not just new associations can form, but that new rules can emerge, and so the generic economy can evolve. This complex open-system process is how economic systems progress through both the development of new generic potentials in individuals and the adaptive growth of economies and societies toward this same end. Economic evolution is driven by generic novelty, and progress is the process of the adoption and retention of the value of these novel generic ideas. Both individual freedom and social coordination are required to originate, adopt and retain the generic novelty that grows both opportunities and wealth.

Glossary

Actualization   The matter-energy manifestation of an idea in a carrier. See *idea, bimodal*.

Adaptation   The process of a carrier fitting into an environment through generic change.

Adoption   Phase 2 of a trajectory. The process of a micro unit accessing and embedding a novel rule for operational use. The meso process of a carrier population change.

Agency   A socially organized rule carrier, such as a firm.

Agent   *Homo sapiens Oeconomicus*.

Association   Ideas that are related. See *connection*.

Austrian economics   The study of the emergent complexity of the market order as a consequence of the interaction of generic rules. Focuses on 0th order market rules.

Axiom   A logical and/or empirical statement that is not questioned in analysis. The (empirical) axioms of evolutionary realism are bimodality, association and process. These ontological axioms underpin the structure of evolutionary economic analysis. See *ontology*.

Behavioral economics   The field of inquiry into the generic rules of the subject.

Bimodal   Ontological property of all existences, in that they are always composed of an idea and an actualization.

Capability   A carrier's ability to attain (generate, selectively retain) competence. See *orders of rules: 2nd order rules, competence*.

Carrier   Actual embodiment of the rule in a matter-energy existence. Carriers include agents, agencies, artefacts and their populations.

Choice, generic   The act of an agent or agency choosing to adopt a rule or not. Generic choice is always in the context of uncertainty with the expectation (that may prove false) of generic profit or generic rent.

Choice, operational   The act of an agent choosing between substitute operations.

Classical economics   Analysis of generic rules from a long run invariant perspective.

Cluster   A system of co-evolving meso trajectories.

Co-evolution   The association between meso trajectories as contemporaneous processes.

Communication   Activities related to the transfer of generic or operational information from one carrier to one or many other carriers.

Competence   A carrier's ability to perform operations. See *orders of rules: 1st order rules, capability*.

Competition   A process of rivalry between micro units to grow knowledge (generic) or to obtain gains from an existing knowledge base (operational).

Complementarity   Generic rules that fit together, or associate.

Complexity, generic   The emergent interaction of (perhaps simple) rules into systems that combine properties of order and chaos, and so are capable of evolution.

Complexity, operational   The pattern of operational outcomes (i.e., in prices and quantities) that display power-law signatures.

Complexity, orders of   The theory of monotonic rank ordering of physical, biological, social and economic systems as based upon the entropy law applied to open systems of knowledge.

Complexity economics   The emerging branch of economics that focuses on the study of the interaction of rules and analysis of the emergent operations that result.

Computational economics   A modeling approach that views the economic system as an explicit rule system. An applied branch of generic analysis.

Connection   Physical component parts or populations that are related. See *association*.

Consumption   An operational process of transformation in which entropy increases through the extraction of order. See *production*.

Coordination   Generic coordination is the fitting together of rules (deep coordination) and populations (surface coordination) into efficacious forms. Operational coordination (allocation) is the fitting together of activities, quantities and prices as based on generic coordination.

Decision   See *economic decision problem*.

Demand   The operational meso aggregate of transactions as based on generic rules. See *supply*.

Development   The macro process of sequences of regimes and regime transitions.

Dynamics, generic   Change in generic rules.

Dynamics, operational   Change in transactions or transformations with respect to given generic rules.

Economic decision problem   How to coordinate and change rules, given the generic opportunity cost of other rules that might also be adopted.

Economic evolution   The rule dynamics changing the deep and surface (generic) structure of the economic system. See *evolution*.

Economic system   The structure and process of generic rules that generate economic operations.

Ecosystem   The system of biological rules and resources that support the generic system.

Efficacy   The quality of rules fitting together so as to have operational effect. See *complementarity*.

Efficiency   The operational rank of substitute rules.

Emergence   A novel property arising into a system in consequence of a specific organization of rules and connections.

Endogeneric   Rule change within the economic system in consequence of itself.

Endogenous growth theory   Generic analysis of macro as if it were an aggregate meso.

Entrepreneur, generic   An agent who introduces novel rules in an uncertain expectation of generic profit. The driver of innovation through enterprise in meso 1.

Entrepreneur, operational   An agent who seeks to obtain operational rents in meso 2 or 3 by exploiting an existing market opportunity.

Environment, generic   Other rules external to a carrier. Includes physical, biological and cultural rules as well as "other" generic rules.

Equilibrium, generic   The state of complete learning in micro and complete adoption in meso that defines a macro order.

Evolution   Differential growth in a rule population through the mechanisms of origination, adoption and retention as processes of variation, selection and replication. See *economic evolution*.

Evolutionary accounting   The generic valuation of a system with reference to 0th, 1st and 2nd order rules. Conventional accounting considers (only) the operational value of given 1st order rules and resources.

Evolutionary game theory   Marginal generic analysis of the co-evolution of connected rule populations with given operational payoffs. See *game theory*.

Evolutionary realism   The ontology of rules, carriers and operations in terms of three ontological axioms: bimodality (the generic-operant distinction), association (micro and macro structure) and process (meso trajectory).

Exogeneric   Rule change within the economic system in consequence of rule change outside the economic system, such as due to terrestrial events.

Finance   The supply of money for rule origination and adoption.

Game theory   Operational analysis of strategic behavior with given generic object rules (payoffs) in terms of the operational interaction based on different behavioral generic rules (strategies). See *evolutionary game theory*.

Generic   The analytic domain of rules and their carrier populations.

Generic analysis   Analysis that is focused on rules and rule populations and how they coordinate and change. Evolutionary economics is generic analysis. See *deep structure, surface structure, operational analysis*.

Generic drift   Change in rule populations due to the sampling effect of selection and adoption.

Generic growth   An increase in the number of rules or an increase in the population of a rule or rules. Equivalent to economic evolution.

Growth   Increase in operations based on a rule or rule system as measured with (operational) output quantities. See *generic growth*.

Histonomics   The analysis that explains the historicity (irrepeatibility, irreversibility) of all actual phenomena. As distinct from history, which provides an exhaustive account of the singular case. Generic analysis is a branch of histonomics.

History, generic   The record of past generic states and how they have changed as the micro, meso and macro map of the growth of knowledge.

History, operational   The record of past transactions and transformations due to the generic rules of the time.

Homo sapiens Oeconomicus   A biologically evolved entity with a mind that is the prime carrier of the economic system and the locus of economic evolution. The evolutionary economic agent as a human being in the process of the origination, adoption and retention of generic rules.

Idea   The ontological form of all generic existence. A rule is the analytical equivalent of the ontological notion of an idea. See *actualization, bimodal*.

Increasing returns   The growth of operational output in consequence of an increase of generic complexity in consequence of a meso trajectory.

Industry   A cluster of co-evolving generic rules as a meso unit.

Information, generic   The knowledge conveyed from one carrier to another concerning a rule.

Information, operational   Signals (such as prices) about the state of the market order.

Innovation   The meso 1 process of originating a rule such that it can be adapted by others, the reward for which is generic profit to the innovator and generic rent to later adopters.

Innovation system   The macro complex of 2nd order rules.

Institution   The state of correlated behavior of a rule population in meso 3. All institutions become institutions via a meso trajectory. Institutions represent stabilized social knowledge.

Institutional economics The study of generic rules in meso 3 from both the micro and macro perspective.

Keynesian economics The study of aggregates of operations as a whole. See also *new Keynesian economics, post-Keynesian economics.*

Knowledge, generic A rule retained by a carrier in micro 3 for effective operational use.

Knowledge, operational The retained operational information (about the rule and its operational context) of a carrier in micro 3.

Learning, generic The adoption or embodiment of a novel generic rule by a subject carrier or populations of carriers for operations.

Learning, operational The adaptation of a generic rule to the conditions of an existing operational environment.

Macro, generic Analysis of the whole economy as a complex system of all meso units (both as rules and populations) in terms of how they are coordinated and how they change.

Macro, operational Analysis of the whole economy as an aggregation of all transactions and transformations in terms of given generic rules.

Market A domain for coordinating rules and for transactions. A market is itself a rule system, and different markets have different rules and rule complexity. A market emerges in meso 1 and becomes an institution in meso 3.

Mechanism The system of 2nd order rules for innovation and evolution. Composed of origination rules, adoption rules and retention rules.

Meso The analytical domain of a rule and its carrier population. All economic evolution involves meso change and re-coordination. Meso is always generic. See *micro, macro.*

Micro, generic The analytical domain of a carrier and its rules. Micro explains meso change by showing how novel rules are originated, adopted and retained by carriers. Micro units are agents and agencies. See *choice, generic.*

Micro, operational The analytic domain of cognition and behavior of the micro unit with respect to transactions and transformations in terms of prices and quantities with given generic rules. See *choice, operational.*

Mind The biologically emergent carrier of generic rules in *Homo sapiens Oeconomicus*. The origin of imagination and the seat of generic evolution.

Monopoly The market form that in meso 1 characterizes generic origination and the onset of competition, and in meso 3 characterizes the end of competition. A source of both generic profit (in meso 1) and operational rents (in meso 3).

Neoclassical economics A general operational analysis based on the assumption of a single invariant subject rule (rational choice) and given resource constraints (scarcity) as defined over given and invariant generic rules (i.e., preferences and technology). See *rationality, operational.*

New-classical economics A general analysis of operational macro as if it were coordinated as an aggregation of generic micro. See *classical economics, neoclassical economics.*

New Keynesian economics Analysis of variation in operational information on the coordination of the whole economy with given generic rules. See *post Keynesian economics.*

Object rules Social and technical rules that organize the things of the economy. See *subject rules.*

Ontology The set of irreducible statements on the status of reality. See *axiom.*

Operation Activities performed on the basis of a rule with respect to resources. See *transaction, transformation.*

Operational analysis Analysis of economic operations in which the generic domain is assumed invariant. Neoclassical economics, for example, is operational analysis.

Order   The generic state of coordination of the whole system of all meso such that rules fit together. See *policy, generic*.

Orders of rules   Hierarchic structure of rules in a micro and macro analysis:

0th order rules are the constitutional rules that determine the total space of possibilities referring to 1st and 2nd order rules.

1st order rules are rules for operations. They are composed of cognitive, behavioral, social and technical rules. Economic evolution is the process of change in 1st order rules.

2nd order rules are rules for changing rules and consist of rules for origination, rules for adoption and rules for retention.

Organization   The state of coordination of rules in a carrier to form a system.

Origination   Phase 1 of a trajectory and a product of the mind. The creation, innovation and emergence of the novel rule.

Phase   An element of a process of a rule trajectory. Generic analysis identifies three phases: origination, adoption and retention.

Policy, generic   Intervention into 0th and 2nd order rules.

Policy, operational   Intervention into 1st order rules to cause reallocation of resources.

Population   The set of actualizations of a rule in carriers. Each rule has a carrier population that changes during meso 2. The measure of a population is adoption frequency as the number of micro trajectories of a rule.

Post-Keynesian economics   Analysis of the whole economy in terms of operational investment coordination, expectations and finance given generic rule coordination.

Production   An operational process of transformation in which entropy is locally decreased through the use of transformation rules (although entropy always globally increases). See *consumption*.

Profit, generic   The captured value of a novel rule by a carrier through meso 1 and 2, and so the reward for introducing a novel generic idea. Synonymous with rewards from Schumpeterian entrepreneurship.

Profit, operational   The expropriated reward to efficient use of resources in meso 3. Synonymous with rewards from managerial efficiency.

Rationality, generic   The quality of efficacious generic choice in a generic environment. See *choice, generic*.

Rationality, operational   The quality of efficiency in operational choice under given generic conditions.

Regime   A complete meso trajectory as (structure) component of macro coordination and as (process) component of macro dynamics.

Regime transition   Process of meso 3 of one meso trajectory giving rise to meso 1 of a new trajectory. The building block of economic development.

Rent, generic   The reward to using a rule in meso 3. The return to knowledge.

Rent, operational   The expropriated reward to manipulation of a market or an unseen market opportunity in meso 3. Includes both arbitrage and monopoly profit, as conventionally understood.

Retention   Phase 3 of a trajectory. The conclusion of the phase of embedding of the rule into the population of carriers for ongoing operational use. The new order has stabilized (macro) as the adoption frequency (meso) and rule stability (micro) have reached a statistical maximum.

Rule   A deductive procedure for operations. What the generic economic system is made of and what changes with economic evolution. See *idea*.

Rule, behavioral   Generic rules that govern human actions and interactions.

Rule, cognitive   Generic rules that govern human thinking.

Rule, social   Generic rules that govern social organizations of humans.

Rule, technical   Generic rules that govern organizations of matter-energy and material forms.

Rule pool   Conceptual analogue of gene pool as applied to the variation in a rule over a meso trajectory.

Schumpeterian economics   The field of inquiry into the process of change in meso populations of object rules. Focuses on 1st and 2nd order rules.

Selection, generic   Differential adoption of generic rules as the outcome of generic choice. A meso 2 process.

Selection, operational   Differential replication of operations as the outcome of operational choice over given generic rules.

Self-organization   The mutual adaptation of meso rule populations to each other by micro generic change. The result is macro order.

Strategy, generic   Micro behavior with respect to a meso trajectory.

Structure, deep   How rules fit together in themselves. The rule-structure of the macro whole.

Structure, surface   The relation between all meso populations constituting a macro whole.

Subject rules   The cognitive and behavioral rules of the agent. See *object rules*.

Substitution   Alternative operational actions with respect to resources.

Supply   The operational aggregate of meso transformations as based on a state of generic rules. See *demand*.

System   A connected set of generic rules with operational function.

Trajectory   The three-phase dynamic of a process in historical time.

Trajectory, macro   The de-coordination, re-coordination and ongoing coordination (order) of a system in consequence of a meso trajectory. A process of structural change.

Trajectory, meso   The origination, adoption and retention of a rule into a population of carriers as a three-phase process.

Trajectory, micro   The origination, adoption and retention of a rule into a micro unit.

Transaction   The operation of transferring an object from one carrier to another, thus crossing the carrier's boundary.

Transformation   The operation of changing resources from one form to another. Transformations occur in the process of production and consumption.

Uncertainty, generic   The state of not knowing the consequences of a rule, the effect of the interaction of rules, or the space of new rules.

Uncertainty, operational   Risk associated with knowing what could happen given generic rules, but not what will happen in specific operational circumstances.

Variation   A change in variety. Given a new rule (meso 1) there is variation in historical time (meso 2) that results in a new meta-state of variety (meso 3).

Variety   The range of difference in a rule pool. Variety depicts the structure of a rule and its carrier population at a point in historical time.

Notes

1 Analytical foundations of evolutionary economics

1 See, for example, Witt (1992, 2003a,b), Dosi and Nelson (1994), Nelson (1995), Vromen (1995), Louçã (1997), Hodgson (1997, 2003), Metcalfe (1998), Loasby (1999), Dosi (2000), Potts (2000), Aruka (2001), Krause (2002), Foster and Metcalfe (2001, 2005), Dopfer (2001, 2005a), Shiozawa (2004), Nishibe (2006). On a comprehensive bibliometric account of recent research trends in evolutionary economics see Silva and Teixeira (2006).
2 See Mirowski (1988, 1989), Dopfer (1988), Louçã (1997).
3 The need for a rethinking of the ontological foundations of economics has been expounded in a number of important contributions, see Lawson (1997, 2003), Mäki (2001), Vromen (2001a), Hodgson (2002). With a view of actually constructing an ontology, a set of ontological propositions (discussed above) has been explicitly introduced in Dopfer (1990, 2001, 2005), and Dopfer and Potts (2004). For similar efforts see Herrmann-Pillath (2001).
4 We use the term "axiom" here (as in previous works) as an ontological term relating to empirical generalization to the level of unquestioned empirical statements. This is not the way it is used in mathematics, nor is it the way that axiom is generally understood in formal analysis. An ontological axiom has to concord not just with a rational basis (which mathematical axioms must) but also with an empirical basis (which mathematical axioms do not).
5 Maynard Smith (1968), Dawkins (1982), Dennett (1995), Hodgson (1997, 2002), Ziman (2000).
6 Although this is not a unique property, as it is well known that other higher chordates also have the ability to culturally transmit "rules," for example, dolphins, apes and dogs. See also Dopfer (2004), Gintis et al. (2005).
7 Maturana and Varela (1980), Damasio (1995), Edelman (1992), Searle (1995).
8 Dosi et al. (2005).
9 Hayek (1952), Shackle (1972, 1979).
10 Plainly, there is much work in the Institutionalist, Austrian, Post Keynesian and Behavioral tradition that does indeed seek to properly integrate the nature and role of the human mind into a theory of economic coordination and change (e.g., Egidi and Rizzello 2004). But our critique remains that these have been mostly partial exercises that have not yet succeeded in providing a general theory that might link the inner workings of the mind to the macrostructure of the whole economy in a co-evolutionary loop. We expect that much of this work might be usefully re-interpreted from the micro meso macro perspective of the mind as a generic carrier.
11 Dopfer (2004). Humans are not only "tool maker" (as anthropologists teach us), but more generally rule-maker.
12 This definition incorporates the Behavioral, Austrian, Institutional definition of rules—for example, Simon (1965), Fields (1984), Earl (1986), Vanberg (1994), Hodgson (1997), Rizzello (1999), Budzinski (2001), Vromen (2004), Ostrom (2005), Lazaric and Raybaut (2005) and others—but seeks to generalize it to a broader and more systematic taxonomy of subject and object rules with the criteria of deductive operational effect.
13 Schumpeter (1942). See also Metcalfe (1998).
14 Georgescu-Roegen (1971).
15 See further Dopfer (2005) on the genealogy of the concept of "generic."
16 For further discussion, see Dopfer and Potts (2004a,b).

17 2nd order rules produce other 2nd order rules such that we get orders of rules accumulating, in the sense of Böhm-Bawerk's notion of the "round-about-ness" of capital. We shall limit our analysis here to the first temporal order of rules. On this rule vintage, including cognitive and behavioral vintage, see Dopfer (2005b: 53–54).

18 Smith (1759), Veblen (1898), Mises (1940), Hayek (1973/1976), Boulding (1978), North (1990), De Soto (2000).

19 See Dopfer et al. (2004) which is entirely constructed without the rule taxonomy either in terms of classes or orders of rules.

20 Note that the concept of human capital is not clear about whether this capital is a 1st order rule to know how to perform some (skilled) operation or whether it is closer to a 2nd order rule to know how to originate, adopt or retain knowledge. A similar imprecision is widely evident in modern endogenous growth theory (e.g., Romer 1990), which defines resources for the growth of knowledge, thus conflating generic 2nd order rules and the operational outcomes of 1st order rules.

21 This distinction is essential. See Dopfer (2004) for a critique of "subjectivist" and "objectivist" fallacies."

22 A proposal for the economics of where rules are carried over a continuum of subject and object carrier possibilities has been suggested by Clark, Morrison and Potts (2005) as an "allocation of complexity" problem in terms of the relative costs of differential embedding of a rule in subjects or objects.

23 Note that this encompasses both rivalrous and nonrivalrous goods.

24 Schumpeter (1912/1934, 1939). While Schumpeter neither distinguished explicitly between the three phases of trajectory nor used the term, he furnished various ideas that are important building blocks for this concept, see Dopfer (2006), Hanusch und Pyka (2006).

25 Freeman and Soete's (1997) classic text offers an excellent study of many large-scale industrial examples of trajectories. See also Dosi (1982), McKelvey (1996), Saviotti (1996, 2003), Mowery and Rosenberg (1998), Freeman and Louçã (2001) and Murmann (2005). The analogous consumer market concept is the product life cycle. However, there are fewer examples of studies of subject rule trajectories such as decision rules (Earl et al. 2006) or social rules such as market institutions (De Soto 2000, Mirowski 2007).

26 Louçã (1997).

27 Potts (2000a).

28 The basic three-phase trajectory can be dissected into various sub-phases depending on the type or specification called for by a particular model. For a trajectory specified by six (3×2) sub-phases discussing the positions of neoclassical, Austrian, Schumpeterian and Nelson/Winter evolutionary economics, for instance Dopfer (1993).

29 See Metcalfe et al. (2006) for discussion of this point. Note also that a logistic process need not actually result in a logistic curve and indeed generally will not if there are other rule populations also changing.

30 Some (e.g., Rogers 1962) argue that this is a four-stage process, distinguishing the adoption phase into two phases corresponding to early and late adoption. Others (e.g., Klepper 1996, Metcalfe et al. 2006) emphasize that the retention phase can also be a phase of rapid decline.

31 As in the work of Alfred Marshall, Frank Knight, Armen Alchian, Jack Downie, Edith Penrose, and others.

32 See Hanusch (1988), Hodgson (1998), Metcalfe (1998), Hanusch and Pyka (2006).

2 Micro meso macro analysis

1 As proposed in Dopfer (2001, 2002, 2005), Dopfer et al. (2004) and Dopfer and Potts (2004a,b).

2 And also post-Keynesian, in the focus on endogenous money/finance and on expectations as components of knowledge (e.g., Shackle 1972, Earl 1990).

3 While there is a sizable contingent of industrial economists among the ranks of evolutionary economists, it is also notable that most others have come from or are associated with macroeconomics rather than micro. There are plainly many exceptions, but in general it is the problems of growth and development, and especially in the historical context, that have engendered evolutionary turns of thought more so than the problems of choice and efficiency.

4 See, for example, Earl and Potts (2004), Earl et al. (2006), Chai et al. (2006), Potts and Morrison (2007), Potts and Dopfer (2006).

5 The classical economists were concerned with the question of why some countries were growing in wealth (e.g., Britain) whereas other countries seemed mired in poverty (e.g., some regions of Europe). Let us immediately note that whatever their answers, they had the right question.

6 This limitation was criticized by Friedrich List (1841), for example, with respect to what later became known as "national systems of innovation" (e.g., Nelson 1993). Neoclassical economics, however, emerged from Mill and Marshall's textbooks which although can be plainly read in their originals as having overriding concern with generic coordination and change, were subsequently adopted and retained without that generality and subtlety.

7 Yet, from the modern perspective, they never developed a proper "model" and so these musings are contemporaneously judged as but pretensions to endogeneity. Yet again, however, they were not wrong about this. But they did struggle to reconcile these sorts of qualitative changes with the model of resource flows they had divined, and so duly established an evasive tradition that continues to this day of mixing closed system quantitative theory with ad hoc accounts of routine excursions into other causes.

8 As was, for example, subsequently developed by Marx (1867) and Veblen (1899).

9 However, classical writers such as Smith, Mill and even Malthus believed firmly in the possibility of increasing "human happiness" on immaterial grounds, and there were no "immutable laws" concerning the potential moral improvement or qualitative change of society.

10 Young (1928) is surely the closest to the spirit of classical analysis in the open generic dimension. The work of Sraffa (1960), for example, is the essence of the closed generic spirit.

11 Note that the so-called Keynesian revolution, which is widely credited with the establishment of modern macroeconomics, reversed this impetus to reassert the primacy of aggregate resource stocks and flows.

12 A growing body of experimental evidence is demolishing this abstraction increasingly; the findings give us an idea of what the price is we have to pay for it in terms of its empirical validity. For example, Falk and Kosfeld (forthcoming), Fehr and Gächter (2000), see also related discussion in Chapter 3.

13 We may of course observe that the history of twentieth-century progress in neoclassical economics then reads as the sequential exercise of re-endogenizing these factors as quantitatively controlled qualitative factors. Exemplars of this approach are, for example, Robert Solow's growth theory, Douglas North's institutions, and Paul Romer's endogenous growth theory.

14 Potts (2000a,b) made the same point in terms of the incompleteness of connections and therefore the possibility of new connections.

15 For example, Schelling (1978).

16 In the same vein focusing on classical and neoclassical economics, Nelson and Winter (1982: 361) wrote: "And it was not a case for a perfect organizational answer to a static and stylized problem, but for a real organizational answer to a real, ambiguous, and ever-changing problem. More than Hayek, but perhaps less than Schumpeter, the classical economists saw the virtues of the system as including an ability to generate a variety of innovations, to screen and select from these, and to assure that in the long run most of the gains would accrue to consumers."

17 See also Vromen (1995, 2001a,b, 2004), Smith (2003, 2005), Witt (2003a).

18 Simon's (1976) concept of bounded rationality in terms of multiple parallel decision heuristics therefore made a radical break from the unitary choice rule of neoclassical economics. Its subsequent reinterpretation as a unitary information partition rather than rules for choice reasserted its neoclassical heritage (e.g., Conlisk 1996 cf. Earl 1990).

19 We may conceive this problem as one of "methodological merism" (derived from the Greek word meros for part) (Dopfer 1986). Indeed the issue is not whether individualism or holism are appropriate forms of modes of analysis of the economy as a whole, but rather whether we conceive of individual entities as parts, meros, of a whole, whether or not we reconstruct the whole from above or below. See also axiom 2 of evolutionary realism.

20 Shackle (1972), Loasby (1976, 1999), Beckenbach and Daskalakis (2003), Earl (1986), Witt (2003a,b).

21 As stated in the preceding note, methodological merism calls for a specification of a component part of a system. This could be the individual, and thus we would have the program of methodological individualism. Our specification of the component part is meso, and so we call it methodological populationism (and thus avoiding the awkward neologism "methodological meso-ism").

22 This distinction is crucial to unpacking the difference between representative agent growth models (e.g., Romer 1990) and population based growth models (see for example, Metcalfe 1997, Metcalfe et al. 2006, Metcalfe and Foster 2005, Foster and Potts 2006).

23 Foster (1987, 2000), Witt (1985), Potts (2000a,b), Boschma and Frenken (2006), Hutter (2001), Pyka and Fagiolo (2007).

24 "The essential point to grasp is that in dealing with capitalism we are dealing with an evolutionary process. ... Capitalism, then, is by nature a form or method of economic change that not only never is but never can be stationary. The fundamental impulse that sets and keeps the capitalist engine in motion comes from the new consumers, the new goods, the new methods of production or transportation, the new markets, and the new forms of industrial organization that capitalist enterprise creates. ... This process of Creative Destruction is the essential fact about capitalism. It is what capitalism consists in and what every capitalist concern has got to live in. ... Every piece of business strategy acquires its true significance only against the background of that process and within the situation created by it. It must be seen in its role in the perennial gale of creative destruction" (Schumpeter 1942: 82–85).

3 Generic micro analysis

1 On the evolutionary theory of the firm and how it carries different sorts of knowledge than individual agents, see Penrose (1959), Cyert and March (1963), Simon (1965), Loasby (1976), Nelson and Winter (1982: chps 3–4), Rumelt (1984), Cohen and Levinthal (1990), Marengo (1992), Langlois and Robertson (1995), Foss and Knudsen (1996), Foss and Loasby (1996), Foss (2001), Potts (2000a: chps 5–6), Langlois (2005), Foster (2006b), Witt (2000), Dietrich (2006), Levinthal (2006).

2 Stigler and Becker (1977).

3 For example, Dosi and Nelson (1994), Winter and Nelson (1973).

4 On HSO as "rule carrier" (rule-maker vs tool-maker) Dopfer (1995, 2004). On the general theme of human agent in evolutionary economics, see Vromen (2001b) and Potts (2000a: ch. 5, 2003), Witt (2003a).

5 Vriend (1996).

6 From the generic viewpoint, human society builds generally on "socially shared imagination" ("socially shared imagined future"), Dopfer (2004), and Foster (2006a) argues that the order of complexity increases as the models of agents include also models of other agents; on the basic paradox of reciprocal expectations (when making predictions) Morgenstern (1928).

7 Romer (1990).

8 Kauffman (1993, 2000) makes a similar argument about the origins of life, but when he extends his thinking to the "self-organizing econosphere" he reverts back to operational definitions in terms of recombinations of resources. This is not wrong, for commodities are indeed used to make commodities and the more there are the greater the possibilities for action, but rather it elides the deeper point, namely that knowledge is used to make knowledge, as Popper (1945), Dennett (1995) and Loasby (1999) explain.

9 Boyd and Richerson (1985).

10 From the beginning of evolutionary biology it was held that man is special because he makes and uses tools or exosomatic instruments. This is now understood to be manifestly untrue, as there is a wide range of animals, including monkeys, beavers, octopi and ants, that regularly make and use "tools."

11 It is tempting to call this difference "culture," in the sense that man is the only animal that creates a comprehensive artificial or cultural environment, but that is just to relabel something already undefined, for what then is culture? However, if we may define culture as the sum of generic rules, including all classes and orders of rules, including rules for changing rules, then we would allow that the difference is culture. But that is effectively just to substitute the word culture for the concept of a rule.

12 If we seek deeper explanation, the scientific domains of evolutionary biology, evolutionary psychology and evolutionary anthropology provide natural micro micro foundations to evolutionary microeconomics. Modern empirical work in the fields of behavioral, experimental and neuroeconomics, for example, also conforms to our notion of human economic behavior explained in terms of a suite of generic rules rather than in terms of a universal and singular notion of objective rationality. Cosmides and Tooby (1994), Darley and Kauffman (1997), Camerer (2003), Gintis et al. (2005), Camerer et al. (2005).

13 What Veblen (1898b) called the instinct of workmanship is but a higher-order version of the same propensity or instinct to adopt and adapt novel rules. Smith's (1776: bk. I, ch. 2) notion of the

propensity to "truck, barter and exchange" can also be understood as the operational expression of this same instinct to truck, barter and exchange rules.

14 Maddison (2001).

15 Whitehead (1925).

16 See Dopfer (2005: 21–29) on the properties of the human brain that facilitate generic evolution. Also Potts (2003) for an argument about genetic potential as derived from evolutionary psychology.

17 This is known generally as symbiosis. But all plants and animals effectively trade and coproduce such that they may be said to have an operational economic system in relation to scarce resources. But this is generically invariant with respect to genetic structures.

18 cf. Bateson (1972).

19 Day (2001), Dopfer (2004).

20 For example, Marx (1867), Schumpeter (1939), Freeman and Perez (1988), Freeman and Soete (1997), Freeman and Louçã (2001).

21 See Loasby (1999), Warsh (2006).

22 Hayek (1945, 1973).

23 This is not a new idea, but rather an integrated view of a vast raft of models of resource-based, competence-based or capability-based theories of the firm. For example, Penrose (1959), Richardson (1960, 1972), Cyert and March (1963), Loasby (1976), Teece (1982), Prahlad and Hammel (1990), Cohen and Levinthal (1990), Langlois (1992), Montgomery (1995), Foss and Knudsen (1996), Nooteboom (2000), Malik (2000), Potts (2000a,b), Schwaninger (2006).

24 Note that this also tracks to different sources of income from the evolutionary perspective which we shall later define with the distinction between generic and operational rent and profit.

25 Potts (2001). This is a position we also attribute to Hayek, as we shall elaborate subsequently.

26 cf. Mokyr (2002: ch. 2).

27 Metcalfe (2004). See also Section 3.2.1 on *Homo sapiens Oeconomicus*.

28 The work of George Akerlof, Michael Spence and Joseph Stiglitz, for example, focuses on the operational consequences of agents having different information about the same choice. But it says nothing of the different knowledge or rules the agents possess, nor how such differences might interact with information differences. Analysis of information asymmetries and the like are all operational concerns that do not yet penetrate to the generic level of analysis because they confuse generic and operant information and generic and operant knowledge.

29 Innovation systems (e.g., Nelson 1993) are 2nd order rule systems that exist between carriers. They are thus external 2nd order rule systems.

30 Yet like all experiments, many will be wrong. But market mechanisms enable us to discover these errors along with the hidden truths they contain in an effective manner. Markets are evolutionary mechanisms in this sense. See Hayek (1945), Potts (2001), Loasby (2001).

31 Pinker (1997), Cosmides and Tooby (1994), Potts (2003).

32 See Dosi et al. (2005) for an excellent survey and analysis.

33 While there is no well-defined science of creativity or entrepreneurship, there is a vast body of literature dealing with these themes that draws on biology, psychology, economics, anthropology, the humanities (especially history, art history and cultural studies), geography, computation theory and artificial intelligence.

34 As for example in endogenous growth models (Romer 1990, Aghion and Howitt 1998).

35 Shackle (1972).

36 Potts (2000), Earl (2003).

37 Loasby (1999).

38 As in the Think-Play-Do model of Dodgson et al. (2005).

39 Hybrid versions, such as Cohen et al. (1972) view a firm as it were a "garbage can" in which problems and solutions rattle around and sometimes match together.

40 Simon (1957, 1968).

41 This would mark an important distinction between evolutionary economics (as based upon generic choice) and an evolutionary approach to sociology, cultural studies, religious studies or politics that would naturally seek to emphasize the absence of generic choice in generic adoption processes. A more comprehensive theory of generic decision-making could, in later theoretic developments, draw on the entire range of interdisciplinary thoughts or experimental evidence extending and deepening the explanatory platform of the theory.

42 Popper (1965, 1972), Loasby (1999).
43 This spans a number of domains, including cognitive and behavioral psychology, evolutionary game theory, non-linear dynamics and complexity theory, computational and experimental economics, the evolutionary theory of the firm, replicator dynamics and others. See Brenner (1999), Dosi et al. (2005).
44 This is to be distinguished from operational learning about the specific conditions of the material environment, such as relating to trades and production. The process of learning about such data is not unimportant, and often crucial in any enterprise setting, yet the focus of the theory of generic adoption is not this but rather the way in which agents and agencies learn to adopt new rules and learn by adopting new rules.
45 The profits of agencies are therefore a basic measure of the generic flow of an open economic system. Since Walras and Keynes, economists are well used to conceptualizing the growth of an economy in terms of the rate of change in income, production or expenditure flow. From the evolutionary perspective this is operational flow, whereas economic evolution is a generic flow of value from a changing stock of knowledge. Yet the problem with this stock-flow metaphor is that knowledge is not a stock but a complex coordinated system, and so when it changes, it changes generically, resulting in operational structural change that is manifest, primarily, in the adoption of a new rule in a micro unit.
46 Smith (1776: bk. 1, pp. 1–3).
47 Including the possibility that it could collapse to zero, which is not generally possible for an economic agent, as there are constitutive rules that engage when an agent makes a sufficiently bad generic rule choice that it is always bailed out; this is not always true for agencies, which may routinely be allowed to die.
48 Inspired by Veblen, Day called it "habituation" (Day 1975).

4 Meso analysis

1 Of course both Marx and Schumpeter plainly recognized the prime importance of competition from the innovation of other agents as a central motivation in the search for new sources of profit. This is called the "Red Queen" hypothesis in evolutionary biology and evolutionary game theory.
2 Ormerod (2005). It is notable that although there are many books and studies on successful innovation, there are very few on failure. Failure is a systematically under-researched area, yet is clearly central to micro meso analysis.
3 The general functional form of an adoption process is analytically represented by the replicator equation or logistic-diffusion curve, which incorporates a logic of feedback between the value of adoption to the marginal adopter and the current state of adoption. See Lotka (1925), Volterra (1926), Dosi (1988), Saviotti (1996), Foster (1997), Metcalfe (1994a,b, 1998, 2005).
4 The absolute generic growth of a rule is measured as a count of the number of adopters of that rule. But more interesting from the evolutionary perspective is the relative generic growth of a rule, as its growth rate compared to other rules. Analysis of a meso trajectory is an analysis of the nominal (or absolute) growth of the rule population, such that it is modeled with other populations held constant.
5 There are various approaches to the theory of the entrepreneur in evolutionary economics (Metcalfe 2004). The George Shackle (1972)/Brian Loasby (1976, 1991) version holds that all choice involves aspects of uncertainty and entrepreneurship, and so all agents are entrepreneurs some of the time. The Schumpeterian (1912) version however focuses on entrepreneurs as a special subgroup of the population, such that some agents are entrepreneurial all of the time. The weakest version is the notion of entrepreneurs as alert to arbitrage opportunities associated with the work of Israel Kirzner (1973) in which some agents are entrepreneurs some of the time (see also Baumol 1990). Our generic view is therefore closest to the Shackle/Loasby approach in the sense that all agents will originate and adopt new rules some of the time.
6 Earl and Potts (2004), Lazaric and Raybaut (2005).
7 David (1985, 2005), Arthur (1989).
8 Popper (1972), Metcalfe (2002).
9 Nelson (1993), Louçã (1997), Metcalfe (1998).
10 Meso 3 is characterized by unit roots in co-integrated variables and stationarity in time series, just as in the efficient markets hypothesis. Indeed, we suggest that such a data signature can be taken as the basic empirical identification of meso 3. See Foster and Potts (2006).

11 This is the sense in which Nelson and Winter (1982) defined routines as "micro" institutions. See also North (1990), Coase (1992), Choi (1993), Vanberg (1994), Langlois and Robertson (1995), Hodgson (1997, 1998b), Loasby (1999, 2000a), Williamson (1985, 2000).

12 This is essentially the same meaning given to an institution in evolutionary game theory in relation to the set of evolutionary stable strategies forming an equilibrium population distribution. It is also similar in essence to the notion of an institution as a commonly accepted (i.e., widely adopted) rule, whether by formal or tacit agreement and enforcement.

13 A particular organism can of course be said to evolve in its neurological structure and immune system, as in the theory of neuronal group selection or in the variation and selection of antibodies, but along the germ line an organism is genetically fixed for the term of its natural life.

14 A point clearly made by Metcalfe (1998).

15 cf. Marshall (1949), who manifestly did conceive of an industry as a population (see Foster 1993).

16 Such as the distance from mean dynamics about some performance indicator in the replicator equation (see Metcalfe 1998).

17 See Menard (1995), Loasby (2000a). On the difference between mechanisms and processes in the context of markets, see Potts (2001).

18 See also Section 4.3.2 below (Variety in Meso) on dynamic (trajectory-based) rule correspondence (Dopfer 2005a,b,c, Foster and Potts 2006a).

19 Mirowski and Somefun (1998), Mirowski (2002, 2007), Potts and Morrison (2007).

20 See Mayr (1975) and Sober (1980) for the biological perspective, and Metcalfe (1998) for its case in economics.

21 For the total set of varied rules we have a "rule pool," Dopfer (2001, 2005); for the related ("surface level") concept of "population thinking" see Metcalfe (2001, 2005). In neoclassical economics, its variety is zero (representativeness, homogeneity); in evolutionary economics it is assumed to be typically larger than zero.

22 Klepper (1996), Klepper and Graddy (1990), Klepper and Simons (1997, 2000).

23 Veblen (1898), Potts (2000a,b), Ormerod and Cook (2003), Hodgson (1993, 2002).

24 Although this is rarely done under such explicit auspices, but more as a by-product of endeavors to map a market or industry.

25 Loasby (1999: 112) argues that "markets are much too important, and much too amenable to economic analysis, to be treated as primitives."

26 Lipsey and Carlaw (2006).

27 Mirowski (2006), McMillan (2002).

28 Dopfer (2005a,b), Foster and Potts (2006b). See also Section 4.3.1.

29 Beyond market size as the sum of operational value, the sum of generic profit and generic rent (over meso 1 and 2) would be a good first approximation. But so too might network measures of centrality or other such structural rather than flow measures. Probably some hybrid index would be best.

30 Barabasi (2002), Ormerod (2005).

31 Indeed, we would suggest that this is an empirical hypothesis that can be tested. Generic analysis and complexity theory would predict that economic evolution should follow a power-law distribution in meso growth patterns.

32 cf. Kondratieff (1935), Schumpeter (1939) or Freeman and Soete (1997), among others, who have studied the velocity of "major" technical-industrial rules.

33 Also Cohen and Levinthal (1990).

34 As, for example, in Binmore (1993, 1998).

35 Note that this is similar in analytic structure to the notion of an agent choosing a strategy in game theory. But generic strategy is 2nd order rules, whereas payoffs are operational consequences of the changes to 1st order rules.

36 Porter (1980, 1990).

37 There are surely immediate welfare theoretic and evolutionary game theoretic implications that might be usefully explored, as the best strategy will depend on the population of other strategies and the profile of payoffs, but we leave that as a task for future work.

38 The transition form meso 2 to 3 is often accompanied by a selection process called "shake-outs" in which a multitude of agencies are merged and whittled into a small number of dominant firms and a few dominant variations of the rule. Klepper and Simons (1997).

39 Simon (1962), Kauffman (1993, 2000), Potts (2000a,b).

5 Macro coordination

1 See axiom 2 of evolutionary realism.

2 A generic equilibrium is defined at the micro level when there is no further learning by carriers, such that potential actualizations minus actual actualizations equals zero.

3 Replicator models such as the Lotka-Volterra equations describe this process. See Maynard Smith (1968), Metcalfe (1998), Chen (2005).

4 Schumpeter (1912) defined an operational equilibrium as the context of the moment of creative destruction as built into a "meso" trajectory, but he never sought to define a generic equilibrium as his starting point (Dopfer 2006). The point is we think that evolutionary economics should be aligning its generic and operant attack not against Schumpeter vs Walras/Marx, but rather in terms of von Neumann as the great operational generalist in his conception of game theory. In his later work (i.e., automata theory) as with Hayek's later work (i.e., generic co-evolution) we observe this generic conception of economic evolution (von Neumann 1966, see also Mirowski 2002). In this respect, we consider our general theory both post-Schumpeterian, post-Hayekian and post-Neumannian.

5 Knight (1921), Schumpeter (1942), Shackle (1972).

6 Schumpeter (1939), King and Levine (1993), Perez (2002), Leathers and Raines (2004).

7 Schumpeter (1912), Knight (1921).

8 Neoclassical economics takes market forms as given for comparative static welfare theory, no explanation of how they emerge from a meso process. They have market forms, but no process.

9 Baumol (1990), Metcalfe (2004).

10 The habits and routines of Veblen or Nelson and Winter are the instruments of this manifest structure, as are the connections between generic rules that Schumpeter and Freeman documented. But in all cases these were composures of evolution, not resting points. Instead, it is the implied connections between stable knowledge bases in general equilibrium theory, evolutionary game theory and input–output theory alike that define the macro order of the coordination of all rules in meso 3. A generic analysis seeks to make these connections and associations explicit.

11 The question naturally arises then whether there is a generic analogue of the operational concept of Pareto equilibrium. If so, this would be the absence of any possible reconfiguration of rules to make the whole system more open. Such a welfare basis for evolutionary analysis is not inconceivable.

12 From the generic perspective, the basic mistake that conventional macroeconomics makes is to suppose, as general equilibrium theory teaches, that coordination is but a one-dimensional problem over n commodity dimensions of that problem. The error is that it only refers to operational coordination (the n dimensions), and ignores generic coordination which although perhaps composed of many parameters, is analytically one dimensional.

13 Georgescu-Roegen (1971), Hayek (1973) and Boulding (1978) are arguably the best examples of general frameworks that seek to allow both subject and object evolution.

14 Although, see Brette and Mehier (2005).

15 If Karl Marx (e.g., 1867) is at one extreme (the subject adapts to the object), then Robert Lucas (e.g., 1988) is at the other (the object adapts to the subject). In evolutionary macro, both are right and both are wrong: the subject and the object co-evolve.

16 Nelson and Winter (1974), Eliasson (1991), Klepper and Simons (1997), Dosi (2000), Loasby (2001), Antonelli (2003), Amendola and Gaffard (2003), Saviotti (2003), Foray (2004), Hoelzl and Foster (2004), Foster and Metcalfe (2005), Pyka and Hanusch (2006).

17 This will also be composed of a generic micro equilibrium such that there is no further learning or experimentation, and in which potential actualizations equal actual actualizations.

18 Note that if there remains the potential for further adoption, such that some meso are not in phase 3, then this is a state of disequilibrium not of coordination failure.

19 This is the essence of what Schumpeter (1942: 82–85) meant by creative destruction. Namely any new idea both destroys the existing value of some extant ideas and creates value for some existing ideas as well as opportunities for new positions. Aghion and Howitt (1992), however, who claim a model of creative destruction, are better described in terms of "operational creative destruction" as compared to the "generic creative destruction" that we, and Schumpeter, refer to. See also Metcalfe (1998), Andersen (2002).

20 It may, and often will, change the relation between complements and substitutes as the simultaneous renewal and disintegration of existing relations between ensembles of knowledge.

21 This phase is often accompanied by a radical divergence in expectations bounded by on the one hand those who believe the novel generic rule has no effect whatsoever, and on the other by those who believe it changes everything in the relevant domain (Shackle 1972, 1979). One of these groups will be correct, but the immediate effect is to compile a chain of speculative revaluation activity that may transform the structure of asset valuations, ownership and strategy of firms (Leijonhufvud 1981). This may then in turn gear consumers up for variously incremental or radical changes in consumption patterns (Earl 1986, Potts 2000b, Earl and Potts 2004).

22 See Kuhn (1962), Lakatos (1978), Popper (1965). See also Shackle (1972), Loasby (1976, 1989, 1991,1999).

23 Some will adopt, some won't. Some will compromise, some vouchsafe, some elide, some partner, and some will find new possibilities again.

24 Just as little empirical work has been directed to the study of failure of ventures and enterprise, so too there has been little work directed to the costs associated with adoption and change (i.e., generic costs). We see these both as a promising theoretical and empirical avenue for future research, especially in behavioral economics and the study of limits to imagination and barriers to adoption.

25 Louçã (1997), Freeman and Louçã (2001).

26 Although in theory, this is exactly the path described by a driver of growth in a new classical model. This is the generally unanalyzed consequence of the assumption of "non-differential" growth, where a new idea, as the outcome of a production function for innovation (e.g., Romer 1986, 1990, 1994) produces a technology shock that "causes" economic growth equally and everywhere as a shift in the production function that transpires effectively without anything else changing. Theoretically, this is a stroke of genius (e.g., see Jones 1995, Aghion and Howitt 1998), but empirically it is less so. In contrast, and in reality, see Metcalfe et al. (2006).

27 This is the assumption implicit in the neo-Walrasian paradigm, for example, Debreu (1959). Again, theoretically elegant and empirically naïve: a contribution to mathematics, not science.

28 The aspect may be central or oblique, and the scale may be magnificent or minor. There does not currently exist a standard measure of centrality or scale about which to measure generic rules, whether novel or embedded. That will need to be rectified if evolutionary economics is to provide not just an historical analysis of what has happened but also a platform for the evaluation of evolution that is happening. Note further that evolutionary biologists have no such qualms because no one ever asks them what species will evolve next. Evolutionary economists, however, do face this challenge, and so need to begin by evaluating what has come before in consistent ways that will allow contemporary estimates of statistical value. Modern medicine represents an interesting intermediate case in that it interferes heavily with natural selection, that is, certain indications nowadays show multifold higher incidences in humans than just a few generations ago (e.g., type 1 diabetes). Here the forecasts refer to a particular socio-biological form of "natural selection."

29 See Lachmann (1986), Kirzner (1997), Loasby (1999), Potts (2001).

30 See Clark et al. (2005) on the allocation of complexity as a model of this process.

31 The fastest time that an evolutionary process can run is in real time. As a computational object, a market economy cannot go faster than that (because if there were an algorithm that could compute that future, it would under generic competition already be applied as a rule). However, it can go slower than that when it artificially disallows economic experiments. See Hayek (1948), Eliasson (1991), Rosenberg (1992), Nelson (1994).

32 cf. Ayres (1944).

33 This approach is based on an analytic methodology long known in engineering, but first introduced to economics by Leijonhufvud (1973) who argued that macroeconomic theory should be based on the study of the ways in which the coordination system can fail in terms of an understanding of how it works at all, rather than a study of failure based upon an implicit presumption that it otherwise works perfectly.

34 Efficacious is not a synonym for efficient, for they are quality references defined from different basis. Efficacious is a sufficiency condition, such that it is the quality of being sufficient for the task (as in Herbert Simon's (1976) notion of procedural rationality). Efficiency is an optimality criterion, such that it is defined with reference to some notion of optimality (cf. substantive rationality). Efficacy is the general quality of evolutionary coordination (Dopfer 2004). See also Potts (2000a: ch. 4) on complexity as the theoretical equivalent of this analytic notion.

35 Genetic drift is a well understood phenomena of population genetics due to the sampling effects of selection. We expect the same phenomena (i.e., generic drift) occurs in economic evolution.

36 As in Keynesian economics with failures of expenditure flows and in New Keynesian economics with failures of prices to convey appropriate information, both of which lead to failures of appropriate operational activity levels. The same argument is also effectively made in neoclassical economics, although without welfare evaluation, in consequence of fluctuations in real business conditions.

37 Or, symmetrically, that the rule environment is under- or over-adopted with respect to the novel rule. The point being that there is no absolute standard by which to judge this.

38 Richardson (1960, 1972).

39 Potts (2000a).

40 There has been relatively little explicit treatment of economic evolution as co-evolution, for example, Gowdy (1994), Lehmann-Waffenschmidt (2006). Yet just as practical economists who do partial economic analysis also understand that there is also a general equilibrium analysis that pertains, all practical evolutionary economists studying the evolution of an industry or sector or some such also understand that this is part of a more general co-evolutionary analysis.

41 Potts (2000a: ch. 2).

42 See also Sections 4.3.1 and 4.3.2.

43 Note that a further implication of the existence of positive feedback clusters, where meso move together symbiotically and with population reinforcement, is the notion of "anti-clusters" of anti-positive feedback between sets of meso. Anti-clusters are the negative effect of an emergent meso on other meso, as the playing of a zero-sum game that does not result in co-evolutionary adaptation, but rather in exclusion, extinction, domination or enslavement.

44 Carlson (1989), Nelson (1993), Malerba and Orsenigo (1996), Brenner (2004).

45 Such a system of associated or complementary goods is associated with consumer lifestyle, consumer knowledge and innovativeness (Earl and Kemp 1999). In the 1970s and 1980s consumer lifestyle studies have mushroomed, but it is only until very recently that the complex demand side has been receiving treatment in evolutionary economics. See also footnote 46.

46 The changing structure of social learning and social consumption and also the complementary aspects of a changing system of goods would be reflected in a changing matrix of co-evolving consumption associations. This is not yet something that economists have been concerned to systematically measure, but evolutionary economists should be very interested in the open-system dynamics of consumption (as with investment) patterns. See Bianchi (1998), Verspagen (2002), Witt (2001, 2003a), Cordes (2005).

47 Cantner and Pyka (1998a,b), Cantner, Hanusch and Westermann (1996), Florida (2002).

48 cf. endogenous growth theory, which, despite its self-given title, has a generically static view of subject and object coordination, an essentially random view of knowledge development and a mostly operational view of the process of coordination and change.

49 For example, Hayek (1973), Kregel (1973), also Foster (1994).

6 Macro dynamics, growth and development

1 Kauffman (1993, 1995, 2000), Potts (2000a), Prigogine (2005), Chen (2005).

2 Simon (1962), Potts (2000a).

3 Loasby (1999).

4 For example, Dosi (1982), Freeman and Soete (1997), Perez (2003).

5 Alchian (1950), Friedman (1953), Hodgson (1993), Nelson (2001).

6 Nelson and Winter (1982).

7 Combining these concepts in a histonomic framework (Dopfer 1985 no ref. in bib., 1986), we obtain a set of theoretic propositions which preclude both a purely "history-driven" and a purely "history-free" (e.g., neoclassical) course of development. On histonomic grounds, the antinomy between theory and history loses its meaning. On the integration of theory and history within evolutionary economics, Witt (2004), Lehmann-Waffenschmidt (2002), Walter (2003). For a notable application of this view to macroeconomics see Foster (1994).

8 Keynes (1936, 1937), Kregel (1973).

9 The likes of Leonard Hurwicz (1973), for example, tried to tame his work into formalisms by effectively collapsing it back into a signal coordination problem of given but distributed agents.

10 Some may say that such a problem is effectively unanalyzable, and based on our current models and methods, they would be right. But we are optimists, and would remind those people that many

great analytical problems that came to be resolved, either through clever algorithms, shifts of dimensionality or sheer computational force, were long thought to be unanalyzable. We have hope that a combination of the further development of multi-agent modeling and the implications of Moore's law may help along the direction of progress. So too may the effects of concentrated resources and institutes (e.g., the Santa Fe Institute and the like) may have similar effects to that of the Cowles Commission and Rand had on the development of general operational models. The history of the resolution of such problems in microbiology and econometric modeling would suggest that it may take decades of further development to crack such problems upon. Who knows? Not us to be sure, but what we do know is that no one has yet provided any impossibility theorems to render the generic coordination problem unanalyzable.

11 As basic evidence, the Schumpeterian framework has been inordinately powerful for the study of technological change and industrial dynamics, and so forth, but has had relatively little impact on macroeconomics and also on microeconomics.

12 As such things did not exist at the time, except for von Neumann (1944–5) and Young (1928).

13 Kaldor (1960), Silverberg and Verspagen (2005). Metcalfe, Foster and Ramlogan (2006), Fagerberg (2002), Llerena and Lorentz (2004).

14 Solow (1956).

7 Generic policy

1 On this, see Nelson (1993), Metcalfe (1995), Wegner (1997, 2005), Elliason (2000), Vosskamp (2001), Schnellenbach (2002, 2005), Koch (2005), Schwerin and Werker (2005), Witt (2003b), Okruch (2003), Dopfer (2005b), David (2005: 175–89).

2 Progress we define as any evolutionary process that corresponds to a welfare criteria set democratically by a community.

3 One could also well imagine policies fostering the acceptance (i.e., adoption) of values like "non-corruption," and relate 2nd order policies to 0th order rules (e.g., in education of young citizens).

4 Note that there are perhaps higher order rules as well, such as origination rules for originating origination rules. The more complex an economic order, the further we may expect the emergence of higher order rules to unfold.

5 Our approach of a "generic economic policy" differs substantially (i.e., ontologically) from the traditional one as pioneered by Jan Tinbergen. He has formulated economic policy in terms of what may be conceived as "Classical Mechanics with an Ethical Dimension" (Dopfer 1988, reply to Jan Tinbergen).

6 The "interdependence of orders" was the major concern of the German ORDO school of Walter Eucken, Wilhelm Röpke, Müller-Armack and others. It emphasized the necessary "interdependence of order," that is, between the order of a market system and the order of a democratic system.

7 See, for example, Sen (1999), Florida (2002).

References

Aghion P, Howitt P (1992) "A model of growth through creative destruction" *Econometrica*, 60: 323–351.

Aghion P, Howitt P (1998) *Endogenous growth theory*. MIT Press: Cambridge, MA.

Alchian A (1950) "Uncertainty, evolution, and economic theory" *Journal of Political Economy*, 58: 211–221.

Alcouffe A, Kuhn T (2004) "Schumpeterian endogenous growth theory and evolutionary economics" *Journal of Evolutionary Economics*, 14: 223–236.

Allen PM (1997) *Cities and regions as self-organizing systems: Models of complexity*. Gordon and Breach: Amsterdam.

Allen PM (2005) "Understanding social and economic systems as evolutionary complex systems," in Dopfer (ed.) (2005) pp. 431–458.

Amendola M, Gaffard J-L (2003) "Persistent unemployment and co-ordination issues: an evolutionary perspective" *Journal of Evolutionary Economics*, 13: 1–27.

Andersen ES (1994) *Evolutionary economics: Post-Schumpeterian contributions*. Pinter: London.

Andersen ES (2002) "Railroadization as Schumpeter's standard case: an evolutionary-ecological account" *Industry and Innovation*, 9: 41–78.

Antonelli C (2003) *The economics of innovation, new technologies and structural change*. Routledge: London.

Arthur WB (1989) "Competing technologies, increasing returns and lock-in by historical events" *Economic Journal*, 99: 116–131.

Arthur WB, Durlauf S, Lane D (1997) *The economy as an evolving complex system II*. Fe Institute Studies in the Science of Complexity, Reading. Addison-Wesley: Massachusetts.

Aruka Y (ed) (2001) *Evolutionary controversies in economics—a new transdisciplinary approach Berlin*. Heidelberg: New York.

Ayres C (1944) *The theory of economic progress*. University of North Carolina Press: Chapel Hill.

Backhouse R (2000) *The ordinary business of life: A history of economics from the ancient world to the twenty-first century*. Princeton University Press: Princeton, NJ.

Bandini S, Manzoni S, Vizzari G (2004), "Multi-agent approach top localization problems: The case of multilayered multi agent situated systems" *Web Intelligence and Agent Systems: An International Journal*, 2/3: 155–166.

Barabasi A (2002) *Linked: The new science of networks*. Perseus: New York.

Barkow J, Cosmides L, Tooby J (1992) *The adapted mind: evolutionary psychology and the generation of culture*. Oxford University Press: New York.

Bateson G (1972) *Step to an ecology of mind*. Ballentine: New York.

Baumol W (1982) "Contestable markets: An uprising in the theory of industry structure" *American Economic Review*, 72: 1–15.

Baumol W (1990) "Entrepreneurship: Productive, unproductive and destructive" *Journal of Political Economy*, 98: 893–921.

Beckenbach F, Daskalakis M (2003) "Invention and innovation as creative problem solving activities" *Volkswirtschaftliche Disussionsbeiträge Universität Kassel*.

Bianchi M (ed.) (1998) *The active consumer: Novelty and surprise in consumer choice*. Routledge: London.

Binmore K (1993) *Game theory and the social contract*. Vol. 1: Playing fair. MIT Press: Cambridge, MA.

Binmore K (1998) *Game theory and the social contract*. Vol. 2: Just playing. MIT Press: Cambridge, MA.

Boschma RA, Frenken K (2006) "Applications of Evolutionary Geography" DRUID *Working Paper* No 06.26.

Boulding K (1978) *Ecodynamics: A new theory of societal evolution*. Sage: Beverley Hills, CA.

Bourgine P, Nadal J (eds) (2004) *Cognitive economics: An interdisciplinary approach*. Springer Verlag: Heidelburg.

Bowles S (1998) "Endogenous preferences: The cultural consequences of markets and other economic institutions" *Journal of Economic Literature*, 36: 75–111.

Boyd R, Richerson P (1980) "Sociobiology, culture and economic theory" *Journal of Economic Behavior and Organization*, 1: 97–121.

Boyd R, Richerson PJ (1985) *Culture and the evolutionary process*. University of Chicago Press: Chicago, IL.

Brenner T (1999) *Modeling learning in economics*. Edward Elgar: Cheltenham.

Brenner T (2004) *Local industrial clusters, existence, emergence and evolution*. Routledge: London.

Brette O, Mehier C (2005) "Veblen's evolutionary economics revisited through the micro-meso-macro framework: The stakes for the analysis of clusters of innovation" STOICA Working Paper N°09–05.

Brooks D, Wiley E (1986) *Evolution as entropy: Towards a unified theory of biology*. University of Chicago Press: Chicago.

Buchanan J, Tullock G (1962) *The calculus of consent: The logical foundations of constitutional democracy*. University of Michigan press: Ann Arbor.

Budzinski O (2001) "Cognitive rules and institutions—on the interrelation of interpersonal and inter-persoanl rules" Universitaet Hannover Discussion Paper 241.

Bünstorf G (2000) "Self-organization and sustainability: Energetics of evolution and implications for ecological economics" *Ecological Economics*, 33: 119–134.

Bünstorf G (2004) *The economics of energy and the production process: An evolutionary approach*. Edward Elgar: Cheltenham.

Caballero R, Hammour M (1994) "The cleansing effects of recessions" *American Economic Review*, 84: 1350–1368.

Caldwell B (2003) *Hayek's challenge*. University of Chicago Press. Chicago.

Camerer C (2003) *Behavioral game theory: Experiments in strategic interaction*. Princeton University Press: Princeton, NJ.

Camerer C, Loewenstein G, Prelec D (2005) "Neuroeconomics: How neuroscience can inform economics" *Journal of Economic Literature*, 43/1: 9–64.

Cantner U, Pyka A (1998a) "Technological evolution: An analysis within the knowledge based approach" *Structural change and Economics Dynamics*, 9/1: 85–107.

Cantner U, Pyka A (1998b) "Absorbing technological spillovers: Simulations in an evolutionary framework" *Industrial and Corporate Change*, 7/2: 369–397.

Cantner U, Hanusch H, Westermann G (1996) "Detecting technological performance and variety—an empirical approach to technological efficiency and dynamics" in E Helmstädter and M Perlman (eds) *Economic Dynamism: Analysis and policy*, University of Michigan Press: Ann Arbor, pp. 223–246.

Carlson B (ed.) (1989) *Industrial dynamics: Technological, organizational and structural changes in industries and firms*. Kluwer Academic: Boston.

Chai A, Earl P, Potts J (2007) "Fashion growth and welfare: An evolutionary approach" *Advances in Austrian Economics*, 10 (Ch. 11):187–207.

Chancellor E (1999) *Devil take the hindmost: A history of financial speculation*. Plum: New York.

Chen (2005) in Dopfer, K (ed.) (2005) "Complex dynamics in economic organisms" *The evolutionary foundations of economics*, Cambridge UP.

Choi YB (1993) *Paradigms and conventions: Uncertainty, decision making and entrepreneurship*. University of Michigan Press: Ann Arbor.

Clark J, Morrison K, Potts J (2005) "The allocation of complexity" School of Economics, mimeo, University of Queensland.

Coase R (1937) "The nature of the firm" *Economica*, 4: 386–405.

Coase R (1992) "The institutional structure of production" *American Economic Review*, 82: 713–719.

Cohen W, Levinthal D (1990) "Absorptive capacity: A new perspective on learning and innovation" *Administrative Science Quarterly*, 35: 128–152.

Cohen W, March J, Olsen J (1972) "A garbage can theory of organizational choice" *Administrative Science Quarterly*, 17: 1–25.

Conlisk J (1996) "Why bounded rationality?" *Journal of Economic Literature*, 34: 669–700.

Cordes C (2005) "Long term tendencies in technological creating: A preference-based approach" *Journal of Evolutionary Economics*, 15/2: 149–168.

Corning P (2003) *Nature's magic: Synergy in evolution and the fate of humankind.* Cambridge University Press: Cambridge.

Corsi M (1991) *Division of labour, technical change and economic growth.* Aldershot: Avebury.

Cosmides L, Tooby J (1994) "Better than rational: Evolutionary psychology and the invisible hand" *American Economic Review*, 84: 327–332.

Cyert R, March J (1963) *A behavioral theory of the firm.* Prentice Hall: Englewood Cliffs, NJ.

Damasio A (1995) *Descarte's Error.* Putnam: New York.

Darley V, Kauffman S (1997) "Natural rationality" in Arthur WB, Durlauf S, Lane D (1997) *The economy as an evolving complex system II.* Fe Institute Studies in the Science of Complexity, Reading. Addison-Wesley: Massachusetts. pp. 45–80.

David PA (1985) "Clio and the economics of QWERTY" *American Economic Review*, 75: 332–337.

David PA (2005) "Path dependence in economic processes: implications for policy analysis in dynamical system contexts" in K Dopfer (ed.) (2005) pp. 151–194.

Dawkins R (1982) *The extended phenotype.* Oxford University Press: Oxford.

Day R (1975) "Adaptive processes and economic theory" In R Day and T Groves (eds) *Adaptive economic models.* Academic press.

Day R (2001) "Adapting, learning and economizing" K. Dopfer (ed.) (2001) pp. 277–298.

De Soto H (2000) *The mystery of capital—why capitalism triumphs in the west and fails everywhere else.* Bantam Press: London.

De Vany H (2004) *Hollywood economics: How extreme uncertainty shapes the film industry.* Routledge: London.

Debreu G (1959) *Theory of value: An axiomatic analysis of economic equilibrium.* Yale University Press: New Haven.

Dennett D (1995) *Darwin's Dangerous Idea.* Simon & Schuster: New York.

Depew B, Weber D (1995) *Darwinism evolving: Systems dynamics and the genealogy of natural selection.* MIT Press: Boston.

Depew B, Weber D (1999) "Natural selection and self-organization" *Biology and Philosophy*, 14: 33–65.

Diamond J (1997) *Guns, germs and steel: The fate of human societies.* WW Norton: New York.

Dietrich M (2006) "The nature of the firm in an evolutionary context" Paper presented at the EAEPE" Conference, Istanbul Nov 2–4 2006.

Dodsgon M, Gann D, Salter A (2005) *Think, play do: Technology, innovation and organization.* Oxford University Press: Oxford.

Dopfer K (ed.) (1976) *Economics in the future: Towards a new paradigm.* Macmillan: London.

Dopfer K (1986) "Causality and consciousness in economics: Concepts of change in orthodox and heterodox economics" *Journal of Economic Issues*, 20: 509–523.

Dopfer K (1988) "Classical mechanics with an ethical dimension" *Journal of Economic Issues*, 22: 675–706.

Dopfer K (1990) "Elemente einer Evolutionsökonomik: Prozess, Struktur und Phasenübergänge" *Studien zur evolutorischen Ökonomik I*, U. Witt (ed.) Duncker & Humblot: Berlin, pp. 19–47.

Dopfer K (1991) "Towards a theory of economic institutions: Synergy and path dependence" *Journal of Economic Issues*, 25: 535–550.

Dopfer K (1993) "The generation of novelty in the economic process: An evolutionary concept" *Entropy and Bioeconomics*, Dragan JC, Seifert EK, Demetrescu MC (eds), Nagard: Milano, pp. 130–153.

Dopfer K (1995) "Evolutionsökonomie" *Lexikon der ökonomischen Bildung*, May H, May U (eds), Oldenbourg: München, Wien, pp. 195–198.

Dopfer K (ed.) (2001) *Evolutionary economics: Program and scope*. Kluwer: London.

Dopfer (2002) "Stufen der Analogiebildung und Ökonomischen Theorieentwicklung—Von der Mechanik zur Selbstorganisation Ökonomischer Prozesse" *Kooperation und interaktives Lernen in der Ökonomie*, Biesecker A, Elsner W, Grenzdörffler K (eds) Peterlang: Frankfurt, AM, pp. 33–52.

Dopfer K (2004) "The economic agent as rule maker and rule user: Homo sapiens Oeconomicus" *Journal of Evolutionary Economics*, 14: 177–195.

Dopfer K (ed.) (2005a) *Evolutionary foundations of economics*. Cambridge University Press: Cambridge.

Dopfer K (2005b) A unified rule theory for economics: Towards a generic approach to self-organisation and evolution Paper presented at the *Second Sino-German Evolutionary Economics Workshop*, 28–31 August 2005.

Dopfer K (ed.) (2005c) *Economics, evolution and the state: The governance of complexity*. Edward Elgar: Cheltenham.

Dopfer K (2006) "The origins of meso economics. Schumpeter's legacy" *Papers on Economics and Evolution*, # 0610.

Dopfer K, Potts J (2004a) "Evolutionary realism: A new ontology for economics" *Journal of Economic Methodology*, 11: 195–212.

Dopfer K, Potts J (2004b) "Micro–meso–macro: A new framework for evolutionary economic analysis" in Metcalfe JS and J Foster (eds) *Evolution and economic complexity*. Edward Elgar: Cheltenham.

Dopfer K, Foster J, Potts J (2004) "Micro meso macro" *Journal of Evolutionary Economics*, 14: 263–279.

Dosi G (1982) "Technological paradigms and technological trajectories" *Research Policy*, 11: 147–162.

Dosi G (1988) "Sources, procedures, and microeconomic effects of innovation" *Journal of Economic Literature*, 26: 1120–71.

Dosi G (1990) "Finance, innovation and industrial change" *Journal of Evolutionary Economics*, 13: 299–319.

Dosi G (2000) *Innovation, organization and economic dynamics: Selected essays*. Edward Elgar: Cheltenham.

Dosi G, Nelson R (1994) "An introduction to evolutionary theories in economics" *Journal of Evolutionary Economics*, 4: 153–172.

Dosi G, Marengo L, Fagiolo G (2005) "Learning in evolutionary environments" in Dopfer (ed.) (2005) pp. 255–338.

Dow S, Earl P (eds) (1999) *Economic organization and economic knowledge: Essays in honour of Brian J Loasby*. Edward Elgar: Cheltenham.

Earl P (1986) *Lifestyle economics: Consumer behaviour in a turbulent world*. Wheatsheaf Books: Brighton.

Earl P (1990) "Economics and psychology: A survey" *Economic Journal*, 100: 718–755.

Earl P (2003) "The entrepreneur as a constructor of connections" *Advances in Austrian Economics*, 6: 113–130.

Earl P, Kemp S (eds) (1999) *The Elgar Companion to consumer research and economic psychology*. Edward Elgar: Cheltenham.

Earl P, Potts J (2004) "The market for preferences" *Cambridge Journal of Economics*, 28: 619–633.

Earl P, Peng TC, Potts J (2006) "Decision rule cascades" Mimeo, School of Economics, University of Queensland.

Earl P, Wakeley T (2005) *Business economics: A contemporary approach*. McGraw-Hill: Maidenhead.

Edelman G (1992) *Bright air, brilliant fire*. Basic Books: New York.

Egidi M, Rizzello S (eds) (2004) *Cognitive economics* (Vols. I&II.) Edward Elgar: Cheltenham.

Eliasson G (1991) "Modeling the experimentally organized economy: Complex dynamics in an empirical micro-macro model of endogenous economic growth" *Journal of Economic Behavior and Organization*, 16: 153–182.

Eliasson G (2000) "Industrial policy, competence blocs and the role of science in economic development" *Journal of Evolutionary Economics*, 10: 217–241.

Eucken W (1952) *Grundsätze der Wirtschaftspolitik*. Mohr Siebeck: Tübingen.

Faber M, Proops J (1993) *Evolution, time, production and environment*. Springer Verlag: Berlin.

Fagerberg J (2002) "A layman's guide to evolutionary economics" Working paper, No. 17, TIK: Oslo.

Fagerberg R (2003) "Schumpeter and the revival of evolutionary economics: An appraisal of the literature" *Journal of Evolutionary Economics*, 13: 125–159.

Falk A, Kosfeld M, "Distrust—the hidden cost of control" IZA DP 1203 (forthcoming in *American Economic Review*).

Fehl U (1994) "Spontaneous Order" in Boetke PJ (ed.) *The Elgar companion to Austrian economics*. Edward Elgar: Aldershot, UK, pp. 197–205.

Fehr E, Gächter S (2000) "Fairness and Retaliation: The Economics of Reciprocity" *Journal of Economic Perspectives*, 14(3): 159–181.

Fields AJ (1984) "Microeconomics, norms and rationality" *Economic Development and Cultural Change*, 32(4): 683–711.

Florida R (2002) *The rise of the creative class*. Basic Books: New York.

Florida R (2005) *The flight of the creative class*. Harper Business: New York.

Foray D (2004) *The economics of knowledge*. MIT Press: Boston.

Foss N (1993) "Theories of the firm: Contractual and competence perspectives" *Journal of Evolutionary Economics*, 3: 127–144.

Foss N (2001) "Leadership, beliefs and coordination: An exploratory discussion" *Industrial and corporate change*, 10/2: 357–388.

Foss N, Knudsen C (eds) (1996) *Towards a competence theory of the firm*. Routledge: London.

Foss N, Loasby B (eds) (1996) *Economic organization, capabilities and coordination: Essays in honour of G. B. Richardson*. Routledge: London.

Foster J (1987) *Evolutionary Macroeconomics*. Unwin Hyman: London.

Foster J (1993) "Economics and the self-organisation approach: Alfred Marshall revisited" *Economic Journal*, 103: 975–991.

Foster J (1994) "Macroeconomic theory" Hodgson GM, Samuels WJ, Tool MR (eds) *The Elgar companion to institutional and evolutionary economics*, Edward Elgar: Cheltenham, pp. 23–29.

Foster J (1997) "The analytical foundations of evolutionary economics: From biological analogy to economic self-organisation" *Structural Change and Economic Dynamics*, 8: 427–451.

Foster J (2000) "Competitive selection, self organization" and Joseph A. Schumpeter" *Journal of Evolutionary Economics*, 10: 311–328.

Foster J (2006a) "From simplistic to complex systems in economics" *Cambridge Journal of Economics*, 29: 873–892.

Foster J (2006b) "Why is economics not a complex systems science" *Journal of Economic Issues*, 40: 1069–1091.

Foster J, Metcalfe JS (eds) (2001) *Frontiers of evolutionary economics*. Edward Elgar: Cheltenham.

Foster J, Metcalfe JS (eds) (2005) *Evolution and economic complexity*. Edward Elgar: Cheltenham.

Foster J, Potts J (2006a) "Complexity, networks and the importance of demand and consumption in economic evolution" in M McKelvey and F Holman (eds) *Flexibility and stability in economic transformation*. Oxford University Press: Oxford, pp. 99–120.

Foster J, Potts J (2006b) "The evolutionary method" Paper presented at the Schumpeter Society Conference, June 21, 2006.

Foster J, Wild P (1999a) "Econometric modeling in the presence of evolutionary change" *Cambridge Journal of Economics*, 23: 749–770.

Foster J, Wild P (1999b) "Detecting self-organizational change in economic processes exhibiting logistic growth" *Journal of Evolutionary Economics*, 9: 109–133.

Freeman C (ed.) (1983) *Long waves in the world economy*. Frances Pinter: London.

Freeman C (1994) "The economics of technical change" *Cambridge Journal of Economics*, 18: 463–514.

Freeman C (2002) "Continental, national and sub-national innovation systems: Complementarity and economic growth" *Research Policy*, 31: 191–211.

Freeman C, Louçã F (2001) *As time goes by: From the industrial revolutions to the information revolution*. Oxford University Press: Oxford.

Freeman C, Perez C (1988) "Structural crises of adjustment, business cycles, and investment behaviour" in Dosi et al. (eds) *Technical change and economic theory*. Pinter: London, pp. 38–66.

Freeman C, Soete L (1997) *The economics of industrial innovation* (3rd edn). Pinter: London.

Friedman M (1953) "The methodology of positive economics" In M. Friedman (1953) *Essays in positive economics*. Chicago University Press: Chicago, pp. 3–43.

Friedman T (2005) *The world is flat: A brief history of the globalized world in the 21st century*. Allen Lane: London.

Georgescu-Roegen N (1971) *The entropy law and the economic process*. Harvard University Press: Cambridge, MA.

Geroski P (2003) *The evolution of new markets*. Oxford University Press: Oxford.

Gintis H (2000) *Game theory evolving: A problem centered introduction to modeling strategic interaction*. Princeton University Press: Princeton, NJ.

Gintis H, Bowles S, Boyd R, Fehr E (2005) *Moral sentiments and material interests: On the foundations of cooperation in economic life*. MIT Press: Cambridge, MA.

Gowdy J (1994) *Coevolutionary economics: The economy of society and environment*. Kluwer Academic Publishers: Boston.

Goyal S, van der Leij M, Morago-Gonzalez J (2006) "Economics: An emerging small world" *Journal of Political Economy*, 114: 403–412.

Hanusch (1988) *Evolutionary economics: Applications of Schumpeter's ideas*. Cup: Cambridge.

Hausmann R, Rodrik D (2003) "Economic development as self-discovery" *Journal of Development Economics*, 72: 603–633.

Hayek FA (1945) "The use of knowledge in society" *American Economic Review*, 35: 519–530.

Hayek FA (1948) "The meaning of competition" In *Individualism and economic order*, University of Chicago Press: Chicago, pp. 92–106.

Hayek FA (1952) *The sensory order*. University of Chicago Press: Chicago.

Hayek FA (1973/1976) *Law, legislation, and liberty: Rules and order*. University of Chicago Press: Chicago.

Hayek FA (1988) *The fatal conceit: The errors of socialism*. University of Chicago Press: Chicago.

Hayek FA (1991) "Spontaneous ('grown') order and organized ('made') order" in Thompson G, Frances J, Lavacic R, Mitchell J (eds) *Markets, Networks and Hierarchies*. Sage: London, pp. 293–305.

Helmstädter E (2003) (ed.) *The economics of knowledge sharing: A new institutional approach*. Edward Elgar: Cheltenham.

Henrich J, Boyd R, Bowles S, Camerer C, Fehr E, Gintis H (2004) *Foundations of human sociality: Economic experiments and ethnographic evidence from fifteen small-scale societies*. Oxford University Press: Oxford.

Herrmann-Pillath C (2001) "On the ontological foundations of evolutionary economics" in Dopfer (ed.) (2001) *Evolutionary Economics*. Kluwer: Dortrecht, pp. 89–139.

Hippel E von (1988) *The sources of innovation*. New York: Oxford University Press.

Hodgson G (1993) *Economics and evolution: Bringing life back into economics*. Polity Press: Cambridge.

Hodgson G (1997) "The ubiquity of habits and rules" *Cambridge Journal of Economics*, 21: 663–684.

Hodgson G (1998a) *The foundations of evolutionary economics: 1890–1973*, International library of critical writings in economics. Edward Elgar: Cheltenham.

Hodgson G (1998b) "The approach of institutional economics" *Journal of Economic Literature*, 36/1: 166–192.

Hodgson G (2002) "Darwinism in economics: From analogy to ontology" *Journal of Evolutionary Economics*, 12: 259–281.

Hodgson G (2003) *How economics forgot history: The problem of historical specificity in social science*. Cambridge University Press: Cambridge.

Hodgson G, Knudsen T (2004) "The firm as an interactor: Firms as vehicles for habits and routines" *Journal of Evolutionary Economics*, 14: 281–307.

Hodgson G, Samuels W, Tool M (eds) (1994) *The Elgar companion to institutional and evolutionary economics*. Edward Elgar: Aldershot.

Hoelzl W, Foster, J (eds) (2004) *Applied evolutionary economics and complexity*. Edward Elgar: Cheltenham.

Holland J (1995) *Hidden order: How adaptation builds complexity*. Perseus Books: Cambridge.

Hurwicz L (1973) "The design of a mechanism for resource allocation" *American Economic Review*, 63/2: 1–30.

Hutter M (2001) "Efficiency, viability and the new rules of the Internet" *European Journal of Law*, 11: 5–22.

Jacobs J (1969) *The economy of cities*. Penguin Books: London.

Jones C (1995) "R&D-based models of economic growth" *Journal of Political Economy*, 103: 759–784.

Kaldor N (1960) *Essays on stability and economic growth*. Duckworth. London.

Kastelle T (2006) "The evolution of the world trade network" Mimeo, School of Business, University of Queensland.

Kauffman S (1993) *The origins of order: Self-organization and selection in evolution*. Oxford University Press: Oxford.

Kauffman S (1995) *At home in the universe: The search for the laws of self-organization and complexity*. Oxford University Press: Oxford.

Kauffman S (2000) *Investigations*. Oxford University Press: New York.

Kay J (2003) *The truth about markets: Why some nations are rich but most remain poor*. Penguin: London.

Keynes JM (1936) *The general theory of employment, interest and money*. Macmillan: London.

Keynes JM (1937) "The general theory of employment" *Journal of Political Economy*, 51: 209–223.

King R, Levine R (1993) "Finance and growth: Schumpeter might be right" *Quarterly Journal of Economics*, 108: 707–737.

Kirman A (1997) "The economy as an evolving network" *Journal of Evolutionary Economics*, 7: 339–353.

Kirzner I (1973) *Competition and entrepreneurship*. University of Chicago Press: Chicago.

Kirzner I (1997) "Entrepreneurial discovery and the competitive market process: An Austrian approach" *Journal of Economic Literature*, 35: 60–85.

Klepper S (1996) "Exit, entry, growth and innovation over the product life cycle" *American Economic Review*, 86: 562–83.

Klepper S, Graddy E (1990) "The evolution of new industries and the determinants of market structure" *Rand Journal of Economics*, 21: 27–44.

Klepper S, Simons K (1997) "Technological extinctions of industrial firms: An enquiry into their nature and causes" *Industrial and Corporate Change*, 6: 379–460.

Klepper S, Simons K (2000) "The making of an oligopoly: Firm survival and technological change in the evolution of the U.S. tire industry" *Journal of Political Economy*, 108: 728–760.

Knight F (1921) *Risk, uncertainty and profit*. Houghton Mifflin: Boston.

Koch (2005) "Economic Policy—a process of communication" in K Dopfer (ed.) *Economics, evolution and the state: the governance of complexity*. Edward Elgar: Cheltenham, pp. 168–189.

Kondratieff N (1935) "The long waves in economic life" *Review of Economic Statistics*, 17/6: 105–115.

Krause G (2002) "Die Geschichte der ökonomischen Theorien. Mainstream und Alternative" *Utopie*, September, 783–803.

Kregel J (1973) *The reconstruction of political economy: an introduction to post-Keynesian economics.* Macmillan: London.

Krugman P (1991) "Increasing returns and economic geography" *Journal of Political Economy*, 99: 483–499.

Kuhn T (1962) *The structure of scientific revolutions.* University of Chicago Press: Chicago.

Lachman L (1986) *The market as an economic process.* Basil Blackwell: Oxford.

Lakatos I (1978) *The methodology of scientific research programmes.* Cambridge University Press: Cambridge.

Lancaster K (1966) "Change and innovation in the technology of consumption" *American Economic Review*, 56: 14–23.

Landes D (1969) *The unbound Prometheus: Technological and industrial development in western Europe from 1750 to the present.* Cambridge University Press: Cambridge.

Landes D (1998) *The wealth and poverty of nations: Why some are so rich and others so poor.* Abacus: London.

Langlois R (1992) "Transaction cost economics in real time" *Industrial and corporate change*, 1: 99–127.

Langlois R (2005) *The dynamics of industrial capitalism: Schumpeter, chandler and the new economy.* Routledge: London.

Langlois R, Robertson P (1995) *Firms, markets and economic change: A dynamic theory of business institutions.* Routledge: London.

Lawson T (1997) *Economics and reality.* Routledge: London.

Lawson T (2003) *Reorienting economics: Economics as social theory.* Routledge: London.

Lazaric N, Raybaut A (2005) "Knowledge, hierarchy and the selection of routines: An interpretative model with group interactions" *Journal of Evolutionary Economics*, 15/4: 393–422.

Leathers C, Raines P (2004) "The Schumpeterian role of financial innovations in the new economy's business cycle" *Cambridge Journal of Economics*, 28: 667–681.

Lehmann-Waffenschmidt M, Schwerin J (1999) "Kontingenz und Strukturähnlichkeit als Charakteristika selbstorganisierender Prozesse in der Ökonomie," Schweitzer F, Silvergerg G (eds) *Selbstorganisation in den Sozialwissenschaften*, Duncker & Humblot: Berlin, pp. 187–208.

Lehmann-Waffenschmidt BC (2006) Industrieevolution und die New Economy. Eine evolutorische Analyse der Beziehung zwischen New Economy and Old Economy aus simulationsanalytischer und wirtschaftshistorischer Perspektive Metropolis: Marburg.

Leibenstein H (1966) "Allocative efficiency vs. X-efficiency" *American Economic Review*, 56: 392–415.

Leibenstein H (1979) "A branch of economics is missing: micro-micro theory" *Journal of Economic Literature*, 17: 477–502.

Leijonhufvud A (1973) "Effective demand failures" *Swedish Journal of Economics*, 75: 27–48.

Leijonhufvud A (1981) *Information and coordination: Essays in macroeconomic theory.* Oxford university Press: Oxford.

Leijonhufvud A (1993) "Towards a not too rational macroeconomics" *Southern Economic Journal*, 60: 1–13.

Levinthal D (2006) "The Neo-Schumpeterian theory of the firm and the strategy field" *Industrial and corporate change*, 15/2: 391–394.

Lindblom C (2002) *The market system: what it is, how it works and what to make of it.* Yale University Press: New Haven.

Lipsey R, Carlaw K, Bekar C (2005) *Economic transformations: general purpose technologies and long-term economic growth.* Oxford University Press: Oxford.

List F (1841) *The national system of political economy.* Longman, Green and Co: London, 1909.

Llerena P, Lorentz A (2004) "Cumulative causation and evolutionary micro-founded technical change: a growth model with integrated economies" *Working Papers of BETA* 2004–08, Strasbourg.

Loasby B (1976) *Choice, complexity and ignorance*. Cambridge University Press: Cambridge.

Loasby B (1989) *The mind and method of the economist*. Edward Elgar: Aldershot.

Loasby B (1991) *Equilibrium and evolution: An exploration of connecting principles in economics*. Manchester University Press: Manchester.

Loasby B (1999) *Knowledge, institutions, and evolution in economics*. London: Routledge.

Loasby B (2000a) "Market institutions and economic evolution" *Journal of Evolutionary Economics*, 10: 297–309.

Loasby B (2000b) "How do we know?" In Earl P, Frowen S (eds) *Economics as an art of thought: Essays in memory of G. L. S. Shackle*. Routledge: London, pp. 1–24.

Loasby B (2001) "Cognition, imagination and institutions in demand creation" *Journal of Evolutionary Economics*, 11: 7–21.

Lotka A (1925) *Elements of physical biology*. Wilkins & Wilkins: Baltimore.

Louçã F (1997) *Turbulence in economics: An evolutionary appraisal of cycles and complexity in historical processes*. Edward Elgar: Cheltenham.

Lucas R (1988) "On the mechanics of economic development" *Journal of Monetary Economics*, 22: 3–42.

Maddison A (2001) *The world economy: A millennial perspective*. OECD: Paris.

Magnusson L (ed.) (1994) *Evolutionary and neo-Schumpeterian approaches to economics*. Kluwer: London.

Mäki U (ed.) (2001) *The economic world view: Studies in the ontology of economics*. Cambridge University Press: Cambridge.

Malerba F (2002) "Sectoral Systems of Innovation" *Research Policy*, 31: 247–264.

Malerba F, Orsenigo L (1995) "Schumpeterian patterns of innovation" *Cambridge Journal of Economics*, 19: 47–65.

Malerba F, Orsenigo L (1996) "The dynamics and evolution of industries" *Industrial and Corporate Change*, 5: 51–87.

Malerba F, Orsenigo L (1997) "Technological regimes and sectoral patterns of innovative activities" *Industrial and Corporate Change*, 6: 83–117.

Malerba F, Orsenigo L (2002) "Innovation and market structure in the dynamics of the pharmaceutical industry and biotechnology: Towards a history friendly model" *Industrial and Corporate Change*, 11: 667–703.

Malerba F, Nelson R, Orsenigo L, Winter S (2001) "History-friendly models: An overview of the case of the computer" *Journal of Artificial Societies and Social Simulation*, 4/3/6.

Malerba F, Nelson R, Orsenigo L, Winter S (2003) "Demand, innovation and the dynamics of market structure: The role of experimental users and diverse preferences" CESPRI working paper No. 135.

Malik F (2000) *Führen, leisten, leben. Wirksames Management für ein neue Zeit*. Deutsche Verlagsanstalt: Stuttgart, München.

Mandelbrot B (2004) *The (mis)behaviour of markets: a fractal view of risk, ruin and reward*. Basic Books: New York.

Marengo L (1992) "Coordination and organizational learning in the firm" *Journal of Evolutionary Economics*, 2: 313–26.

Marshall A (1949) *The principles of economics* (8th edn.) Macmillan: London.

Marx K (1867) *Capital: The process of production of capital*. Progress Publishers: Moscow.

Maturana H, Varela F (1980) "Autopoiesis and cognition: The realization of the living" in Cohen R, Wartofsky M (eds) *Boston studies in the philosophy of science*, Vol. 42, D. Reidel Publishing Co.: Dordecht.

Maynard Smith J (1968) *Mathematical ideas in biology*. Cambridge University Press: Cambridge.

Mayr E (1975) *Evolution and the diversity of life*. Harvard university Press. Cambridge.

McKelvey M (1996) *Evolutionary innovations: The business of biotechnology*. Oxford University Press: Oxford.

McMillan (2002) *Reinventing the bazaar: A natural history of markets*. W.W. Norton: New York.

Menard C (1995) "Markets as institutions vs organizations as markets: Disentangling some fundamental concepts" *Journal of Economic Behavior and Organization*, 28: 161–182.

Metcalfe JS (1994a) "Competition, Fisher's principle and increasing returns in the selection process" *Journal of Evolutionary Economics*, 4: 327–346.

Metcalfe JS (1994b) "Evolutionary economics and technology policy" *Economic Journal*, 104: 918–931.

Metcalfe JS (1995) "Technology systems and technology policy in an evolutionary framework" *Cambridge Journal of Economics*, 19: 25–47.

Metcalfe JS (1998) *Evolutionary economics and creative destruction*. Routledge: London.

Metcalfe JS (2001) "Evolutionary approaches to population thinking and the problem of growth and development" in Dopfer (ed.) (2001) *Evolutionary Economics*. Kluwer: Dortrecht, pp. 141–164.

Metcalfe JS (2002) "Knowledge of growth and the growth of knowledge" *Journal of Evolutionary Economics*, 12: 3–15.

Metcalfe JS (2003) "Equilibrium and evolutionary foundations of competition and technology policy: New perspectives on the division of labour and the innovation process" In Pelikan and Wegner (2003) pp. 162–190.

Metcalfe JS (2004) "The entrepreneur and the style of modern economics" *Journal of Evolutionary Economics*, 14: 157–175.

Metcalfe JS (2005) "Evolutionary concepts in relation to evolutionary economics" in Dopfer (ed) (2005) pp. 391–430.

Metcalfe JS, Foster J, Ramlogan R (2006) "Adaptive economic growth" *Cambridge Journal of Economics*, 30: 7–32.

Minsky H (1975) *John Maynard Keynes*. Columbia University Press: New York.

Mirowski P (1988) *Against mechanism: Protecting economics from science*. Rowman & Littlefield: Totowa, NJ.

Mirowski P (1989) *More heat than light: Economics as social physics*. Cambridge University Press: New York.

Mirowski P (2002) *Machine dreams: How economics became a cyborg science*. Cambridge University Press: New York.

Mirowski P (2007) "Markets come to bits: Evolution, computation and markomata in economic science" *Journal of Economic Behavior and Organization*, 63/2: 209–242.

Mirowski P, Somefun K (1998) "Markets as evolving computational entities" *Journal of Evolutionary Economics*, 8: 329–356.

Mises L (1940) *Human action*. Hodge: London

Mokyr J (1990) *The lever of riches*. Oxford University Press: New York.

Mokyr J (2002) *The gifts of Athena: Historical origins of the knowledge economy*. Princeton University Press: Princeton, NJ.

Monod J (1972) *Chance and necessity: An essay on the natural philosophy of modern biology*. Collins: London.

Montgomery C (1995) *Resource-based and evolutionary theories of the firm: Toward a synthesis*. Kluwer: Boston.

Morgenstern O. (1928) *Wirtschaftsprognose. Eine Untersuchung ihrer Voraussetzungen und Möglichkeiten*. Springer Verlag: Wien.

Mowery D, Rosenberg N (1998) *Paths of innovation: Technical change in 20th century America*. Cambridge University Press: Cambridge.

Murmann JP (2004) *Knowledge and competitive advantage: The coevolution of firms, technology and national systems*. Cambridge University Press: Cambridge.

Nelson R (1993) *National innovation systems: A comparative analysis*. Oxford University Press: New York.

Nelson R (1994) "The co-evolution of technology, industrial structure, and supporting institutions" *Industrial and Corporate Change*, 3: 47–63.

Nelson R (1995) "Recent evolutionary theorizing about economic change" *Journal of Economic Literature*, 33: 48–90.

Nelson R (2001) "Evolutionary perspectives on economic growth" in Dopfer K (ed.) (2001) *Evolutionary Economics*. Kluwer: Dordrecht, pp. 165–193.

Nelson R (2002) "On the uneven evolution of human know-how" *Research Policy*, 31: 213–231.

Nelson R, Winter S (1974) "Neoclassical vs evolutionary theories of economic growth: critique and prospectus" *Economic Journal*, 84: 886–905.

Nelson R, Winter S (1982) *An evolutionary theory of economic change*. Harvard University Press: Cambridge, MA.

Neumann J von (1944–5) "A model of general equilibrium" *Review of Economic Studies*, 13: 1–9.

Neumann J von, Burks A (1966) *Theory of self-reproducing automata*. University of Illinois Press: Urbana, IL. [JvN manuscript from 1946].

Ng YK (1986) *Mesoeconomics: A micro–macro analysis*. Harvester Wheatsheaf: New York.

Nishibe M (2006) "Redefining evolutionary economics" *Evolutionary Institutional Economics Review*, 3/1: 3–25.

Nooteboom B (2000) *Learning and innovation in organizations and economies*. Oxford University Press: Oxford.

North D (1990) *Institutions, institutional change and economic performance*. Cambridge University Press: Cambridge.

Okruch S (2003) "Knowledge and economic policy: A plea for political experimentalism" in Pelikan and Wegner (2003) pp. 67–95.

Ormerod P (1999) *Butterfly economics: A new general theory about social and economic behaviour*. Pantheon Books: London.

Ormerod P (2005) *Why most things fail: Evolution, extinction and economics*. Faber & Faber: London.

Ormerod P, Cook W (2003) Power law distributions of the frequency of demises of US firms. *Physica A*, 324: 207–212.

Ostrom E (2005) *Understanding institutional diversity* Princeton University Press: Princeton.

Parra, CM (2005) "Rules and Knowledge" *Evolutionary and Institutional Economics Review*, 2/1: 81–111.

Pelikan P, Wegner G (eds) (2003) *The evolutionary analysis of economic policy*. Edward Elgar: Cheltenham.

Penrose E (1959) *Theory of the growth of the firm*. Oxford University Press: Oxford.

Perez C (2003) *Technological revolutions and financial capital: The dynamics of bubbles and golden ages*. Edward Elgar: Cheltenham.

Pinker S (1997) *How the mind works*. WW Norton: New York.

Popper K (1945) *The open society and its enemies*. Routledge: London.

Popper K (1965) *Conjectures and refutations: The growth of scientific knowledge*. Harper & Row: New York.

Popper K (1972) *Objective knowledge: An evolutionary approach*. The Clarendon Press: Oxford.

Porter M (1980) *Competitive strategy*. Free Press: New York.

Porter M (1990) *The competitive advantage of nations*. Free Press: New York.

Potts J (2000a) *The new evolutionary microeconomics: Complexity, competence and adaptive behaviour*. Edward Elgar: Cheltenham.

Potts J (2000b) "Uncertainty, complexity and imagination" in Earl P, Frowen S (eds) *Economics as an art of thought*. Routledge: London. pp. 187–213.

Potts J (2001) "Knowledge and markets" *Journal of Evolutionary Economics*, 11: 413–431.

Potts J (2003) "Toward an evolutionary theory of *Homo Economicus*: The concept of universal nomadism" In J Laurent (ed.) *Evolutionary Economics and Human Nature*. Edward Elgar: Cheltenham, pp. 195–216.

Potts J (2004) "Liberty Bubbles" *Policy*, 20/3: 15–21.

Potts J, Dopfer K (2006) "An evolutionary theory of rent and profit" Paper presented at the Schumpeter Society Conference, June 21, 2006.

Potts J, Morrison K (2007) "Meso comes to markets" *Journal of Economic Behavior and Organization*, 63/2: 307–312.

Prahlad C, Hamel G (1990) "The core competencies of the corporation" *Harvard Business Review*, 66: 79–91.

Prigogine (2005) The rediscovery of value and the opening of economics in Dopfer, K (ed.) (2005) *The evolutionary foundations of economics*, Cambridge UP.

Pyka, A (2002) "Innovation Networks in Economics—From the incentive-based to the knowledge-based Approaches" *European Journal of Innovation Management*, 5/3, 152–163.

Pyka A, Fagiolo G (2007) "Agent-based modeling: A methodology for Neo-Schumpeterian economics" in Hanusch H and Pyka A (eds) *The Elgar companion to Neo-Schumpeterian Economics*. Edward Elgar: Cheltenham.

Pyka A, Hanusch H (eds) (2006) *Applied evolutionary economics and the knowledge-based economy*. Edward Elgar: Cheltenham.

Richardson G (1960) *Information and investment*. Oxford University Press: Oxford.

Richardson G (1972) "The organization of industry" *Economic Journal*, 82: 883–896.

Richerson P, Boyd R (2000) "Complex societies: The evolutionary dynamics of a crude superorganism" *Human Nature*, 10: 253–289.

Rizzello S (1999) *The economics of the mind*. Edward Elgar: Cheltenham.

Robbins L (1935) *An essay on the nature and significance of economic science*. Macmillan: London.

Robson A (2002) "Evolution and human nature" *Journal of Economic Perspectives*, 16: 89–106.

Rogers EM (1962) *Diffusion of innovations*. Free Press: New York.

Romer P (1986) "Increasing returns and long run growth" *Journal of Political Economy*, 94: 1002–1038.

Romer P (1990) "Endogenous technological change" *Journal of Political Economy*, 98: S71–S102.

Romer P (1994) "The origins of endogenous growth" *Journal of Economic Perspectives*, 8: 3–22.

Rosenberg N (1992) "Economic experiments" *Industrial and Corporate Change*, 1: 181–204.

Rumelt R (1984) "Towards a strategic theory of the firm" in R Lamb (ed.) *Competitive Strategic Management*. Prentice Hall: Englewood Cliffs, NJ, pp. 556–70.

Ryle G (1949) *The concept of mind*. University of Chicago Press: Chicago.

Sahlins M (1972) *Stone age economics*. Aldine: Chicago.

Samuelson P (1947) *Foundations of economic analysis*. Harvard University Press: Cambridge, MA.

Saviotti P (1996) *Technological evolution, variety and the economy*. Edward Elgar: Cheltenham.

Saviotti P (ed.) (2003) *Applied evolutionary economics—New empirical methods and simulation techniques*. Edward Elgar: Cheltenham.

Schelling T (1978) *Micro-motives and macro-behavior*. W.W. Norton: New York.

Schnellenbach J (2002) "New political economy, scientism and knowledge. A critique form a Hayekian perspective" *American Journal of Economics and Sociology*, 61: 193–216.

Schnellenbach J (2005) "The Dahrendorf hypothesis and its implications for the theory of Economic Theory" *Cambridge Journal of Economics*, 29: 997–1009.

Schumpeter J (1912/1934) *The theory of economic development*. Harvard University Press, Cambridge, MA.

Schumpeter J (1928) "The instability of capitalism" *Economic Journal*, 38: 361–368.

Schumpeter J (1939) *Business cycles*. McGraw-Hill: New York.

Schumpeter J (1942) *Capitalism, socialism and democracy*. Harper & Row: New York.

Schwaninger M (2006) *Intelligent organizations*. Springer: Berlin, Heidelberg, New York.

Schwerin J, Werker C (2005), "Innovation and the learning policy maker—an evolutionary approach based on historical experience" in Dopfer K (ed.) (2005c) *Economics, evolution and the state. The governance of complexity*.

Searle J (1995) *The construction of social reality*. The Free Press: New york.

Sen A (1999) *Development as freedom*. Oxford University Press: Oxford.

Shackle G (1972) *Epistemics and economics*. Cambridge University Press: Cambridge.

Shackle G (1974) *Keynesian kaleidics*. Edinburgh University Press: Edinburgh.

Shackle G (1979) *Imagination and the nature of choice*. Edinburgh University Press: Edinburgh.

Shapiro C, Varian H (1999) *Information rules: A strategic guide to the network economy*. Harvard Business School Press: Boston.

Shiller R (2000) *Irrational exuberance*. Princeton University Press: Princeton.

Shiozawa Y (2004) "Evolutionary economics in the 21st century: A manifesto" *Evolutionary and Institutional Economic Review*, 1/1: 5–47.

Silva ST, Teixeira AC (2006) "On the divergence of research paths in evolutionary economics: a comprehensive bibliometric account" *Papers on Economics & Evolution #0624.*

Silverberg G, Verspagen B (2005) "A percolation model of innovation in complex technology spaces" *Journal of Economic Dynamics and Control*, 29: 225–244.

Simon H (1957) *Models of man*. Wiley: New York.

Simon H (1962) "The architecture of complexity" *Proceedings of the American Philosophical Society*, 106: 467–482.

Simon H (1965) *Administrative behavior*. Free Press: New York.

Simon H (1968) *Sciences of the artificial*. MIT Press: Cambridge, MA.

Simon H (1976) "From substantive to procedural rationality" in S Latsis (ed.) *Method and Appraisal in Economics*. Cambridge University Press: Cambridge.

Smith A ([1759] 1976a) *The theory of moral sentiments* in D Raphael and A Macfie (eds). Oxford University Press: Oxford.

Smith A ([1776] 1976b) *An inquiry into the nature and causes of the wealth of nations* in R Campbell, A Skinner and W Todd (eds). Oxford University Press: Oxford.

Smith V (2003) "Constructivist and ecological rationality in economics" *American Economic Review*, 93: 465–508.

Smith V (2005) "Hayek and experimental economics" *Review of Austrian Economics*, 18: 135–144.

Sober E (1980) "Evolution, population thinking and essentialism" *Philosophy of Science*, 47: 350–383.

Solow R (1956) "A contribution to the theory of economic growth" *Quarterly Journal of Economics*, 70: 65–94.

Solow R (1994) "Perspectives on growth theory" *Journal of Economic Perspectives*, 8: 45–54.

Sraffa P (1960) *The production of commodities by means of commodities*. Cambridge University Press: Cambridge.

Steedman I (2001) *Consumption takes time*. Routledge: London.

Stigler G, Becker G (1977) "De gustibus non est disputandum" *American Economic Review*, 67: 76–90

Straton A (2005) "A complex systems approach to the value of ecological resources" *Ecological Economics*, 56: 402–411.

Teece D (1982) "Towards an economic theory of the multiproduct firm" *Journal of Economic Behavior and Organization*, 3: 39–63

Tesfatsion L (2002) "Agent based computational economics: growing economies from the bottom-up" *Artificial Life*, 8: 55–82.

Vanberg V (1994) *Rules and choice in economics*. Routledge: London.

Veblen T (1898a) "Why is economics not an evolutionary science" *Quarterly Journal of Economics*, 12: 373–397.

Veblen T (1898b) "The instinct of workmanship and the irksomeness of labor" *American Journal of Sociology*, 4/2: 187–201.

Veblen T (1899) *The theory of the leisure class*. Modern Library: New York.

Velupillai K (2000) *Computable economics*. Oxford University Press: Oxford.

Velupillai K (2005) "The unreasonable ineffectiveness of mathematics in economics" *Cambridge Journal of Economics*, 29: 849–872.

Verspagen B (2002) "Evolutionary macroeconomics: A synthesis between neo-Schumpeterian and post-Keynesian lines of thought" *Electronic Journal of Evolutionary Modeling and Economic Dynamics*. www.e-jemed.org/1007

Volterra V (1926) "Fluctuations in the abundance of a species considered mathematically" *Nature*, 118: 558–560.

Vosskamp R (2001) "Evolutorische Finanzwissenschaft" in M Lehmann-Waffenschmidt (ed.), *Perspektiven des Wandels.* Metropolis: Marburg.

Vriend N (1996) "Rational behavior and economic theory" *Journal of Economic Behavior and Organization*, 29: 263–285.

Vromen J (1995) *Economic evolution: An inquiry into the foundations of new institutional economics.* Routledge: London.

Vromen J (2001a) "Ontological commitments of evolutionary economics" in Mäki U (ed.) *The Economic world view: Studies in the ontology of economics.* Cambridge University Press: Cambridge, pp. 189–224.

Vromen J (2001b) "The human agent in evolutionary economics" in Laurent J, Nightingale J (eds) *Darwinism and evolutionary economics.* Edward Elgar: Cheltenham, pp. 184–208.

Vromen J (2004) "Conjectural revisionary economic ontology: Outline of an ambitious research agenda for evolutionary economics" *Journal of Economic Methodology*, 11/2: 213–247.

Walter R (2003) "Zum Verhältnis der Wirtschaftsgeschichte und evolutorischer Ökonomik" in Dopfer, K (ed.), *Studien zur Evolutorischen Ökonomik VII*, 113–131.

Warsh D (2006) *Knowledge and the wealth of nations: A story of economic discovery.* W.W. Norton: New York.

Watts D, Strogatz S (1998) "Collective dynamics of small-world Networks" *Nature*, 393: 440–442.

Wegner G (1997) "Economic policy from an evolutionary perspective: A new approach" *Journal of Institutional and Theoretical Economics*, 153: 485–509.

Wegner G (2003) "Evolutionary markets and the design of institutional policy" in Pelikan and Wegner (2003) pp. 46–66.

Weisbuch G, Kirman A, Herreiner D (2000) "Market organization and trading relationships" *Economic Journal*, 110: 411–436.

Whitehead AN (1925) *Science and the modern world.* Mentor: New York.

Williamson O (1985) *The economic institutions of capitalism.* Free Press: New York.

Williamson O (2000) "The new institutional economics: Taking stock, looking ahead" *Journal of Economic Literature*, 38: 595–613.

Winter S, Nelson R (1973) "In search of useful theory of innovation" *Research Policy*, 6: 36–76.

Witt U (1985) "Coordination of individual economic activities as an evolving process of self-organization" *Economie Appliquée,* 37: 569–595.

Witt U (1992) "Evolutionary concepts in economics" *Eastern Economic Journal*, 18: 405–420.

Witt U (ed.) (1993) *Evolutionary economics.* Edward Elgar: Aldershot.

Witt U (1997) "Self-organization and economics: What is new?" *Structural Change and Economic Dynamics*, 8: 489–507.

Witt U (2000) "Changing cognitive frames—changing organizational forms: An entrepreneurial theory of organizational development" *Industrial and Corporate Change*, 9: 733–755.

Witt U (2001) "Learning to consume—A theory of wants and the growth of demand" *Journal of Evolutionary Economics*, 11: 23–36.

Witt U (2003a) *The evolving economy: Essays on the evolutionary approach to economics.* Edward Elgar: Cheltenham.

Witt U (2003b) "Economic policy making in evolutionary perspective" *Journal of Evolutionary Economics*, 13: 77–94.

Witt U (2004) "Evolution und Geschichte—die ungeliebten Bräute der Ökonomik" *Institutioneller Wandel, Marktprozesse und dynamische Wirtschaftspolitik*, Lehmann-Waffenschmidt M, Ebner A, Fornahl D (eds). Metropolis: Marburg, pp. 31–51.

Wohlgemuth M (1999) "Democracy as a discovery procedure. Toward an Austrian economics of the political process" Max-Planck-Institute for Research into Economic Systems, Discussion paper 17/99.

Wohlmuth K (1999) "Global Competition and Asian Economic Development. Some Neo-Schumpeterian Approaches and their Relevance" *IWIM* Nr 63.

Wright R (2000) *Non-zero: The logic of human density.* Pantheon: New York.

Yergin D, Stanislaw J (1998) *The commanding heights: The battle for the world economy*. Simon & Schuster: New York.

Young A (1928) "Increasing returns in economic progress" *Economic Journal*, 38: 527–542.

Young P (1998) *Individual strategy and social structure: An evolutionary theory of institutions*. Princeton University Press: Princeton.

Ziman J (ed.) (1994) *Prometheus bound: Science in a dynamic steady state*. Cambridge University Press: Cambridge.

Ziman J (ed.) (2000) *Technological innovation as an evolutionary process*. Cambridge University Press: Cambridge.

Index